Microsoft Azure AI Fundamentals AI-900 Exam Guide

Gain proficiency in Azure AI and machine learning concepts and services to excel in the AI-900 exam

Aaron Guilmette

Steve Miles

Microsoft Azure AI Fundamentals AI-900 Exam Guide

Copyright © 2024 Packt Publishing

All rights reserved. No part of this book may be reproduced, stored in a retrieval system, or transmitted in any form or by any means, without the prior written permission of the publisher, except in the case of brief quotations embedded in critical articles or reviews.

Every effort has been made in the preparation of this book to ensure the accuracy of the information presented. However, the information contained in this book is sold without warranty, either express or implied. Neither the authors, nor Packt Publishing or its dealers and distributors, will be held liable for any damages caused or alleged to have been caused directly or indirectly by this book.

Packt Publishing has endeavored to provide trademark information about all of the companies and products mentioned in this book by the appropriate use of capitals. However, Packt Publishing cannot guarantee the accuracy of this information.

Associate Group Product Manager: Niranjan Naikwadi
Publishing Product Manager: Surbhi Suman
Book Project Manager: Ashwin Kharwa
Senior Editor: Divya Vijayan
Technical Editor: Irfa Ansari
Copy Editor: Safis Editing
Proofreader: Divya Vijayan
Indexer: Tejal Daruwale Soni
Production Designer: Prafulla Nikalje
Senior DevRel Marketing Executive: Vinishka Kalra, Kunal Raj

First published: May 2024
Production reference: 1170524

Published by Packt Publishing Ltd.

Grosvenor House
11 St Paul's Square
Birmingham
B3 1RB, UK

ISBN 978-1-83588-566-6

www.packtpub.com

I'd like to thank my long-suffering girlfriend, Christine, who has put up with my book deadlines for the last 14 books. She's the real hero. Also, I'd like to thank my kids—Liberty, Hudson, Anderson, Glory, and Victory—without them, I'd probably be able to retire sooner to a tropical location with umbrella drinks.

– *Aaron Guilmette*

I'd like to thank the people who have supported me professionally and at home, especially my wife, Pippa, aka Mrs Smiles, and my family. Also, apologies to my two four-legged family members, Henry and Lilly, for their missed walks while I have been locked away at evenings and weekends writing.

– *Steve Miles*

Foreword

Artificial intelligence (**AI**) is transforming the world in unprecedented ways. From enhancing customer experiences to automating business processes, AI enables organizations to achieve more with fewer resources and less time. However, AI is not a magic bullet that can solve any problem without human guidance and expertise. To harness the full potential of AI, you need to understand its core concepts, principles, and applications, as well as the ethical and social implications of using it.

This is where **Microsoft Azure AI** comes in. Azure AI offers a comprehensive set of cloud services and tools that enable you to build, deploy, and manage AI solutions at scale. Whether you want to create intelligent chatbots, analyze images and videos, generate natural language, or make predictions based on data, Azure AI provides the necessary services. It also integrates with other Azure services, such as **Azure Data**, **Azure DevOps**, and **Azure Security**, to offer a seamless and secure end-to-end AI development life cycle.

But how do you kickstart your journey with Azure AI? How do you choose the appropriate service for your specific use case? How do you design, implement, and optimize your AI solutions? How do you ensure that your AI solutions are ethical, responsible, and trustworthy? These are some of the questions that this book, *Microsoft Azure AI Fundamentals (AI-900) Exam Guide*, aims to address.

I've collaborated with Steve Miles for several years, and have worked as a technical reviewer for all his books, and enjoying each one. Steve's books are packed with amazing content, going above and beyond in clarifying complex matters, having detailed diagrams for clarity, and bringing in a lot of his own practical knowledge and great skill set. In my job as a Microsoft Technical Trainer, I often refer to his material when learners ask me for additional content for certification preparation.

This book serves as a comprehensive guide to prepare you for the Microsoft Azure AI Fundamentals certification exam (AI-900). This exam is designed to assess your foundational knowledge of AI and machine learning concepts, as well as your ability to use Azure AI services to implement AI solutions. By passing this exam, you will demonstrate your competence and confidence in using Azure AI, earning you a valuable credential that can boost your career prospects and credibility.

This book covers all the topics and objectives of the AI-900 exam, with clear explanations, practical examples, and self-assessment questions. You will learn about the following topics:

- The principles and concepts of AI and machine learning, such as supervised and unsupervised learning, deep learning, computer vision, natural language processing, conversational AI, and anomaly detection
- The features and capabilities of Azure AI services, such as **Azure Cognitive Services**, **Azure AI Bot Service**, **Azure Machine Learning**, and **Azure Cognitive Search**

- The best practices and considerations for designing, implementing, and optimizing AI solutions using Azure AI services, such as choosing the right service, data preparation, model training and deployment, performance monitoring, and security and privacy
- The ethical and social aspects of AI, such as the principles of responsible AI, the risks and challenges of AI, and the tools and frameworks for ensuring fairness, reliability, accountability, and transparency of AI solutions

By reading this book, you will not only prepare for the AI-900 exam but also establish a solid foundation of Azure AI for your future AI projects and endeavors. You will also cultivate a critical and responsible mindset that enables you to leverage AI for positive outcomes and avoid its pitfalls.

AI is a powerful and exciting field that offers endless possibilities and opportunities. With Azure AI, you can unleash your creativity and innovation to develop AI solutions that can make a positive impact on your organization and society. Whether you are a beginner or an experienced professional, this book will help you in achieving your Azure AI goals and aspirations.

I hope you enjoy reading this book and learning from it as much as I did. I wish you all the best in your AI-900 exam and for your Azure AI journey.

Peter De Tender

Microsoft Technical Trainer,

Microsoft Corp, Redmond.

Contributors

About the authors

Aaron Guilmette is a principal architect at Planet Technologies, an award-winning Microsoft Partner focused on dragging public sector public sector customers into the modern era. Previously, he worked at Microsoft as a senior program manager for Microsoft 365 Customer Experience. As the author of over a dozen IT books, he specializes in identity, messaging, and automation technologies. When he's not writing books or tools for his customers, trying to teach one of his kids to drive, or making tacos with his girlfriend, Aaron can be found tinkering with cars. You can visit his blog at `https://aka.ms/aaronblog` or connect with him on LinkedIn at `https://www.linkedin.com/in/aaronguilmette`.

Steve Miles is CTO at Westcoast Cloud, part of a multi-billion turnover IT distributor based in the UK and Ireland. Steve is a Microsoft **Most Valuable Professional** (**MVP**), **Microsoft Certified Trainer** (**MCT**), and an Alibaba Cloud MVP. He has 25+ years of technology experience and a previous military career in engineering, signals, and communications. Among other books, Steve is the author of the #1 Amazon best-selling AZ-900 certification title *Microsoft Azure Fundamentals and Beyond*. His books can be found on his author profile on Amazon at `https://www.amazon.com/stores/Steve-Miles/author/B09NDJ1RC8`.

Like Aaron, Steve is also a petrolhead, and can also be found tinkering with cars when he is not writing. You can connect with him on LinkedIn at `https://www.linkedin.com/in/stevemiles70/`.

About the reviewers

Peter De Tender has an extensive background in architecting, deploying, managing, and training Microsoft technologies, dating back to Windows NT4 Server in 1996, all the way to the latest and modern cloud solutions available in Azure today. With a passion for cloud architecture, DevOps, app modernization, and AI solutions, Peter always has a story to share on how to optimize your enterprise-ready cloud workloads.

Peter was an Azure MVP for 5 years, has been an MCT for 13+ years, and is still actively involved in the community as a public speaker, technical writer, book author, and publisher.

You can follow Peter on Twitter/X (@pdtit) and read his technical blog adventures at `http://www.007ffflearning.com`.

Jetro WILS is a cloud and information security advisor who began providing managed IT services as a teenager. He's a certified Microsoft cybersecurity architect, Azure solutions architect, and MCT.

"For 18 years, I've been active in various tech companies in Belgium. From developer to business analyst to product manager to cloud specialist, I've experienced digital evolution first-hand. I've seen the rise of cloud technology fundamentally change business operations, yet many organizations struggle to adopt the cloud securely. Also, Europe adds more legislation yearly, making it harder to maintain compliance."

Jetro is the founder of BlueDragon Security (`www.bluedragonsecurity.com`), where he helps organizations operate safely in the cloud.

Syed Mohamed Thameem Nizamudeen is a pioneer and subject matter expert (SME) in application modernization and cloud computing. He holds multiple industry certifications in Azure, AWS, GCP, Oracle, PMP, and CSM. Syed has over a decade of experience in product development, architecture, scalability, and modernization. He has worked with Oracle, leading top technology advisory firms like PwC and Ernst & Young, and other contemporary application enterprises. Syed is a skilled and dedicated technology management executive, leveraging his 15+ years of experience in designing and developing high-demand On-Premise/Commercial Off-The-Shelf Software/SaaS solutions.

I am honored to have served as a technical reviewer for the AI Exam Guide. This role has allowed me to contribute to shaping content that is both enlightening and essential for anyone looking to navigate the complex world of artificial intelligence. I extend my heartfelt thanks to the authors and editorial team for their collaborative spirit and dedication to excellence.

Table of Contents

Preface — xv

Part 1: Identify Features of Common AI Workloads

1

Identify Features of Common AI Workloads — 3

Making the Most Out of this Book – Your Certification and Beyond — 4
Identify features of data monitoring and anomaly detection workloads — 5
Identify features of content moderation and personalization workloads — 6
Identify computer vision workloads — 9
Identify natural language processing workloads — 10
Identify document inteliigence workloads — 12
Summary — 14
Exam Readiness Drill — 15
Working On Timing — 16

2

Identify the Guiding Principles for Responsible AI — 17

Understanding ethical principles — 18
Describe considerations for accountability — 18
Describe considerations for inclusiveness — 19
Describe considerations for reliability and safety — 20
Understand explainable principles — 21
Describe considerations for fairness — 21
Describe considerations for transparency — 22
Describe considerations for privacy and security — 23
Summary — 24
Exam Readiness Drill – Chapter Review Questions — 24
Exam Readiness Drill — 25
Working On Timing — 26

Part 2: Describe the Fundamental Principles of Machine Learning on Azure

3

Identify Common Machine Learning Techniques 29

Understanding machine learning terminology	30
Training	30
Inferencing	34
Identify regression machine learning scenarios	35
Example	35
Evaluation metrics	39
Applications	41
Identify classification machine learning scenarios	41
Binary classification	41
Multiclass classification	48
Identify clustering machine learning scenarios	52

Example	53
Evaluation metrics	55
Applications	57
Identify features of deep learning techniques	57
Example	59
Applications	59
Summary	61
Exam Readiness Drill – Chapter Review Questions	61
Exam Readiness Drill	62
Working On Timing	63

4

Describe Core Machine Learning Concepts 65

Identify features and labels in a dataset for machine learning	65
Identifying features in a dataset	66
Identifying labels in a dataset	69
Describe how training and validation datasets are used in machine learning	71
Training set	71
Validation set	72

Summary	73
Exam Readiness Drill – Chapter Review Questions	73
Exam Readiness Drill	74
Working On Timing	75

5

Describe Azure Machine Learning Capabilities — 77

What is Azure ML?	77	Describe model management and deployment capabilities in Azure ML	90
Describe capabilities of AutoML	79		
AutoML use cases	80	Model management and deployment capabilities	90
Training, validation, and test scenarios	82	MLOps	92
Feature engineering	82		
Ensemble models	82	Build a machine learning model in Azure ML	94
Describe data and compute services for data science and machine learning	84	Creating a machine learning workspace	94
		Using AutoML to train a model	96
Compute	84	Reviewing and selecting the best model	105
Data	85	Deploying and testing the model	106
Datastore	86	Testing the deployed model service	106
Environments	87	Teardown	107
Model	88		
Workspaces	88	Summary	108
Subscription	89	Exam Readiness Drill – Chapter Review Questions	108
Storage account	89		
Key Vault	89	Exam Readiness Drill	109
Application Insights	89	Working On Timing	110
Container Registry	90		

Part 3: Describe Features of Computer Vision Workloads on Azure

6

Identify Common Types of Computer Vision Solutions — 113

Introduction to CV solutions	114	Identify features of object detection solutions	120
Image processing	114		
CV ML	115	Identify features of OCR solutions	123
Identify features of image classification solutions	118	Identify features of facial detection and facial analysis solutions	126
		Facial detection	126

Facial analysis	128	Exam Readiness Drill – Chapter Review Questions	130
Facial recognition	129	Exam Readiness Drill	131
Summary	**130**	Working On Timing	132

7

Identify Azure Tools and Services for Computer Vision Tasks

Technical requirements	**134**	Facial detection	145
Describe capabilities of the Azure AI Vision service	**135**	Responsible AI	149
		Describe capabilities of the Azure AI Video Indexer service	**149**
Image classification	136		
Object detection	139	**Summary**	**151**
OCR solutions	142	**Exam Readiness Drill – Chapter Review Questions**	**152**
Describe the capabilities of the Azure AI Face service	**143**		
		Exam Readiness Drill	153
Getting started	144	Working On Timing	154

Part 4: Describe Features of Natural Language Processing (NLP) Workloads on Azure

8

Identify Features of Common NLP Workload Scenarios   157

Introduction to NLP	**158**	**Identify features and uses for language modeling**	**166**
NLP concepts	159		
NLP scenarios	161	Conversational language understanding (CLU)	167
Identify features and uses for key phrase extraction	**162**	Conversational AI	167
Identify features and uses for entity recognition	**164**	**Identify features and uses for speech recognition and synthesis**	**168**
Identify features and uses for sentiment analysis	**165**	Speech recognition	168
		Speech synthesis	169

Identify features and uses for translation	171	Exam Readiness Drill – Chapter Review Questions	172
Summary	172	Exam Readiness Drill	173
		Working On Timing	174

9

Identify Azure Tools and Services for NLP Workloads — 175

Technical requirements	175	Azure AI Speech Studio	181
Describe capabilities of the Azure AI Language service	176	Describe capabilities of the Azure AI Translator service	183
Text analysis	177	Summary	184
Conversational language understanding	177	Exam Readiness Drill – Chapter Review Questions	184
Question-answering	178		
Azure AI Language Studio	179	Exam Readiness Drill	185
Describe capabilities of the Azure AI Speech service	181	Working On Timing	186

Part 5: Describe Features of Generative AI Workloads on Azure

10

Identify Features of Generative AI Solutions — 189

What is Generative AI?	189	Music creation	199
Identify Features of Generative AI models	190	Synthetic data generation	200
		Code generation	200
What's a transformer model and how does it work?	191	Voice generation and transformation	201
How does generative AI put all this together?	195	Drug discovery and chemical synthesis	201
		Personalized content and recommendation systems	202
Identify common scenarios for generative AI	197	Maintenance analysis	202
Image generation	197	Copilots	202
Text generation	198	Deepfake creation and detection	202
		Quality control	203

Identify Responsible AI considerations for generative AI	203	Summary	209
		Exam Readiness Drill – Chapter Review Questions	209
Identify	204	Exam Readiness Drill	211
Measure	205	Working On Timing	211
Mitigate	206		
Operate	208		

11

Identify Capabilities of Azure OpenAI Service 213

What is Azure OpenAI Service?	213	Describe code generation capabilities of Azure OpenAI Service	232
What's included?	214		
What's the difference between Azure AI and Azure OpenAI services?	215	Describe image generation capabilities of Azure OpenAI Service	236
Accessing Azure OpenAI services	216	Summary	236
Describe natural language generation capabilities of Azure OpenAI Service	229	Exam Readiness Drill – Chapter Review Questions	237
		Exam Readiness Drill	238
		Working On Timing	239

12

Accessing the Online Practice Resources 241

How to Access These Resources	241	A Clean, Simple Cert Practice Experience	245
Purchased from Packt Store (packtpub.com)	241	Practice Questions	246
Packt+ Subscription	241	Flashcards	248
Purchased from Amazon and Other Sources	241	Exam Tips	249
		Chapter Review Questions	249
Troubleshooting Tips	245	Share Feedback	250
Practice Resources – A Quick Tour	245	Back to the Book	250

Index 253

Other Books You May Enjoy 264

Preface

The AI-900 certification exam, also known as the Microsoft Azure AI Fundamentals exam, is designed to validate foundational knowledge of **artificial intelligence** (**AI**) concepts and how they are implemented in Microsoft Azure.

The AI-900 exam has been updated a few times to include new technologies as they emerge and enter the Azure space—and this edition of the exam is no different. AI-900 now includes a focus on the new OpenAI services available as part of an Azure subscription.

Who this book is for

This book is intended for individuals who are interested in gaining a basic understanding of AI and its applications in Azure but who may not have extensive technical experience in the field. This includes business stakeholders, decision-makers, and technical professionals who are new to AI technologies.

The content in this book assumes you have no knowledge of any machine learning or AI concepts (though it certainly helps with understanding some of the more complex topics).

What this book covers

Chapter 1, *Identify Features of Common AI Workloads*, introduces some of the basic concepts of AI in the Azure platform space.

Chapter 2, *Identify the Guiding Principles for Responsible AI*, explains Microsoft's principles for responsible AI, such as transparency and inclusiveness.

Chapter 3, *Identify Common Machine Learning Techniques*, explores machine learning techniques, such as clustering and regression.

Chapter 4, *Describe Core Machine Learning Concepts*, expands on the concepts of machine learning techniques with explanations of features, labels, training, and validation.

Chapter 5, *Describe Azure Machine Learning Capabilities*, focuses on the power of **automated machine learning** (**AutoML**) as well as the functional resources necessary for enabling machine learning in Azure.

Chapter 6, *Identify Common Types of Computer Vision Solutions*, introduces the concepts behind computer vision, such as optical character recognition and object detection.

Chapter 7, *Identify Azure Tools and Services for Computer Vision Tasks*, expands on the basics of computer vision with services such as Azure AI Vision and Azure AI Face.

Chapter 8, Identify Features of Common NLP Workload Scenarios, introduces the core foundational workload uses for natural language processing, such as sentiment analysis, translation, and key phrase extraction.

Chapter 9, Identify Azure Tools and Services for NLP Workloads, provides information about Azure's natural language processing solutions, such as the Azure AI Translator and Azure AI Language services.

Chapter 10, Identify Features of Generative AI Solutions, explains the broad features and use cases for generative AI models.

Chapter 11, Identify Capabilities of Azure OpenAI Service, highlights the powerful features of Azure OpenAI Service, including text content and image generation.

Chapter 12, Accessing the Online Practice Resources.

To get the most out of this book

To make the most of your studying experience, we recommend the following components:

- Azure tenant with free trial subscriptions (`https://azure.microsoft.com/en-us/free/ai-services/`)
- Register for OpenAI access (`https://aka.ms/oai/access`)

If you are using the digital version of this book, we advise you to type the code yourself or access the code from the book's GitHub repository (a link is available in the next section). Doing so will help you avoid any potential errors related to the copying and pasting of code.

Online Practice Resources

With this book, you will unlock unlimited access to our online exam-prep platform (Figure 0.1). This is your place to practice everything you learn in the book.

> **How to access the resources**
> To learn how to access these resources, head over to *Chapter 12, Accessing the Online Resources*, at the end of the book.

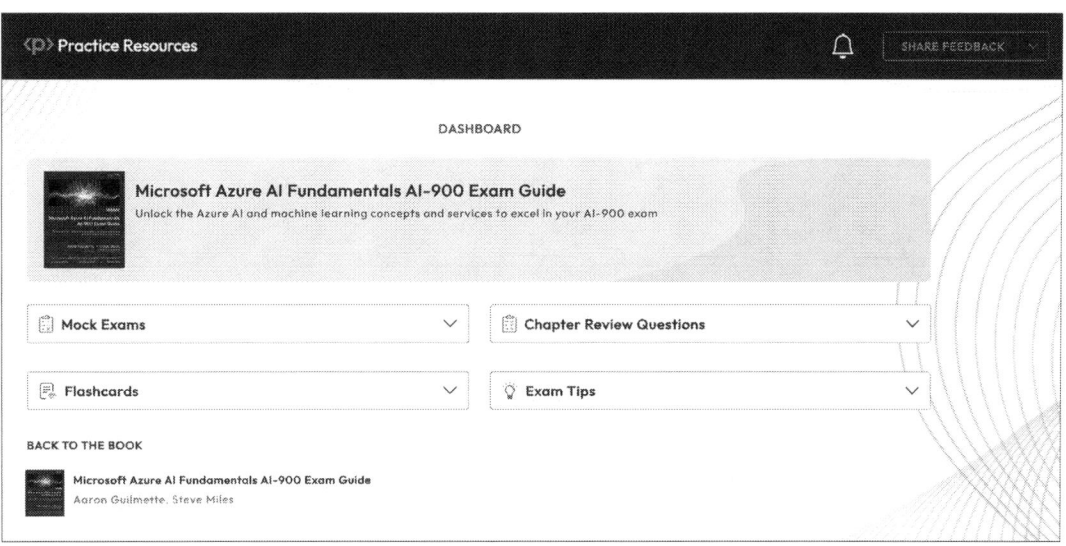

Figure 0.1: Dashboard interface of the online practice resources

Download the example code files

You can download the example code files for this book from GitHub at `https://github.com/PacktPublishing/Microsoft-Azure-AI-Fundamentals-AI-900-Exam-Guide`. If there's an update to the code, it will be updated in the GitHub repository.

We also have other code bundles from our rich catalog of books and videos available at `https://github.com/PacktPublishing/`. Check them out!

Conventions used

There are a number of text conventions used throughout this book.

`Code in text`: Indicates code words in text, database table names, folder names, filenames, file extensions, pathnames, dummy URLs, user input, and Twitter handles. Here is an example: "Mount the downloaded `WebStorm-10*.dmg` disk image file as another disk in your system."

A block of code is set as follows:

```
[
    {
            "recognitionModel": "recognition_01",
            "faceRectangle": {
            "width": 144,
            "height": 209,
            "left": 305,
            "top": 473
    },
```

Bold: Indicates a new term, an important word, or words that you see onscreen. For instance, words in menus or dialog boxes appear in **bold**. Here is an example: "Select **System info** from the **Administration** panel."

> **Tips or important notes**
> Appear like this.

Get in touch

Feedback from our readers is always welcome.

General feedback: If you have questions about any aspect of this book, email us at customercare@packtpub.com and mention the book title in the subject of your message.

Errata: Although we have taken every care to ensure the accuracy of our content, mistakes do happen. If you have found a mistake in this book, we would be grateful if you would report this to us. Please visit www.packtpub.com/support/errata and fill in the form.

Piracy: If you come across any illegal copies of our works in any form on the internet, we would be grateful if you would provide us with the location address or website name. Please contact us at copyright@packt.com with a link to the material.

If you are interested in becoming an author: If there is a topic that you have expertise in and you are interested in either writing or contributing to a book, please visit authors.packtpub.com.

Share Your Thoughts

Once you've read *Microsoft Azure AI Fundamentals AI-900 Exam Guide*, we'd love to hear your thoughts! Scan the QR code below to go straight to the Amazon review page for this book and share your feedback.

https://packt.link/r/1835885675

Your review is important to us and the tech community and will help us make sure we're delivering excellent quality content.

Download a free PDF copy of this book

Thanks for purchasing this book!

Do you like to read on the go but are unable to carry your print books everywhere?

Is your eBook purchase not compatible with the device of your choice?

Don't worry, now with every Packt book you get a DRM-free PDF version of that book at no cost.

Read anywhere, any place, on any device. Search, copy, and paste code from your favorite technical books directly into your application.

The perks don't stop there, you can get exclusive access to discounts, newsletters, and great free content in your inbox daily

Follow these simple steps to get the benefits:

1. Scan the QR code or visit the link below

`https://packt.link/free-ebook/9781835885666`

2. Submit your proof of purchase
3. That's it! We'll send your free PDF and other benefits to your email directly

Part 1: Identify Features of Common AI Workloads

In this first part of the book, you will be introduced to foundational concepts of **artificial intelligence (AI)** workloads as well as Microsoft's principles for responsible AI development.

This part includes the following chapters:

- *Chapter 1, Identify Features of Common AI Workloads*
- *Chapter 2, Identify the Guiding Principles for Responsible AI*

1
Identify Features of Common AI Workloads

Welcome to the world of **artificial intelligence** (**AI**)!

When you think of AI, what comes to mind? If you've watched sci-fi movies, your mind might conjure images of walking and talking human-like androids from movies such as *Blade Runner* or *Terminator*. Or perhaps you think of just a voice, such as the HAL 9000 in *2001: A Space Odyssey* or Tony Stark's seemingly all-knowing computational butler, Jarvis, as featured in *Iron Man*.

While that future is still a ways off, there are some pretty amazing things that AI can do right now. Artificial intelligence is software technology that imitates certain human capabilities, such as interpreting images and language or predicting outcomes of scenarios based on historical data and patterns.

In this book, you'll learn about the broad range of AI technologies and capabilities that are available inside the Microsoft Azure platform. And, throughout this book, you'll be exposed to examples, demos, and labs that show you how Azure AI services can be used to help address both simple and complex business scenarios.

The objectives and skills we'll cover in this chapter include the following:

- Identify features of data monitoring and anomaly detection workloads
- Identify features of content moderation and personalization workloads
- Identify computer vision workloads
- Identify natural language processing workloads
- Identify Knowledge Mining workloads
- Identify document intelligence workloads
- Identify features of generative AI workloads

Identify Features of Common AI Workloads

By the end of this chapter, you should be able to discuss the features and capabilities of AI workloads and capabilities available in Microsoft Azure.

Get ready for your first steps on this exciting journey!

> **Note**
> Azure Cognitive Services was rolled up into the new Azure AI Services family branding. Neither pricing nor capabilities have changed as a result of the branding change.

Before we move on to the topics of this chapter, have a look at the following section.

Making the Most Out of this Book – Your Certification and Beyond

This book and its accompanying online resources are designed to be a complete preparation tool for your **Microsoft Azure AI Fundamentals AI-900 Exam**.

The book is written in a way that you can apply everything you've learned here even after your certification. The online practice resources that come with this book (*Figure 1.1*) are designed to improve your test-taking skills. They are loaded with timed mock exams, interactive flashcards, and exam tips to help you work on your exam readiness from now till your test day.

> **Before You Proceed**
> To learn how to access these resources, head over to *Chapter 12, Accessing the Online Practice Resources*, at the end of the book.

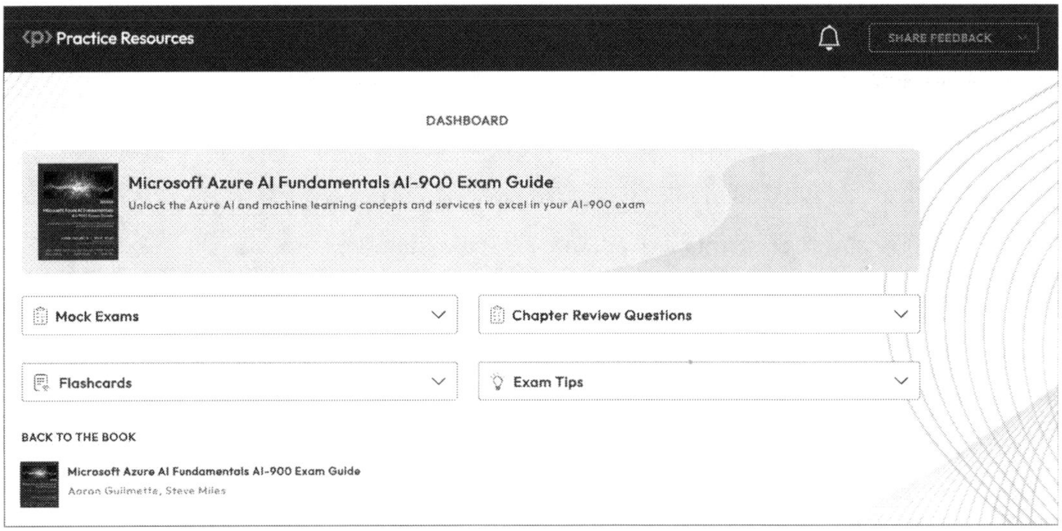

Figure 1.1 – Dashboard interface of the online practice resources

Read each section thoroughly.

Here are some tips on how to make the most out of this book so that you can clear your certification and retain your knowledge beyond your exam:

1. **Make ample notes**: You can use your favorite online note-taking tool or use a physical notebook. The free online resources also give you access to an online version of this book. Click the BACK TO THE BOOK link from the Dashboard to access the book in **Packt Reader**. You can highlight specific sections of the book there.

2. **Chapter Review Questions**: At the end of this chapter, you'll find a link to review questions for this chapter. These are designed to test your knowledge of the chapter. Aim to score at least **75%** before moving on to the next chapter. You'll find detailed instructions on how to make the most of these questions at the end of this chapter in the *Exam Readiness Drill – Chapter Review Questions* section. That way, you improve your exam-taking skills after each chapter, rather than at the end.

3. **Flashcards**: After you've gone through the book and scored **75%** more in each of the chapter review questions, start reviewing the online flashcards. They will help you memorize key concepts.

4. **Mock Exams**: Solve the mock exams that come with the book till your exam day. If you get some answers wrong, go back to the book and revisit the concepts you're weak in.

5. **Exam Tips**: Review these from time to time to improve your exam readiness even further.

Identify features of data monitoring and anomaly detection workloads

Anomaly Detector is an AI service equipped with a suite of **application programming interfaces** (**APIs**) designed to empower users in monitoring and identifying anomalies within their time series data, even with limited **machine learning** (**ML**) expertise. Whether you require **batch validation** (a method for checking a model's efficacy using a subset of training data) or real-time **inference** (making predictions using machine learning models), Anomaly Detector has you covered.

> What's time series data?
>
> Time series data refers to a type of data where observations are collected or recorded over regular intervals of time. These observations are typically ordered chronologically, with each data point associated with a specific time stamp. Time series data is common in various areas such as finance, economics, weather forecasting, and sales.

This service offers two primary functionalities:

- Univariate anomaly detection
- Multivariate anomaly detection

Univariate anomaly detection allows users to identify anomalies in a single variable, such as revenue or cost, without the need for extensive ML knowledge. The model selection process is automated based on patterns in the data itself, ensuring optimal performance regardless of industry, scenario, or data volume. By leveraging time series data, the API establishes boundaries for anomaly detection, determines expected values, and then identifies anomalous data points.

On the other hand, **multivariate anomaly detection** APIs enable developers to integrate advanced AI capabilities for detecting anomalies across groups of metrics, eliminating the requirement for ML expertise or previously labeled data. These APIs automatically account for dependencies and inter-correlations between signals, crucial for safeguarding complex systems such as software applications, servers, factory machines, and spacecraft from failures.

In the real world, multivariate anomaly detection is frequently used to help identify things such as credit card transaction fraud. By training on data such as places you normally shop, locations you normally travel, and the average size of transactions, financial institutions can detect when your credit card has been compromised and alert you right away.

> **Exam tip**
> Multivariate anomaly detection can correlate up to 300 signals.

When deviations occur beyond the usual range of signal interactions, the multivariate anomaly detection feature acts as a seasoned expert, promptly identifying anomalies. The underlying AI models are trained and tailored using user data to address the unique requirements of their business. With the addition of these APIs, developers can seamlessly integrate multivariate time series anomaly detection capabilities into predictive maintenance solutions, AIOps monitoring solutions for complex enterprise software, or business intelligence tools.

Next, we'll look at features of content moderation and personalization.

Identify features of content moderation and personalization workloads

Using AI to monitor and moderate content is also a growing task area. Content moderation refers to the process of screening user-generated content to ensure it adheres to certain standards or guidelines. The moderation APIs give AI developers ways to submit content for programmatic evaluation.

> **Note**
> The legacy Azure **Content Moderator** has been slated for retirement in February 2027. While it is still available, Microsoft recommends developers start switching to Azure AI **Content Safety**, which includes more robust features.

Azure AI Content Safety offers a comprehensive solution for detecting harmful content, encompassing both user-generated and AI-generated material across applications and services. This suite includes text and image APIs, along with an interactive Content Safety Studio, providing developers with the tools to identify and mitigate potentially harmful content effectively.

Content moderation plays a critical role in various industries, ensuring compliance with regulations and maintaining a safe environment for users. Scenarios where content moderation services are essential include online marketplaces, gaming companies, social messaging platforms, enterprise media, and K-12 education solutions.

The service offers different types of analysis through its APIs, including text and image analysis for sexual content, violence, hate speech, and self-harm, along with newer functionalities such as jailbreak risk detection and protected material text detection.

Azure AI **Content Safety Studio** serves as a powerful online tool for handling offensive or risky content, equipped with advanced content moderation ML models. It allows users to customize workflows, upload their own content, and utilize pre-built AI models and blocklists provided by Microsoft, ensuring comprehensive coverage of harmful content.

With Content Safety Studio, businesses can establish moderation workflows, continuously monitor and improve content moderation performance, and meet the specific content requirements of their industries. The platform simplifies operations, enabling quick validation of different solutions and facilitating efficient content moderation without the need for extensive model development.

Additionally, you can configure filters and thresholds for different types of potentially harmful content. Depending on the scenarios, you can tweak the filter settings to be more or less permissive, and then test samples of content against the filters to ensure the right type of content is getting blocked, as shown in *Figure 1.1*:

8 Identify Features of Common AI Workloads

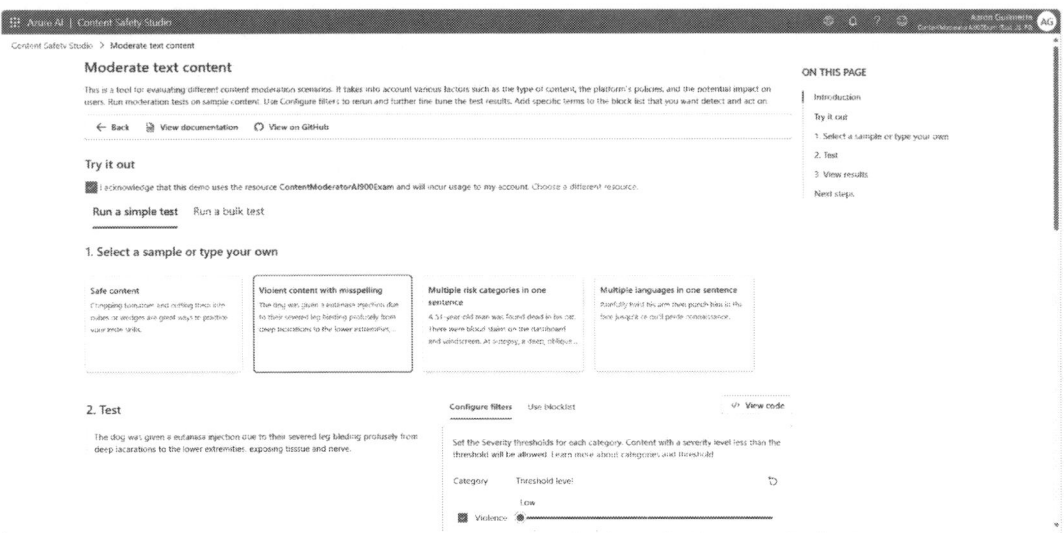

Figure 1.2 – Evaluating text in Content Safety Studio

Key features of **Content Safety Studio** include the ability to moderate text and image content, monitor online activity, and access detailed response information such as category distribution, latency, and error detection. Its user-friendly interface empowers developers to configure content filters, manage blocklists of prohibited terms, and implement moderation tools directly into their applications, streamlining workflow processes and enhancing content safety measures.

> **Further exploration**
>
> You can take a test drive of Content Safe Studio (part of Azure AI Cognitive Services) here: `https://contentsafety.cognitive.azure.com/`.

Azure also contains personalization services called the **AI Personalizer**. Like content moderation, the personalizer analyzes content. However, instead of making decisions about a content's safety or possible offensiveness, it's used to make predictions on user behaviors, such as the following:

- Using recent choice data or items already viewed, will the customer make a purchase?
- Based on the things viewed already, what other products or articles might be interesting to the user?
- Where should an advertisement be placed for optimal exposure?
- How should a popup notification be deployed to maximize visibility or response?
- Are there other data points available from partner or affiliate organizations that could be used to help make better decisions?

The Azure Personalizer works through the use of **reinforcement learning** (a type of machine learning) by assigning a point value (**reward**) for actions or choices that a user can make based on the current context of their session (location, items viewed, device, previous browsing history, or other information that the service has been able to gather). With this information, the personalizer service can then make automated decisions on what content to present to the user to encourage a particular choice or response.

> Note
>
> The Azure Personalizer has been deprecated and will be taken offline in October 2026. As of this writing, new Personalizer resources can no longer be created.
>
> For more information on Azure Personalizer service, see the following: `https://learn.microsoft.com/en-us/azure/ai-services/personalizer/what-is-personalizer`.

In the next section, we'll review the high-level features of computer vision.

Identify computer vision workloads

Azure's **AI Vision** (also referred to as **computer vision**) service offers access to cutting-edge algorithms designed to process images and provide relevant information based on specific visual features.

The service boasts several key functionalities:

- **Optical character recognition (OCR)**: This feature enables the extraction of text from images, including both printed and handwritten text from various sources such as photos and documents. Utilizing deep-learning-based models, the OCR service works across different surfaces and backgrounds, including business documents, invoices, receipts, posters, business cards, letters, and whiteboards. Additionally, it supports multiple languages for extracting printed text.

- **Image analysis**: The image analysis service extracts a wide range of visual features from images, including objects, faces, adult content, and automatically generated text descriptions.

- **Face recognition**: The face service provides AI algorithms for detecting, recognizing, and analyzing human faces within images. This capability finds application in various scenarios such as identification, touchless access control, and privacy protection through face blurring.

- **Spatial analysis**: The spatial analysis service analyzes the presence and movement of individuals within video feeds, generating events that can trigger responses in other systems.

Some of the common uses or features for computer vision might include generating captions of images (such as "*dog retrieves frisbee in a park*") or providing an analysis for objects detected in an image (such as a *dog*, a *frisbee*, the *outdoors*, a *tree*, or *grass*). When detecting objects, the Azure AI Vision service also returns information on **confidence** (or how sure the service is of the detection).

Azure AI Vision is particularly relevant for **digital asset management** (**DAM**) scenarios. DAM involves organizing, storing, and retrieving rich media assets while managing digital rights and permissions. For example, a stock photography service may design a digital asset management system to apply AI-generated descriptions of photographs, enabling customers to search for images.

Overall, Azure AI Vision provides a robust platform for leveraging advanced image processing capabilities to enhance digital asset management and various other applications.

Next, we'll look at the features and capabilities for processing language in Azure.

Identify natural language processing workloads

Natural language processing (**NLP**) is a branch of AI focused on comprehending and responding to human language. The goal of NLP is to allow computers to interpret text similarly to humans and provide realistic dialogue and responses. Several popular and common consumer AI-based services, such as OpenAI's ChatGPT or predictive text on a smartphone, use natural language processing to help understand input and context.

NLP is a building block for many other AI services, such as text analytics, which extract information from unstructured text. Examples of NLP applications include sentiment analysis for product marketing campaigns on social media, document summarization in a catalog search application, and extracting brands and company names from text.

Azure AI Language, a cloud-based service, offers tools for understanding and analyzing text. It features sentiment analysis, key phrase identification, text summarization, and conversational language understanding capabilities. These capabilities can help organizations process volumes of internal and customer-generated data to help make information more accessible and digestible as well as highlight patterns or anomalies that need to be addressed.

Azure AI Language has the following features and sub-services:

- **Text Analytics**: This feature provides sentiment analysis, key phrase extraction, named entity recognition (identifying and categorizing items of interest), and language detection. It allows applications to understand the context, evaluate the sentiment of written text, identify important concepts, and recognize entities such as people, locations, and organizations.

- **Translator**: This feature offers real-time, multi-language translation capabilities, supporting text translation across dozens of languages. It's designed for scenarios that require quick and accurate translations, such as content localization and multilingual customer support.

- **Language Understanding** (**LUIS**): LUIS is a machine learning-based service used to build natural language understanding into apps, bots, and **Internet of Things** (**IoT**) devices. It allows developers to define custom **intents** (representations of actions that a user wants to perform) and **entities** (parameters required to execute the action) relevant to their application's domain and provides models that can understand user inputs in natural language.

> **Note**
> Microsoft has announced that LUIS will be retired on October 1, 2025. Microsoft recommends that organizations begin migrating to Conversational Language Understanding.

- **Conversational Language Understanding**: This service provides tools to build conversational AI applications that can understand and respond to user queries in a natural way. It helps in developing sophisticated chatbots and virtual assistants that can engage with users conversationally.
- **QnA Maker**: This feature enables the creation of a conversational question-and-answer layer over your data, making it easy to build and maintain knowledge bases from your content, such as websites, documents, and FAQs.
- **Custom text**: This allows for the creation of customized NLP models tailored to specific industries or business needs. You can build custom classification, entity recognition, and single/multi-label classification models based on your unique datasets.
- **Decision AI**: Though not strictly limited to language processing, this feature integrates with the language service to aid in making informed decisions based on the text analysis, enhancing the decision-making processes within applications.

Azure AI Language was previously known as **Text Analytics**.

Identify Knowledge Mining workloads

You can think of knowledge mining a bit like an AI-powered search engine. Traditional search engines easily catalog and index traditional text pages. However, they may be less capable of ingesting unstructured data, such as directories of documents, spreadsheets, presentations, and images, and answering search queries for it.

Azure's **AI Knowledge Mining** is a comprehensive suite of tools and services designed to extract valuable insights and knowledge from large volumes of unstructured data, such as documents, images, videos, and audio files. This suite leverages advanced artificial intelligence technologies, including natural language processing, computer vision, and machine learning, to enable organizations to understand their volumes of data.

Let's look at the key feature of Azure's AI Knowledge Mining:

- **Powerful text analytics capabilities**: Using state-of-the-art NLP algorithms, organizations can extract entities, key phrases, and sentiment from textual data, enabling them to identify important concepts and trends within their documents. Additionally, Azure's AI Knowledge Mining offers entity recognition and linking, allowing organizations to identify and resolve references to entities such as people, organizations, and locations across their documents.

- **Document processing capabilities**: This includes OCR for extracting text from scanned documents and images, as well as document classification and entity extraction for organizing and structuring large document collections. With these features, organizations can efficiently process and analyze large volumes of documents, enabling them to uncover valuable insights and knowledge.
- **Search capabilities**: It allows users to quickly and easily search across their entire document repository. Leveraging AI-powered indexing and search algorithms, organizations can find relevant information within their documents, regardless of format or language. Additionally, Azure's AI Knowledge Mining supports faceted search, enabling users to filter search results based on specific criteria such as document type, date, or sentiment.

Azure's AI Knowledge Mining also includes advanced data visualization tools, enabling organizations to visualize their data and insights in meaningful and informative ways. With support for interactive dashboards, charts, and graphs, organizations can gain deeper insights into their data and communicate findings more effectively.

Azure **AI Search**, a key component of Azure's AI Knowledge Mining capability, leverages capabilities such as computer vision for text and object identification as well as natural language processing to extract data from large volumes of information. When using all of these capabilities together, knowledge mining allows users to search vast amounts of unstructured information and surface insights for making decisions.

Azure also has strong capabilities around document automation and text extraction, which we'll look at in the next section.

Identify document intelligence workloads

Azure **AI Document Intelligence** (formerly known as Azure **Form Recognizer**) is a set of capabilities that allows automation to make decisions based on extracted text.

For example, it might be very easy for a human to look at a receipt or an invoice and determine what it is, what the different data fields mean (such as a subtotal or an address) and insert them accordingly into a database or perform some other activity with them. This type of business process automation is very difficult for traditional computer systems to do. AI-enabled document intelligence can be used to bridge that gap to identify certain types of data and map them to appropriate fields.

Azure **AI Document Intelligence** is a comprehensive suite of tools and services designed to streamline document processing tasks using advanced artificial intelligence technologies. This service enables organizations to extract valuable insights from various types of documents, including scanned images, PDFs, and digital files, with remarkable accuracy and efficiency.

At the core of Azure AI Document Intelligence are advanced OCR capabilities. These capabilities allow for the extraction of text from images and documents, whether they are printed or handwritten. By leveraging deep learning-based models, Azure AI Document Intelligence can accurately interpret text across diverse surfaces and backgrounds, including business documents, invoices, receipts, posters, and more. Additionally, the OCR functionality supports multiple languages, ensuring broad applicability across different regions and industries.

Beyond simple text extraction, Azure AI Document Intelligence offers a range of features for sophisticated document analysis. For instance, it includes tools for entity recognition, enabling the identification and extraction of key entities such as names, dates, addresses, and organizations from documents. This capability is invaluable for tasks such as information retrieval, data entry automation, and content classification.

Another powerful aspect of Azure AI Document Intelligence is its ability to perform semantic analysis on documents. This involves extracting meaningful insights from the content of documents, such as identifying themes, topics, and sentiments. By analyzing the context and semantics of text, organizations can gain deeper understanding and actionable intelligence from their document repositories.

In this last section, we'll look at some of the newest and most popular AI workloads on the market that assist in content creation.

Identify features of generative AI workloads

If you've been paying attention to the media over the last year or so, you've probably seen some examples of **generative AI** tools such as ChatGPT, Bing Image Creator, and Midjourney. All of these types of tools are able to generate new content (hence the term *generative AI*) as the result of a natural language instructive input, also known as a **prompt**.

Azure AI Generative AI is a set of tools and services within the Azure AI ecosystem designed to enable the creation of new content, such as images, text, audio, and videos, based on existing data patterns. This cutting-edge technology leverages deep learning techniques to mimic human creativity and generate content that is realistic and relevant to specific use cases.

Azure AI Generative AI can be used to generate high-quality images. Using **generative adversarial networks** (**GANs**) and other advanced techniques, Azure AI can create realistic images that closely resemble those found in real-world scenarios. This capability has various applications across industries, including creating synthetic training data for machine learning models, generating realistic product images for e-commerce platforms, and producing lifelike graphics for video games and virtual environments.

Another important aspect of Azure AI Generative AI is its text generation capabilities. By training language models on large corpora of text data, Azure AI can generate coherent and contextually relevant text passages that mimic human writing styles. This feature is particularly useful for tasks such as automated content creation, chatbot development, and natural language generation.

Furthermore, Azure AI Generative AI includes features for fine-tuning and customizing generated content. By providing controls for adjusting parameters such as style, tone, and content, users can tailor the output of generative models to meet their specific requirements. This flexibility allows for the creation of highly customized and personalized content across a wide range of domains.

Generative AI can also be used to assist in the development or review of application code and scripting.

Overall, Azure AI Generative AI offers a powerful set of tools and services for creating artificial intelligence models capable of generating new and innovative content. By leveraging deep learning techniques and advanced algorithms, Azure AI enables organizations to harness the power of generative AI to unlock new possibilities in content creation, storytelling, and creative expression.

Summary

In this chapter, you learned about the core features of Azure AI workloads and services, including computer vision, document intelligence, and generative AI. Each of the workloads in Azure AI's cognitive services portfolio offer capabilities to help accelerate understanding organization data and advance business use cases.

In the next chapter, you'll learn about Microsoft's commitment to responsible AI.

Exam Readiness Drill – Chapter Review Questions

Apart from a solid understanding of key concepts, being able to think quickly under time pressure is a skill that will help you ace your certification exam. That is why working on these skills early on in your learning journey is key.

Chapter review questions are designed to improve your test-taking skills progressively with each chapter you learn and review your understanding of key concepts in the chapter at the same time. You'll find these at the end of each chapter.

> **Before You Proceed**
>
> If you don't have a Packt Library subscription or you haven't purchased this book from the Packt store, you will need to unlock the online resources to access the exam readiness drills. Unlocking is free and needs to be done only once. To learn how to do that, head over to the chapter titled *Chapter 12, Accessing the Online Resources*.

To open the Chapter Review Questions for this chapter, perform the following steps:

1. Click the link – `https://packt.link/AI-900_CH01`.

    Alternatively, you can scan the following QR code (*Figure 1.2*):

Figure 1.3 – QR code that opens Chapter Review Questions for logged-in users

2. Once you log in, you'll see a page similar to the one shown in *Figure 1.3*:

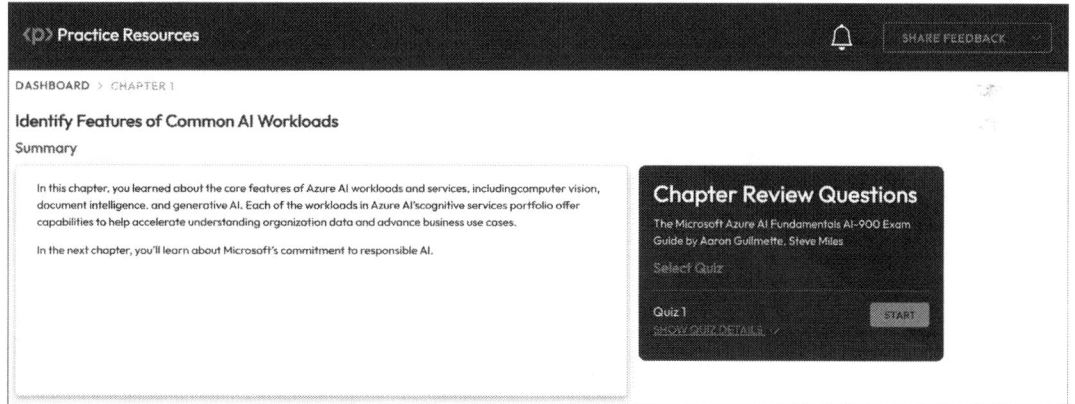

Figure 1.4 – Chapter Review Questions for Chapter 1

3. Once ready, start the following practice drills, re-attempting the quiz multiple times.

Exam Readiness Drill

For the first three attempts, don't worry about the time limit.

ATTEMPT 1

The first time, aim for at least **40%**. Look at the answers you got wrong and read the relevant sections in the chapter again to fix your learning gaps.

ATTEMPT 2

The second time, aim for at least **60%**. Look at the answers you got wrong and read the relevant sections in the chapter again to fix any remaining learning gaps.

ATTEMPT 3

The third time, aim for at least **75%**. Once you score 75% or more, you start working on your timing.

> **Tip**
> You may take more than **three** attempts to reach 75%. That's okay. Just review the relevant sections in the chapter till you get there.

Working On Timing

Your aim is to keep the score the same while trying to answer these questions as quickly as possible. Here's an example of how your next attempts should look like:

Attempt	Score	Time Taken
Attempt 5	77%	21 mins 30 seconds
Attempt 6	78%	18 mins 34 seconds
Attempt 7	76%	14 mins 44 seconds

Table 1.1 – Sample timing practice drills on the online platform

> **Note**
> The time limits shown in the above table are just examples. Set your own time limits with each attempt based on the time limit of the quiz on the website.

With each new attempt, your score should stay above **75%** while your "time taken" to complete should "decrease". Repeat as many attempts as you want till you feel confident dealing with the time pressure.

2
Identify the Guiding Principles for Responsible AI

While AI can do some amazing things, it also has the potential to be part of truly terrible things—which is exactly what this chapter will try to address.

How do we (as practitioners, developers, and consumers) protect against either intentional or unintentional malicious manipulation? Microsoft, for its part, has developed a set of six principles for the responsible development and implementation of AI-based solutions.

Microsoft has termed these principles its **guiding principles for responsible AI**.

The objectives and skills we'll cover in this chapter include the following:

- Describe considerations for accountability
- Describe considerations for inclusiveness
- Describe considerations for reliability and safety
- Describe considerations for fairness
- Describe considerations for transparency
- Describe considerations for privacy and security

These principles are divided into two categories or perspectives: **ethical** and **explainable**. We'll examine these two categories and how the principles fit into them. By the end of this chapter, you should be able to articulate how AI can be developed and implemented in a responsible manner.

Understanding ethical principles

The first category or perspective on responsible AI usage and development is that of ethical principles. From an ethical perspective, AI implementations should include the following considerations:

- Require accountability for designers and implementers
- Exhibit inclusivity
- Ensure the output doesn't cause harm

Let's look at how those ethical considerations map to Microsoft's principles.

Describe considerations for accountability

Microsoft's accountability principle in responsible AI development emphasizes the importance of transparency, fairness, and oversight throughout the AI development lifecycle. This principle underscores the need for individuals and organizations involved in designing and deploying AI systems to be accountable for the actions and decisions of these systems, particularly as they evolve toward greater autonomy.

To achieve accountability, Microsoft advocates for the establishment of internal review bodies within organizations to provide oversight, insights, and guidance on AI development and deployment. These bodies play a crucial role in ensuring that AI systems meet ethical and legal standards, and that they align with the organization's governance and organizational principles.

Central to Microsoft's accountability principle is the requirement for organizations to assess the impact of AI systems on people, organizations, and society. This involves completing impact assessments early in the development process to evaluate potential risks and ethical considerations associated with the system's intended uses. Regular reviews and updates of these assessments are also mandated to ensure ongoing compliance and adherence to responsible AI principles.

Microsoft emphasizes the importance of transparency and communication with stakeholders regarding the capabilities and limitations of AI systems. This includes providing documentation to customers about the intended uses of the system as well as evidence demonstrating its fitness for purpose. In cases where evidence is lacking or refutes the system's suitability for a particular use, Microsoft advocates for prompt action to rectify the issue and communicate transparently with customers.

The accountability principle encompasses a comprehensive framework for ensuring transparency, fairness, and ethical oversight throughout the AI lifecycle. By adhering to these principles, Microsoft aims to build trust with stakeholders and promote the responsible use of AI technologies for the benefit of society.

Describe considerations for inclusiveness

Inclusive AI mandates the consideration of all peoples' experiences across the breadth of humanity. Adopting inclusive design practices enables developers to proactively identify and address potential barriers that might otherwise inadvertently exclude people.

AI systems are meant to empower and engage everyone, bringing benefits to all sectors of society, irrespective of physical ability, gender, sexual orientation, ethnicity, or other factors. Microsoft's commitment to inclusiveness in responsible AI development underscores the imperative of designing and deploying AI technologies in a manner that fosters diversity, equity, and inclusion. This principle reflects Microsoft's dedication to creating AI systems that are accessible and advantageous to all individuals, regardless of their background, identity, or abilities. Examples of inclusivity might include leveraging speech-to-text, text-to-speech, and visual recognition technologies to empower individuals with hearing, visual, and other sensory impairments. Actively seeking ways to include others commonly overlooked is a key component of inclusive design.

Central to Microsoft's inclusiveness principle is the acknowledgment of AI's potential to either exacerbate or mitigate existing inequalities. By prioritizing inclusivity in AI development, Microsoft aims to counter historical biases and promote fair and equitable outcomes for all users. This involves considering the diverse needs and perspectives of different demographic groups throughout the AI lifecycle.

A pivotal aspect of Microsoft's approach to inclusiveness in AI development is the promotion of diversity within the teams responsible for creating AI technologies. By fostering diverse teams representing various backgrounds, experiences, and viewpoints, Microsoft seeks to mitigate bias risks and ensure that AI systems are designed with inclusivity in mind. This diversity enables teams to identify and address potential biases and blind spots that might otherwise be overlooked. This same type of inclusivity exhibited in the design of the core technology should be extended to organizations leveraging AI to create solutions to ensure multiple viewpoints are considered.

Additionally, Microsoft advocates for inclusive design practices prioritizing accessibility and usability for all individuals, including those with disabilities or special needs. This entails integrating features such as alternative input methods, voice recognition, and screen readers into AI systems to ensure accessibility for individuals with diverse abilities.

Moreover, Microsoft emphasizes engaging with diverse stakeholders throughout the AI development process, including community organizations, advocacy groups, and individuals from marginalized communities. This collaboration facilitates gathering feedback and insights to inform the design and deployment of AI technologies, ensuring responsiveness to the needs and concerns of all users.

Microsoft's commitment to inclusiveness in responsible AI development underscores its dedication to building AI technologies that are inclusive, equitable, and accessible to all individuals. By prioritizing diversity, equity, and inclusion across the AI lifecycle, Microsoft aims to leverage AI's potential to drive positive social change and create a more inclusive future for everyone.

Describe considerations for reliability and safety

Microsoft's responsible AI principle of reliability and safety is foundational to ensuring that AI technologies are not only dependable but also safe for users and society at large. This principle emphasizes the necessity of developing AI systems that consistently deliver accurate results while minimizing the potential for harm or unintended consequences. At its core, it reflects Microsoft's commitment to building AI technologies that users can trust and rely on with confidence.

A crucial aspect of this principle is the rigorous testing and validation processes that organizations must establish to ensure that AI systems operate safely across a wide range of scenarios and conditions. By integrating methods such as A/B testing and champion/challenger approaches, organizations can effectively evaluate the performance of their AI systems and identify and address potential safety hazards or biases before deployment.

Microsoft underscores the importance of prioritizing safety within AI systems and mitigating risks to users and society. This involves proactive identification and mitigation of safety hazards, including biases, errors, or security vulnerabilities, to enhance user trust and confidence in AI-driven solutions. By promoting safety, Microsoft aims to build AI technologies that not only perform as intended but also prioritize the well-being of users.

By prioritizing transparency and accountability, Microsoft strongly promotes documenting the decision-making process, data sources, and algorithmic logic behind AI systems. This transparency enables effective oversight and auditability, empowering users and regulators to hold AI systems (and their creators) accountable for their actions and decisions.

Continuous monitoring and evaluation are essential components of Microsoft's strategy to maintain reliability and safety in AI systems. By implementing feedback mechanisms and continuous improvement processes, organizations can detect and address potential issues or failures in real time, ensuring that AI systems remain reliable and safe throughout their lifecycle. This proactive approach fosters a culture of continuous learning and adaptation, further enhancing the reliability and safety of AI technologies over time.

The commitment to reliability and safety in AI development underscores the importance in building trustworthy and dependable AI systems. By prioritizing transparency, accountability, and continuous improvement, Microsoft and other organizations can enhance user trust and confidence in AI-driven solutions while minimizing the risk of harm or unintended consequences.

These principles help ensure that AI solutions are developed in a way that is ethical, prioritizing inclusiveness and harm avoidance to benefit the people using the systems. In the next section, we'll look at principles that help people understand how an AI solution arrived at its conclusion.

Understand explainable principles

The concept of explainability in AI is crucial for data scientists, auditors, and business decision makers. It enables these stakeholders to understand and justify the decisions made by AI systems and the reasoning behind them. In terms of Microsoft's responsible AI principles, explainability covers three principles:

- Fairness, or the ability for the system to make decisions that don't discriminate or apply a bias toward groups or individuals based on identifiers such as gender, race, religion, or sexual orientation
- Transparency in understanding how a model arrived at its result
- Securing the data inputs and outputs to protect the privacy of both organization and personal data

Explainability is vital for ensuring compliance with company policies, industry standards, and government regulations. For data scientists, it involves being able to explain how they achieved specific levels of accuracy and what factors influenced the outcome. Auditors require tools that can validate AI models to comply with company policies, while business decision makers aim to build trust by providing transparent models.

Describe considerations for fairness

Microsoft's fairness principle in responsible AI development is crucial to ensure that AI systems do not discriminate or express bias against individuals based on gender, race, sexual orientation, or religion. To achieve this, Microsoft provides an AI fairness checklist that offers guidance across various stages of AI system development, including envisioning, prototyping, building, launching, and evolving. This checklist includes recommended due-diligence activities to minimize the impact of unfairness in the system.

> **Further reading**
>
> Organizations are encouraged to use the Fairlearn toolkit to closely assess the fairness of their models throughout the development process, making fairness assessment an integral part of data science workflows. You can learn more about Fairlearn at `https://fairlearn.org/` and read the original Microsoft Fairlearn research paper at `https://www.microsoft.com/en-us/research/publication/fairlearn-a-toolkit-for-assessing-and-improving-fairness-in-ai/`.

Microsoft's fairness principle highlights the importance it places on promoting equal opportunities and outcomes for all individuals, irrespective of their background or identity. It emphasizes the need to mitigate biases and ensure that AI technologies do not exacerbate existing inequalities within society. This involves proactive measures to identify, mitigate, and monitor biases throughout the AI lifecycle, including implementing fairness-aware algorithms and conducting bias assessments.

Ongoing monitoring and evaluation play a vital role in detecting and addressing potential biases or unfairness in real-time. In its Responsible AI Standard, Microsoft emphasizes the importance of feedback mechanisms, reporting, and continuous improvement to ensure that AI systems remain fair and equitable throughout their lifecycle. By fostering a culture of continuous learning and adaptation, Microsoft aims to enhance the fairness and equity of AI technologies over time.

> **Further reading**
> You can read Microsoft's Responsible AI Standard document at `https://query.prod.cms.rt.microsoft.com/cms/api/am/binary/RE5cmFl`.

Transparency and accountability are essential components of Microsoft's approach to ensuring fairness in AI systems. Microsoft advocates for documenting data sources, decision-making processes, and algorithmic logic to enable effective oversight and auditability. By promoting transparency in understanding the algorithms for fairness, adopting Microsoft's responsible AI principles provides users and regulators the means to hold AI systems accountable for their actions and decisions.

Describe considerations for transparency

Up to this point, you've seen the concept of transparency woven throughout several of Microsoft's responsible AI principles. Microsoft's responsible AI principle of transparency is key to ensuring that AI systems are accountable, understandable, and trustworthy. It involves providing visibility into the inner workings of AI systems, including their data sources, decision-making processes, and algorithmic logic. By promoting transparency, Microsoft aims to empower users, regulators, and stakeholders to comprehend and scrutinize AI systems, thereby fostering trust and accountability in their operation.

At its core, Microsoft's transparency principle acknowledges users' rights to understand how AI systems make decisions that impact them. This encompasses comprehending the factors influencing recommendations, predictions, and outcomes generated by AI models—as well as the fact that AI models are being used to deliver those results. Transparency enables users to make informed decisions and assess the reliability and fairness of AI-driven solutions.

Transparency extends to documenting the data used to train AI models, ensuring its quality, diversity, and representativeness. This enables users to evaluate the robustness and generalizability of AI systems across different demographics and use cases. Additionally, transparency encompasses the methods employed for data collection, labeling, and processing, ensuring accountability and fairness in handling sensitive information.

Microsoft advocates for clear and accessible communication about AI systems to facilitate understanding among diverse audiences. This includes providing documentation, explanations, and user interfaces that are easy to comprehend and navigate. By demystifying AI technologies, Microsoft aims to bridge the gap between technical experts and non-experts, promoting transparency and inclusivity in the AI ecosystem.

Microsoft's transparency principle reaffirms the company's dedication to building AI systems that are transparent, accountable, and understandable to users and stakeholders. By prioritizing transparency throughout the AI lifecycle, Microsoft seeks to enhance trust, foster collaboration, and promote responsible AI development.

Describe considerations for privacy and security

As both our personal and business lives move more online, data (and being assured of its security and our privacy) becomes an increasingly important commodity. Microsoft's responsible AI principle of privacy and security is important to ensuring that AI systems uphold individuals' rights to privacy and safeguard sensitive information from unauthorized access or misuse. This principle emphasizes the importance of protecting personal data throughout the AI lifecycle, from data collection to processing and storage. By prioritizing privacy and security, Microsoft aims to build AI systems that inspire trust and confidence among users and stakeholders.

The principle of privacy and security acknowledges the significance of preserving individuals' privacy rights in the digital age. This entails implementing robust security measures to prevent data breaches, unauthorized access, and other security threats that could compromise personal information. By protecting privacy, Microsoft seeks to uphold both ethical standards and legal obligations.

Microsoft supports privacy-preserving technologies and practices that enable AI systems to analyze and derive insights from data without compromising individuals' privacy. This includes techniques such as **differential privacy**, **federated learning**, and **homomorphic encryption**, which enable data analysis while preserving the confidentiality of sensitive information. By integrating privacy-preserving technologies, Microsoft aims to mitigate privacy risks and enhance user confidence in AI-driven solutions.

> **What is homomorphic encryption?**
> Homomorphic encryption is a new type of encryption technology that allows computations and calculations to be performed on encrypted data without actually decrypting the data first. Because the data isn't decrypted, potentially sensitive data isn't exposed.

Privacy and security considerations extend beyond technical measures to encompass organizational policies, governance frameworks, and regulatory compliance. Microsoft emphasizes the importance of adopting a privacy-by-design approach, where privacy considerations are embedded into the design and development of AI systems from the outset. This involves conducting privacy impact assessments, implementing privacy-enhancing controls, and ensuring transparency about data practices and usage.

> **What is differential privacy?**
>
> Differential privacy is an obfuscation technique that introduces statistical noise into each result to mask data points—typically, data points that could be used to identify an individual or group of people. The noise is small enough to protect individuals but not large enough to make a statistical impact. For more information on differential privacy concepts, see `https://cloudblogs.microsoft.com/opensource/2020/05/19/new-differential-privacy-platform-microsoft-harvard-opendp/`.

Transparency and accountability also play an important role in the privacy and security space. Transparency is necessary in all phases of data handling practices, including clear communication about data collection, processing purposes, and user rights.

Summary

In this chapter, you learned about Microsoft's guiding principles for responsible AI development and usage, including accountability, inclusiveness, fairness, and transparency. In order to live up to the vision of empowering individuals, AI and AI-based solutions must be developed in a way that benefits society.

In the next chapter, you'll discover common machine learning techniques.

Exam Readiness Drill – Chapter Review Questions

Apart from a solid understanding of key concepts, being able to think quickly under time pressure is a skill that will help you ace your certification exam. That is why working on these skills early on in your learning journey is key.

Chapter review questions are designed to improve your test-taking skills progressively with each chapter you learn and review your understanding of key concepts in the chapter at the same time. You'll find these at the end of each chapter.

> **Before You Proceeds**
>
> If you don't have a Packt Library subscription or you haven't purchased this book from the Packt store, you will need to unlock the online resources to access the exam readiness drills. Unlocking is free and needs to be done only once. To learn how to do that, head over to the chapter titled *Chapter 12, Accessing the Online Resources*.

To open the Chapter Review Questions for this chapter, perform the following steps:

1. Click the link – `https://packt.link/AI-900_CH02`.

    Alternatively, you can scan the following QR code (*Figure 2.1*):

Figure 2.1– QR code that opens Chapter Review Questions for logged-in users

2. Once you log in, you'll see a page similar to the one shown in *Figure 2.2*:

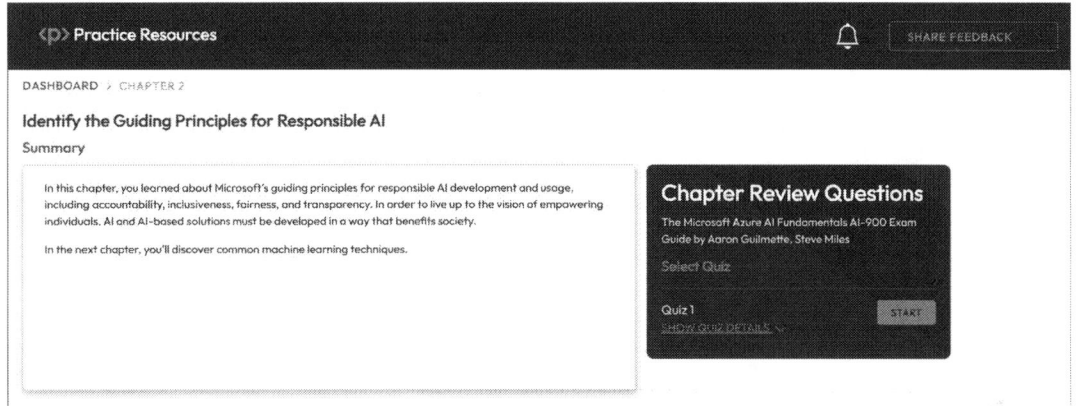

Figure 2.2 – Chapter Review Questions for Chapter 2

3. Once ready, start the following practice drills, re-attempting the quiz multiple times.

Exam Readiness Drill

For the first three attempts, don't worry about the time limit.

ATTEMPT 1

The first time, aim for at least **40%**. Look at the answers you got wrong and read the relevant sections in the chapter again to fix your learning gaps.

ATTEMPT 2

The second time, aim for at least **60%**. Look at the answers you got wrong and read the relevant sections in the chapter again to fix any remaining learning gaps.

ATTEMPT 3

The third time, aim for at least **75%**. Once you score 75% or more, you start working on your timing.

> **Tip**
> You may take more than **three** attempts to reach 75%. That's okay. Just review the relevant sections in the chapter till you get there.

Working On Timing

Your aim is to keep the score the same while trying to answer these questions as quickly as possible. Here's an example of how your next attempts should look like:

Attempt	Score	Time Taken
Attempt 5	77%	21 mins 30 seconds
Attempt 6	78%	18 mins 34 seconds
Attempt 7	76%	14 mins 44 seconds

Table 2.1 – Sample timing practice drills on the online platform

> **Note**
> The time limits shown in the above table are just examples. Set your own time limits with each attempt based on the time limit of the quiz on the website.

With each new attempt, your score should stay above **75%** while your "time taken" to complete should "decrease". Repeat as many attempts as you want till you feel confident dealing with the time pressure.

Part 2: Describe the Fundamental Principles of Machine Learning on Azure

After learning about some of the foundational concepts and workloads of AI, it's time to delve into the principles behind machine learning—and, more specifically, machine learning on Azure. You'll learn about machine learning concepts and capabilities.

This part includes the following chapters:

- *Chapter 3, Identify Common Machine Learning Techniques*
- *Chapter 4, Describe Core Machine Learning Concepts*
- *Chapter 5, Describe Azure Machine Learning Capabilities*

3

Identify Common Machine Learning Techniques

So far, we've introduced you to AI technologies (such as computer vision or generative AI) as well as Microsoft's principles for responsible AI. Now, it's time to start talking about the substance of AI.

One of the most important questions you might have about AI is how AI manages to know what it does. Just as humans learn, AI systems have been designed to be capable of learning. And, just like humans learn through a variety of mechanisms (such as memorization and practice or repetition), AI systems also learn through different techniques and scenarios.

To be honest, though, the term **machine learning** is a bit of a misnomer. Since computers aren't exactly sentient at this point, one might argue that they're not capable of really learning. What they are capable of, however, is something quite useful: examining vast data sets to establish patterns and predict outcomes. Humans can sometimes be pretty good at recognizing patterns for small data sets. Once the data set includes tens of thousands or millions of data points, it becomes much more difficult for a human to keep up—and this is where machine learning excels.

The core idea of machine learning is looking at these vast data sets and predicting outcomes or values of similar actions or scenarios. Examples of machine learning might include the following:

- A power company combining historical weather patterns and historical energy usage to estimate the load on an electric grid
- An insurance company using miles driven, whether driven hours are daylight or nighttime, and driver age to predict the likelihood of an accident
- A biologist researcher using visual data of animals to automate the identification of known species observed on cameras and highlight potentially unknown species

In each of these cases, an AI system is trained on known data sets and then either asked questions or exposed to new data and is instructed to apply its past observations on the new data or queries to come up with new outputs or results.

In this chapter, we'll cover some of the high-level concepts related to machine learning. The objectives and skills we'll cover in this chapter include the following:

- Identify regression machine learning scenarios
- Identify classification machine learning scenarios
- Identify clustering machine learning scenarios
- Identify features of deep learning techniques

By the end of this chapter, you should be able to identify and describe some of the common machine learning scenarios.

First, let's establish a little background information on machine learning.

Understanding machine learning terminology

As you've already learned, machine learning is another way to think about predicting outcomes based on observed data sets.

Machine learning models are essentially software applications that use mathematical functions to calculate output values based on input values. This process involves two main phases: **training** and **inferencing**.

Training

During training, the model learns to predict output values based on input values by analyzing past observations. These past observations include both the **features** (input values) and **labels** (output values).

In a typical scenario, features are represented as variables denoted by x, while labels are denoted by y. Features can consist of multiple values, forming a **vector** represented by *[x1, x2, x3, ...],y*. For example, in predicting bottled water sales based on weather, weather measurements are features (x) and the number of bottles sold is the label (y).

An **algorithm** is then applied to the data to establish a relationship between the features and labels, creating a calculation to predict the label based on the features. The choice of algorithm depends on the type of predictive problem being addressed. The outcome is a **model** represented by a function *f*, where $y = f(x)$.

> **What are vectors and algorithms, anyway?**
>
> Vectors, foundational units of algebra, are essentially **tuples** (or collections) of values. These groups of values can be thought of as being similar to an array, though tuples can contain mixed data types such as strings, floating point numbers, and integers.
>
> At a high level, an algorithm is a set of functions, rules, formulas, or processes that an AI system uses to analyze data, discover insights, and predict outcomes. Algorithms represent the math that enables machine learning.

The learning part of machine learning can be divided into two types: **supervised** and **unsupervised**. Each of these types has a variety of algorithms and processes associated with them.

Supervised machine learning techniques

Supervised machine learning encompasses algorithms that learn from data containing both input features and corresponding target labels. The goal is to uncover patterns that link the input features to their outcomes, enabling the model to forecast outcomes for new, unseen data. Let's look at types of supervised learning techniques:

Regression

Regression-based learning is designed to identify and understand the relationship between independent and dependent variables and is frequently used to make business projections. Regression is a type of supervised learning where the output is a continuous number. Examples include the following:

- Predicting bottled water sales based on weather conditions such as temperature
- Estimating a dealership's vehicle sales prices from amount of available inventory and previous sales prices

Classification

Classification uses an algorithm to assign the training data to categories. Classification identifies or recognizes entities in the training data and attempts to draw conclusions about how the entities are defined or labeled. Classification involves categorizing data points into distinct classes:

- **Binary classification**: This predicts one of two possible outcomes. Examples include diagnosing diabetes from health metrics, assessing loan default risk from financial history, and predicting marketing response from consumer profiles.
- **Multiclass classification**: This predicts which one of several classes an observation belongs to. For instance, classifying an animal species based on physical features or a movie's genre from its production details. Unlike binary classification, a single observation in multiclass classification is assigned to one exclusive category.

Algorithms

As you've already learned, algorithms are the mathematical formulas used to process data. From a supervised learning perspective, these algorithms are commonly used:

- **AdaBoost** and **gradient boosting**: These methods enhance the accuracy of simple models by aggregating them into a more robust model. By sequentially correcting errors of a basic model using additional weak models, they collectively improve prediction accuracy. Boosting models can be applied to both classification and regression problems.

- **Artificial Neural Networks** (**ANNs**): ANNs are inspired by the human brain's neural networks and are foundational to deep learning. They process data through interconnected units called neurons, learning to recognize patterns and make decisions over time. ANNs are used in a variety of contexts, such as natural language processing, speech and image recognition, and game-playing (such as chess and Go).

- **Decision trees**: These algorithms predict outcomes or classify data by breaking down decisions into a tree-like structure of choices. Decision trees are transparent, making them easier to understand and validate compared to more opaque models such as neural networks. You might picture a decision tree as a type of flow chart, as shown in *Figure 3.1*:

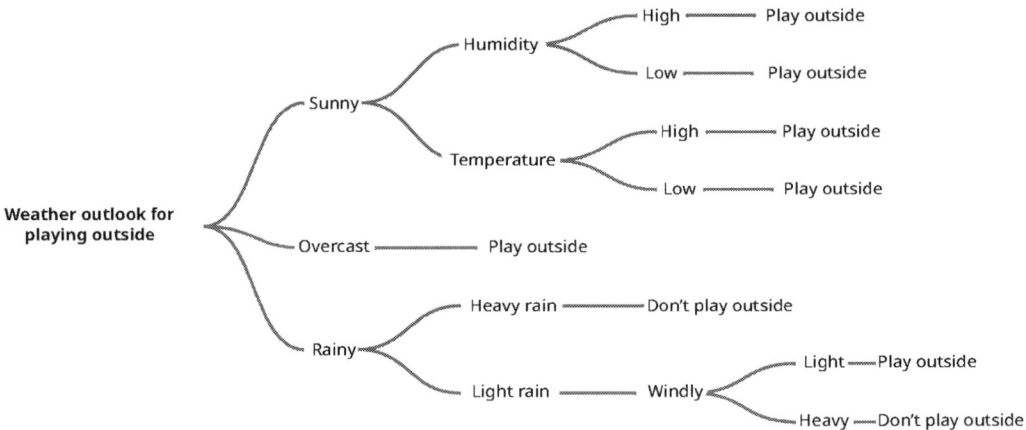

Figure 3.1 – Example of a simple decision tree

- **Dimensionality reduction**: This technique reduces the complexity of data by decreasing the number of input features, focusing on retaining only the most relevant information. Principal component analysis is a common method used for this purpose.

- **K-Nearest Neighbor** (**KNN**): KNN classifies data points based on the closest neighboring points in the data set. It calculates the distance (often Euclidean) between points and assigns a category based on the most common category among its nearest neighbors. KNN makes predictions based on the majority or average value of the nearest data points.

- **Linear regression**: This approach models the relationship between a dependent variable and one or more independent variables to predict continuous outcomes. Simple linear regression involves just one independent and one dependent variable. An example of a linear regression might be predicting house prices based on its square footage.

- **Logistic regression**: Used for binary outcomes (e.g., yes/no, true/false), logistic regression models the probability of a categorical dependent variable based on one or more independent variables, ideal for binary classification tasks. Logistic regression can be used in spam email detection by building a model based on the features of messages such as keywords that indicate spam content, source IP address, length of the email, volume of misspelled words, or other characteristics.

- **Naïve Bayes**: Based on Bayes' theorem, this technique assumes independence among predictors and is effective for text classification, spam detection, and recommendation systems. Variants include multinomial, Bernoulli, and Gaussian Naïve Bayes. Bayes algorithms are frequently used in text classification tasks such as spam detection and sentiment analysis.

- **Random forests**: This ensemble method uses multiple decision trees to make more reliable and accurate predictions by averaging their results, effectively reducing overfitting and variance in predictions. A common use case of a random forest algorithm might be detecting if a customer is likely to leave a subscription service (or churn) based on a number of features (number of calls made to support, length of calls, length of subscription service, telemetry data of how often the service used). Each of those features can be evaluated in a decision tree and then used together to predict a customer's churn potential.

- **Support Vector Machines (SVM)**: SVMs are used for classification and regression by finding the optimal boundary (hyperplane) that maximizes the margin or distance between different classes of data points, enhancing the model's discriminative power. Imagine you have a collection of points on a graph that you need to divide into two groups. An SVM would determine how to draw a line that best separates them. The optimal line path would be one that divides the points on the plane, maximizing the gaps between the line and points. See *Figure 3.2* for a very simple example:

Figure 3.2 – Simple representation of a support vector machine model

> **Further reading**
>
> While you won't see all of these individual algorithms on the AI-900 exam, they're neat to learn about. You can explore the basic mathematical concepts behind many of these algorithms at sites such as `https://machinelearningmastery.com/a-tour-of-machine-learning-algorithms/` and `https://www.kdnuggets.com/a-beginner-guide-to-the-top-10-machine-learning-algorithms`.

Unsupervised machine learning techniques

Unsupervised learning models are trained on data without labels, aiming to find underlying patterns or groupings in the data based on similarities.

Clustering is a primary technique in unsupervised learning that groups data points based on feature similarities. Examples include categorizing different types of flowers or segmenting customers by purchasing habits. Unlike classification, clustering does not require pre-defined categories; the algorithm identifies these groups autonomously. Clustering can also be a preliminary step to define classes for a subsequent classification model, such as segmenting customers into categories for targeted marketing strategies.

Semi-supervised machine learning techniques

Semi-supervised learning occupies a space between supervised and unsupervised learning. This technique combines both aspects of supervised learning (providing labeled input data) as well as unsupervised learning (training with unlabeled data).

Inferencing

Once the training phase is complete, the model can be used for **inferencing** or making predictions. The model acts as a software program encapsulating the learned function, allowing users to input feature values and receive predictions of corresponding labels. The predicted label is represented by $\hat{y}$ (pronounced "y-hat") to distinguish it from observed values.

Understanding machine learning involves grasping these fundamental concepts of training and inferencing, as well as recognizing the role of algorithms in establishing predictive relationships between features and labels. By applying mathematical functions to data, machine learning models can make predictions and facilitate decision-making in various domains, from weather forecasting to medical diagnosis.

Identify regression machine learning scenarios

Regression models aim to forecast numerical outcomes using training data that encompasses input features along with their corresponding target values. The development of a regression model, as with any supervised learning approach, unfolds through several cycles. In each cycle, you select a suitable algorithm—often configurable with various parameters—to build the model. You then assess how well the model predicts outcomes and adjust it by experimenting with alternative algorithms and tuning the parameters. This iterative process continues until the model reaches a satisfactory level of prediction accuracy.

The overall process for regression training is as follows:

1. Divide the training data randomly to form a training set for model development, reserving a portion for model validation. For example, consider setting aside 30-50% of the training data to test against later.
2. Employ a fitting algorithm, such as linear regression for regression models, to construct the model based on the training set.
3. Then, use the set aside validation data from *step 1* to evaluate the model's effectiveness by making predictions and comparing these predicted values against the actual labels in the validation set.
4. Summarize the discrepancies between predicted and actual values to derive a performance metric reflecting the model's prediction accuracy.
5. Iterate this train–validate–evaluate cycle, experimenting with various algorithms and settings, until the model's performance matches your expectations.

Through these steps, you can build regression models to predict a number of real-world scenarios.

Example

Earlier, we discussed an example of predicting bottled water sales based on how warm it is. To see how regression training works, let's dive into the bottled water sales example.

Let's say you want to predict, based on the outside temperature, how many bottles of water you anticipate selling. This would be important to you as a vendor since it helps you understand how much you need to stock to meet the demand.

First, you need to gather historical data that will be used to train the model (as well as validate the model later). Take the following sample data set in *Table 3.1*—it captures two critical pieces of data: how many bottles of water sold (y) at a given temperature (x):

Sample	Temperature (x)	Bottled water sales (y)
1	50	0
2	53	1
3	62	5
4	63	7
5	65	9
6	68	12
7	70	18
8	74	22
9	77	28
10	84	36
11	64	7
12	78	33
13	81	34
14	79	31
15	54	2

Table 3.1 – Bottled water sales

The next step is to select the amount of data that we'll use for training and the amount we'll set aside for validation and testing. Let's go ahead and take the first 10 rows for training our fictional model, leaving the last 5 rows for validation.

In this case, an easy way to understand the relationship between temperature and bottles of water sold is to plot them on a simple graph, as shown in *Figure 3.3*.

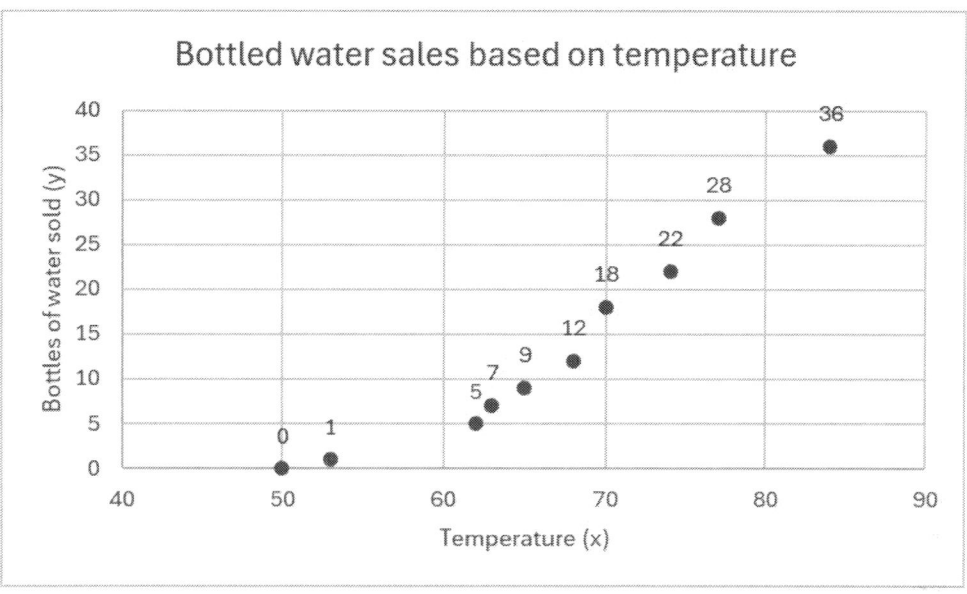

Figure 3.3 – Temperature and bottles of water sold plotted on a graph

Through the training process, an algorithm applies a formula or function to calculate the value of *y* from the value of *x*. In this case, the algorithm used would be one of linear regression—one that calculates a straight line through the points. See *Figure 3.4*:

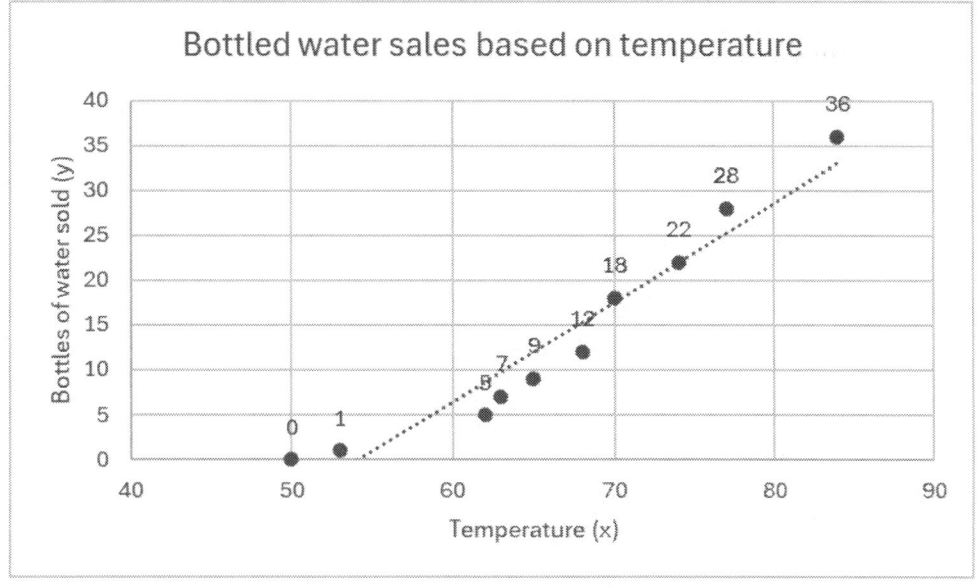

Figure 3.4 – Linear regression

As you can see from the graph, for every degree of change, the historical data trends upward. The slope can be expressed using the equation $y = 1.11x - 60.02$, where x is the temperature and y is the number of water bottles sold. Put another way, starting at 60 degrees, for every 1 degree increase in temperature, the number of water bottles sold increases by 1.11.

Given this formula that's been developed, the next step is to test the formula based on the remaining data in the training set. In this example, the additional data left in the training set has been plotted on the same graph and a linear regression run against them as well:

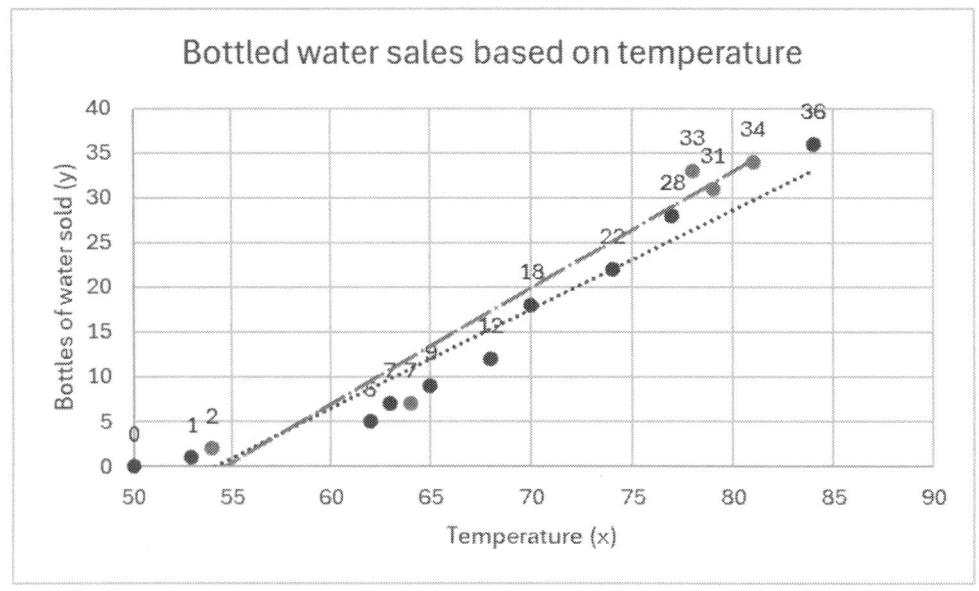

Figure 3.5 – Validation data set composited on to original graph

To test the formula, you could take a value from the held back training data (such as 81 degrees) and project the number of water bottles sold by calculating $y = 1.11(81) - 60.02$, which results in 30 water bottles (or 29.91 rounded up to the next whole number).

You can repeat that process for every temperature value held back in the data set, using the function to calculate a prediction for the number of water bottles sold. See *Table 3.2* for an example:

Sample	Temperature	Bottles of water sold	Prediction
11	64	7	12
12	78	33	27
13	81	34	29
14	79	31	28
15	54	2	0

Table 3.2 – Predicting the water bottles sold with the training data

How do you express the accuracy of the model? If you're not sure how accurate your model is, read on! There are a few metrics that can be used to help understand how accurate (or inaccurate) the model and its predictions are.

Evaluation metrics

Evaluation metrics are statistical formulas used to evaluate the validity of predictions against a data set.

Mean Absolute Error (MAE)

This **mean absolute error** (**MAE**) represents how many units of variance there are (either positive or negative) on average. For example, in sample *11* from *Table 3.2*, the prediction was to sell 12 bottles of water. The actual value sold (based on the training data) was seven, meaning that the prediction was five units higher than actual. This variance is known as the **absolute error**. In sample 12, the prediction was for 27 bottles to be sold, but the actual number sold was 33 (6 units higher, or an absolute error of 6).

To calculate the MAE, add up all the absolute error values and divide by the number of samples in the validation set. In this case:

Sample	Bottles of water sold	Prediction ($\hat{y}$)	Absolute error
11	7	12	5
12	33	27	6
13	34	29	5
14	31	28	4
15	2	0	2

Table 3.3 – Absolute error table

The total of all of the absolute errors is 22, and the number of items in the validation set was 5, resulting in an MAE for the validation set of 4.4 (22 divided by 5).

Mean squared error

One of the drawbacks of the mean absolute error is that it treats all discrepancies equally. While the overall average error rate may be acceptable, there are industries or scenarios where it's more desirable to have more (but smaller) errors as opposed to fewer (but larger) errors. For example, with fresh produce, it's very undesirable to overstock because you have a higher likelihood of having to throw away larger quantities of expired food.

The **mean squared error** (MSE) functions as a measure of the quality of the model itself. This metric gives individual errors more weight—and larger error predictions in the training data result in a much higher MSE.

To calculate this, each absolute error value is squared, and then the sum of those values is averaged. Using the training data output in *Table 3.3*, the mean squared error value is 21.2, highlighting the fact that the model may need tweaking or more training data.

Root Mean Squared Error (RMSE)

The next metric is **root mean squared error**, which is the square root of the MSE. While the MSE provides a measure of the quality of the predictor function, the RMSE is converted back to the original unit, making it a little easier to interpret and communicate the model's performance. RMSE is sensitive to outliers and gives relatively high weight to large errors. Like MSE, a smaller RMSE indicates a better fit.

With our validation data set, the RMSE is 4.6.

Coefficient of determination

The **coefficient of determination**, known as R^2, measures how well a statistical model predicts the actual outcome. It's a score between 0 and 1 that tells us the percentage of the variation in our target variable (what we're trying to predict) that can be explained by the model. A score of 1 means the model predicts perfectly, with no difference between predicted and actual values, while a score of 0 means the model doesn't explain any of the variation.

An R^2 closer to 1 indicates a model that fits our data well, suggesting a strong relationship between our input variables and the outcome. However, a high R^2 alone doesn't guarantee that the model is accurate or useful for making predictions, especially in complex models with many variables. It's essential to look beyond R^2 to ensure the model isn't just fitting the noise in our data (overfitting), which could lead to misleading results. So, while R^2 is a helpful indicator of model fit, it's just one piece of the puzzle in evaluating a model's performance.

The coefficient of determination for our sample validation data set is 0.898—essentially 89.8% accurate.

Based on that, it appears that our model may be pretty good (for bottled water). Since bottled water isn't as perishable of a product as say, strawberries, stocking a little extra water likely won't result in a product loss.

If, however, we were talking about more volatile products, you would probably perform some **iterative training** (that is repeated training sessions) by varying the input data sets, regression algorithms, and algorithm **hyperparameters** (parameters that control how the algorithm works, as opposed to the data supplied to the algorithm) to come up with a function that more accurately predicts the sales outcomes.

Applications

So where is regression machine learning useful? As you can see from the bottled water example, it's useful for making a number of predictions, especially when projecting sales, quotas, housing prices, stock prices, and other forecasting activities. It's also useful in analyzing user trends for advertising or media services.

Identify classification machine learning scenarios

Classification is a supervised machine learning technique that essentially puts values into groups (classes) based on a criteria. There are two main types of classification techniques: binary and multiclass. Let's look at both of them.

Binary classification

You may have heard the terminology **binary** before and know that it's the language of ones and zeroes that computers use to process information. Binary simply means that a data item can be set to one of two values. For example, 0 or 1 and true or false are binary selections.

In the machine learning context, binary classification works similarly—using the value of a feature (x, just like in regression machine learning), the model predicts whether a label (y) is 0 or 1. Binary classification categories data into mutually exclusive groups based on the feature data.

Example

Let's look at a sample data set that might be used for training a binary classification model on whether a patient might be at risk of heart disease based on their LDL cholesterol level. Just like the regressive data set we looked at earlier, we'll have a feature (x) column containing data measurements and a corresponding label (y):

Patient ID	LDL cholesterol level (x) (measured in mg/DL)	Heart disease (y) 0 = no, 1 = yes
1	100	0
2	87	0
3	132	0
4	159	1
5	152	1
6	171	1
7	188	1
8	161	0
9	118	0
10	141	0
11	102	1
12	144	0
13	155	1
14	167	1
15	142	1

Table 3.4 – Binary classification data for heart disease patients

Just as with the regression model techniques, there are many algorithms that can be used with binary classification. One popular algorithm is *logistic regression* (which, despite its name, is not an algorithm for regression-based models), which is typically identified by its sigmoid (S-shaped) function graph depicting values between 0 and 1. See *Figure 3.6*:

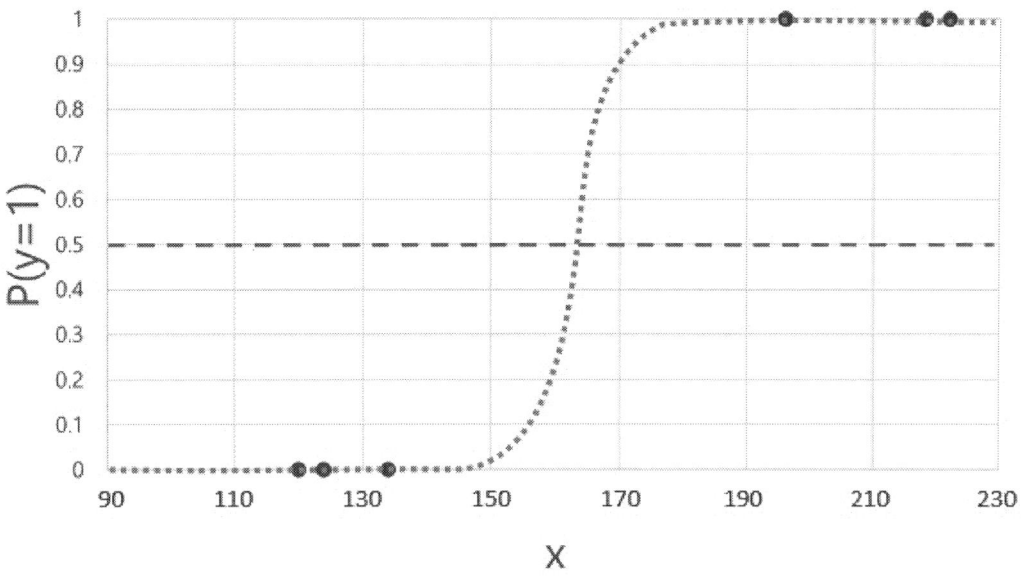

Figure 3.6 – An example of a Sigmoid function graph

Like a regression algorithm, the resultant function can be expressed mathematically. In the graph, the *y* axis represents the probability of a label being true (ranked 0 to 1), using the following expression:

f(x) = P(y=1 | x)

The training data set in *Table 3.4* shows seven patients that definitely do not have heart disease and eight patients that do. The graph depicted in *Figure 3.6* also shows an optional horizontal line that can indicate the **threshold** at which a prediction switches from false to true.

As with the regression model training, you should divide the dataset into two selections: one piece to be used for training and the other for validation.

Plugging the data into a simple binary classification function, you may plot a graph similar to the one in *Figure 3.7*.

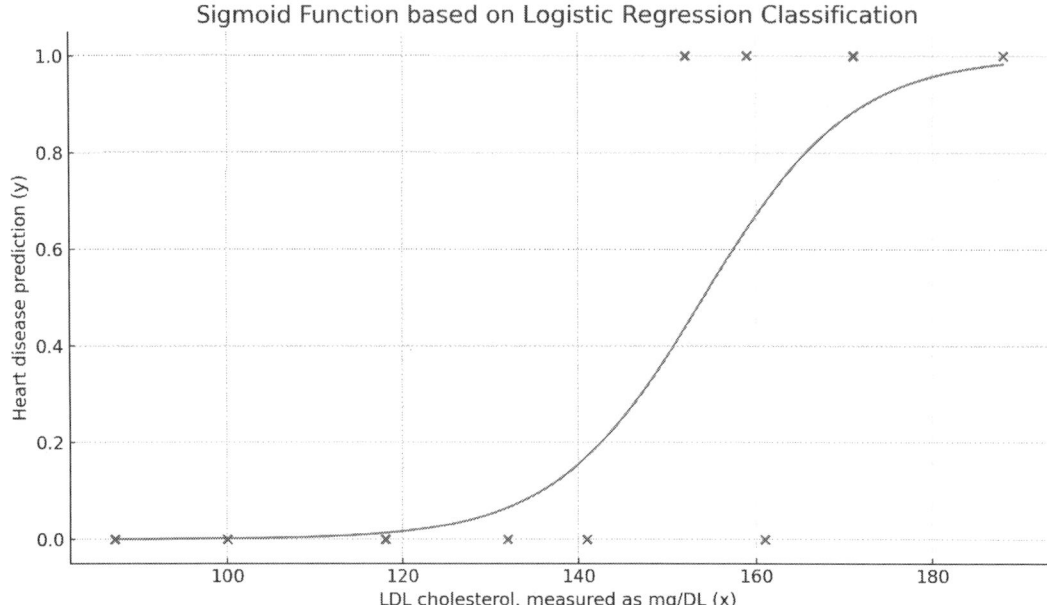

Figure 3.7 – A sample binary classification graph

In *Figure 3.7*, the plotted points indicate the patient's LDL cholesterol reading (plotted along the *x* axis)., and their location on the *y* axis indicates if the patient had heart disease or not, where 0 represents "no" and 1 represents "yes."

Using the same method for validating the algorithm with the reserved training data as we did with regression training, you can do the same thing with binary classification. With the model created, predicting heart disease based on the features (LDL cholesterol levels) should be easy:

Patient ID	LDL cholesterol level (x) (measured in mg/DL)	Prediction ($\hat{y}$)	Heart disease (y) 0 = no, 1 = yes
11	102	0	1
12	144	0	0
13	155	1	1
14	167	1	1
15	142	0	1

Table 3.5 – Predictions for heart disease based on cholesterol

Next, let's look at how to evaluate the data.

Evaluation metrics

When evaluating a model, it's important to be able to determine not only *where* the predictions were right and wrong but to understand *how* they were right or wrong. These results can be expressed in a graph called a **confusion matrix** or **confusion diagram**, as shown in *Figure 3.8*:

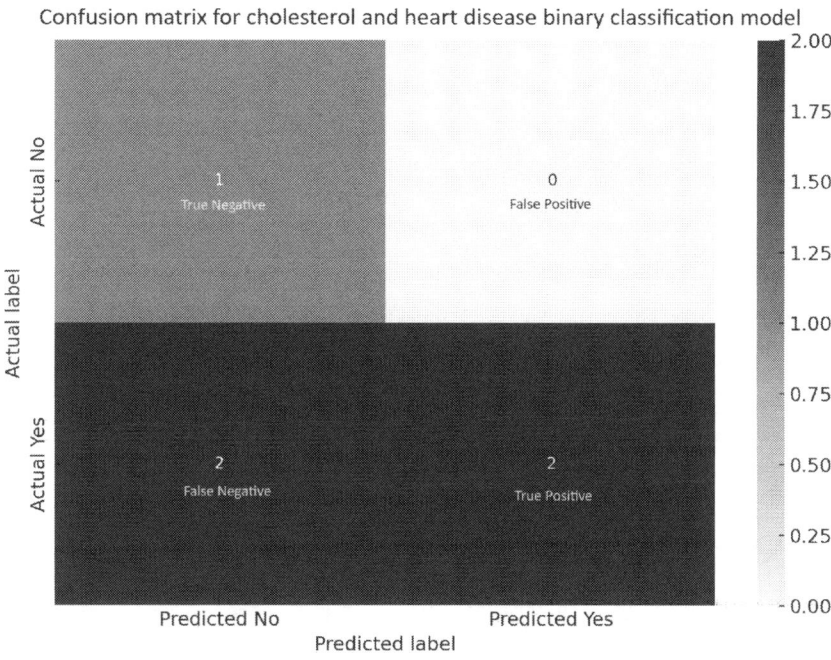

Figure 3.8 – Confusion matrix

The data is broken into four categories:

- **Actual Yes**: The training data said the patient had heart disease
- **Actual No**: The training data said the patient did not have heart disease
- **Predicted Yes**: The model predicted based on the cholesterol level that the patient would have heart disease
- **Predicted No**: The model predicted based on the cholesterol level that the patient would not have heart disease

Those are then laid out on a quadrant, and the intersections are labelled accordingly:

	Predicted No	**Predicted Yes**
Actual No	True negative	False positive
Actual Yes	False negative	True positive

Table 3.6 – Confusion matrix table

Here's how to interpret the values:

- **True Negatives** (**TN**): This is the number of instances where the model correctly predicted the absence of the condition (class 0). In our case, this would represent the number of patients correctly identified as not being at risk for heart disease.
- **False Positives** (**FP**): This is the number of instances where the model incorrectly predicted the presence of the condition (class 1). In our case, this would represent the number of patients incorrectly identified as being at risk for heart disease when they are not.
- **False Negatives** (**FN**): This is the number of instances where the model incorrectly predicted the absence of the condition (class 0). In our case, this would represent the number of patients who are actually at risk for heart disease but were incorrectly identified as not being at risk.
- **True Positives** (**TP**): This is the number of instances where the model correctly predicted the presence of the condition (class 1). In our case, this would represent the number of patients correctly identified as being at risk for heart disease.

These data points (the true negatives, true positives, false positives, and false negatives) can then be used to further evaluate how accurate the model is using several metrics.

Accuracy

Accuracy is used to describe how often the model is correct in general. The formula or computing accuracy is *(TP + TN) / (total)*. In this case, the accuracy of the model is 60%.

Recall

Recall (sometimes called **sensitivity**) indicates how well the model identifies the positive class (1, or in this case, patients at risk of heart disease). The formula is *TP / (TP + FN)*. The recall for class 1 (with heart disease) is 50%.

Precision

Precision is an indicator of how often the model is right for each class prediction. For the positive class, this formula is TP / (TP + FP). For class 1 (heart disease), the model correctly predicts 100% of the time.

Specificity

Specificity measures how often a model is right for the negative class (0, or in this case, patients without heart disease). The formula is *TN / (TN + FP)*. This model's specificity for the negative class is 33%, indicating that it is only correct 33% of the time when predicting that a patient will not have heart disease.

If there were discrepancies in prediction versus actual data, it could suggest areas where the model might need improvement, such as collecting more diverse data, using a different model, or tuning the existing model. Understanding where the model fails can help in reducing false positives (incorrectly predicting risk where there is none) and false negatives (missing out on identifying actual risk), which are particularly critical in medical diagnostics.

Applications

Binary classifications are most useful when there are a limited number of factors influencing a true or false outcome. It is common in fields such as medicine, biology, technology, and chemistry when you're trying to determine a yes/no or true/false result based on a small set of variables.

Common real-world examples of binary classification include the following:

- **Email spam detection**: Classifying emails as either spam or not spam. This is one of the most common applications of binary classification, used by email services to filter out unwanted messages.

- **Medical diagnosis**: Diagnosing patients with a disease or condition as either positive (having the disease) or negative (not having the disease). For example, binary classification models can be used to detect the presence of a tumor as malignant or benign based on medical imaging.

- **Credit approval**: Deciding whether to approve or decline a credit application. Financial institutions use binary classification algorithms to predict whether an applicant is likely to default on a loan.

- **Churn prediction**: Predicting whether a customer will churn (leave) or stay with a company or service. Companies use binary classification to identify at-risk customers and develop strategies to retain them.

- **Fraud detection**: Identifying transactions as fraudulent or legitimate. Banks and financial institutions use binary classification models to detect suspicious activities and prevent fraud.

- **Sentiment analysis**: Determining whether a piece of text (such as a product review or social media post) expresses a positive or negative sentiment. This is widely used in marketing and customer service to gauge public opinion and customer satisfaction.

- **Malware detection**: Classifying files or programs as malicious or safe, used by cybersecurity systems to protect computers and networks from viruses and other malicious software.

Multiclass classification

Shifting gears a little bit, let's look at multiclass classification. Like binary classification, it's a probability method that assigns a classification based on a feature. However, instead of using a single feature or a binary label (true/false, 0/1), it can use multiple features and multiple classifications. The underlying ideas are the same, but let's just look at a quick example of how it works.

Example

In this example, we'll be evaluating peppers and their heat (or Scoville heat unit rating). Every pepper has a heat rating, ranked in Scoville units, that describes how spicy it is.

The data in *Table 3.7* depicts a variety of peppers and their average Scoville heat units:

Scoville heat units	Pepper
1,500,000 – 2,200,000	Carolina Reaper
1,000,000 – 1,500,000	Trinidad Scorpion
855,000 – 1,000,000	Ghost pepper
350,000 – 577,000	Red Savina Habanero
100,000 – 350,000	Habanero
70,000 – 100,000	Charleston hot
30,000 – 50,000	Cayenne pepper
10,000 – 23,000	Serrano pepper
8,000 – 10,000	Hungarian pepper
2,000 – 7,000	Jalapeno pepper
0-100	Bell pepper

Table 3.7 – Selected peppers and their Scoville heat unit ratings

Now, just like the binary classification training, let's generate a sample table of features (Scoville heat unit ratings) and labels (peppers):

ID	Scoville heat unit (x)	Pepper (y)
1	1,900,000	Carolina reaper
2	10	Bell
3	2,850	Jalapeno
4	447,700	Red Savina
5	8,700	Hungarian
6	127,000	Habanero
7	88,000	Charleston hot
8	289,000	Habanero
9	0	Bell
10	900,000	Ghost
11	1,250,000	Scorpion
12	11,000	Serrano
13	42,000	Cayenne
14	7,000	Jalapeno
15	2,200,000	Carolina Reaper

Table 3.8 – Scoville rating sample data

Once the training data is assembled, it's time to use an algorithm to fit the training data to a function that will calculate the probability for our classes. There are 11 possible answers (classes) for our data set based on our training data. They're zero-indexed, meaning they're numbered from 0 to 10.

The most common algorithms in multiclass classification models are **one-vs-rest (OvR)** and **multinominal** algorithms.

- **One-vs-Rest (OvR) or One-vs-All (OvA)**: With this algorithm, you train a binary classification function for each class individually. Each function targets a specific class compared to any of the other classes in the set. In this case, since there are 11 pepper types represented, the algorithm would create 11 binary classification functions. Like the binary classifications previously, the algorithm produces a sigmoid function. The outcome of this model predicts the class for the function that results in the highest probability output. OvR or OvA strategies could be applied, for example, in a Carolina Reaper vs. all classifier—essentially determining if an element is a Carolina Reaper or not.
- **Multinomial**: This algorithm approaches the problem differently, creating a single function with a multivalued (or vector) output. This vector can contain a probability distribution across all the potential classes, though it's really designed for mutually exclusive data sets (for example, if a pepper's Scoville rating can't expand into another pepper's range). With a vector containing multiple elements, each class element is scored individually between 0 and 1, with the total adding up to 1.

These types of models may need more information to reliably predict. For example, review the sample data in *Table 3.7* for the Scoville pepper ratings. As you can see, there are a few instances where a pepper might have a similar heat rating to another pepper (either milder or spicier). A larger training data set would help the model understand concepts of frequency to help more accurately predict and select an appropriate classification strategy (depending on the factors you want to identify) would help you be most successful in this classification methodology.

Evaluation metrics

Since multiclass classification can really be looked at as an extension of binary classification (in many cases), the same techniques and terminology apply.

For example, with the training data, you could develop a confusion matrix. The layout is very similar to the confusion matrix for binary classification—it's just got more labels to deal with, as shown in *Figure 3.9*:

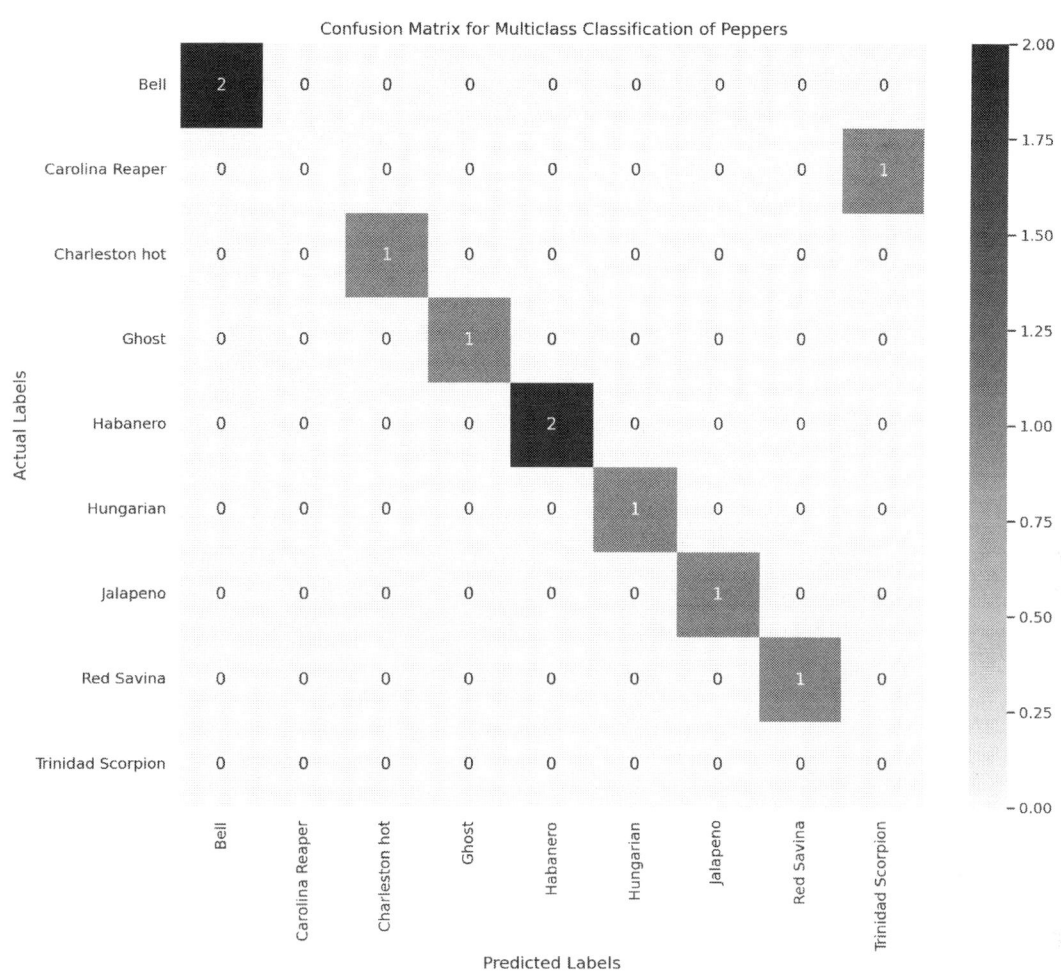

Figure 3.9 – Multiclass confusion matrix based on Scoville pepper data

Applications

Multiclass classification refers to the scenarios where you need to classify items into more than two categories. Unlike binary classification, which differentiates between two classes (such as yes/no or true/false), multiclass classification deals with situations where there are three or more classes.

Potential use cases include the following:

- **Predicting animal types**: Suppose you have a dataset containing images of animals and you want to classify each image as a dog, cat, bird, or fish. This is a multiclass classification problem with four classes.

- **Weather forecasting**: If you're predicting whether the weather will be sunny, cloudy, rainy, or snowy, you're dealing with multiclass classification.
- **Handwritten numeral recognition**: A classic example is the MNIST dataset, where the task is to classify images of handwritten digits into 10 classes (0 through 9).
- **Medical diagnosis**: Suppose a particular diagnostic test can indicate one of several different diseases. If you're developing a model to predict which specific disease (out of a possible set) a patient might have based on their symptoms and test results, you're engaging in multiclass classification.

In multiclass classification, techniques and metrics are slightly different from binary classification in that you have to consider how the model performs across all the different classes (not just two), but overall the process is very similar. Metrics such as precision and recall are calculated for each class and then averaged in some way (such as micro, macro, or weighted average) to understand the overall performance.

A classification's F1 score is a measure used to summarize the overall accuracy of a class. Previously, you learned about **precision** (ratio of correctly predicted positive observations to the total positives using the formula $P = TP / (TP+FP)$) and recall (ratio of correctly predicted positive observations to all the observations in the class, calculated using the formula $R = TP / (TP +FN)$).

An F1 score is calculated using the formula $F1 = 2 * (P * R) / (P + R)$.

Up to this point, you've been learning about **supervised learning** scenarios such as binary and multiclass classification. Next, we'll be shifting to unsupervised scenarios.

Identify clustering machine learning scenarios

Clustering is an unsupervised machine learning scenario where algorithms are employed to try to identify patterns in data. Unlike supervised learning, where training data has labels and features, unsupervised learning does not. The main goal of clustering is to be able to let the machine learning algorithms discover natural groupings within the data based on the similarities in the data points themselves.

Just as supervised learning had its algorithms, there are several popular algorithms available to use with clustering scenarios:

- **K-means clustering**: This algorithm partitions the data into *K* distinct, non-overlapping subsets (or clusters) based on the mean distance from the centroid of each cluster. The value of *K* needs to be specified beforehand.
- **Hierarchical clustering**: Builds a hierarchy of clusters either with a bottom-up approach (agglomerative) or a top-down approach (divisive). It does not require pre-specification of the number of clusters.
- **Density-Based Spatial Clustering of Applications with Noise (DBSCAN)**: Forms clusters based on the density of data points, capable of discovering clusters of arbitrary shape and handling noise and outliers effectively.

Example

Let's say we have some sample data from grocery shoppers; 15 shoppers have put the items (or features, in this case) depicted in *Table 3.9* in their baskets:

Basket Id	Bread (x1)	Milk (x2)	Eggs (x3)	Bananas (x4)	Chicken (x5)	Apples (x6)	Cheese (x7)	Tomatoes (x8)	Potatoes (x9)	Onions (x10)	Coffee (x11)	Lettuce (x12)
1	1	1	1	1	1	0	0	0	1	1	1	0
2	1	1	0	1	0	1	0	1	0	1	1	0
3	1	1	1	0	1	1	1	0	1	1	1	1
4	1	1	1	1	1	1	1	1	1	1	1	1
5	1	0	1	0	0	0	0	0	0	0	0	0
6	0	1	1	0	1	0	1	1	0	1	1	1
7	1	1	0	1	1	0	1	1	0	1	1	0
8	1	0	1	0	1	0	1	0	1	1	1	1
9	0	0	1	1	1	0	0	1	1	1	0	0
10	1	1	1	0	1	1	0	1	1	1	1	1
11	1	0	1	0	1	0	0	1	0	1	0	1
12	1	1	0	1	1	0	1	1	0	0	1	1
13	1	1	1	0	0	0	1	1	1	0	0	1
14	0	0	1	0	0	1	0	0	1	1	0	1
15	0	1	1	1	0	1	0	0	0	0	1	0

Table 3.9 – Example shopping baskets of food

In this example, we can instruct a K-means algorithm to partition the data into three groups of shopping baskets. Based on the output, we end up with the following three clusters:

- Cluster 0: Baskets 2, 5, 12, 15
- Cluster 1: Baskets 5, 9, 11, 14
- Cluster 2: Baskets 1, 3, 4, 6, 8, 10, 13

Here's how the K-means algorithm was applied to the dataset of grocery items purchased by shoppers:

1. First, the grocery items (such as bread, milk, eggs, etc.) were represented in a format suitable for machine learning algorithms. This was done using a binary representation where each item was encoded as 0 (not purchased) or 1 (purchased), as shown in *Table 3.9*. This binary matrix forms the dataset where each row represents a shopping basket and each column represents a different grocery item.

2. Next, we chose a number of clusters (or groups) that would be used for grouping the items. In this case, we set K to three, meaning we decided to group the shopping baskets into three distinct clusters based on the items they contained. The choice of K can be influenced by domain knowledge, experimentation, or other techniques and algorithms.

3. Once the prerequisites for the process are set, we then choose some random points on a graph. These points, called **centroids**, are the center points of the clusters being formed. In our case, three shopping baskets were randomly chosen as the initial centroids.

4. Each shopping basket (or row of our dataset) was then assigned to the nearest centroid. The "nearest" is typically determined by calculating the distance between the basket and each centroid. Each basket is assigned to the cluster whose centroid is closest to it, forming three initial clusters based on the current centroids.

> **Go the distance**
>
> There are many different methods for determining distance in clustering. The three most common types of distance calculations are **Euclidean**, **Hamming**, **Manhattan**, **Minkowski**, and **Jaccard**. Each type of distance is used for different types of data (for example, binary data versus linear or continuous numerical data). The good news is that none of these things appear on the exam, so you don't need to learn them. However, if you want to explore different mathematical foundations for determining clustering distance, see `https://www.displayr.com/understanding-cluster-analysis-a-comprehensive-guide/`.

5. Once all baskets have been assigned to clusters, the centroids of these clusters are recalculated. This is done by taking the mean (or average) of all baskets in each cluster. Since our data is binary, this average may not be exactly 0 or 1; it represents the proportion of baskets in the cluster that contain each item.

6. The steps of assigning baskets to the nearest centroid and then updating the centroids based on the current cluster memberships were repeated. With each iteration, baskets might shift from one cluster to another as the centroids change.

7. This process was repeated until the centroids no longer changed significantly between iterations, meaning that the clusters had stabilized and the algorithm had converged. This is the stopping criterion for K-means.

8. Once the algorithm converged, each shopping basket was assigned to one of the three clusters based on the items it contained. The final clusters represent groups of shopping baskets that are similar to each other based on the presence or absence of certain items.

In the context of our grocery item dataset, applying K-means allowed us to group shopping baskets into clusters that could potentially reflect different types of shopping patterns or preferences among customers. For example, one cluster might represent weekly staple shopping (including items such as bread, milk, and eggs), another might represent fresh produce shopping (including items such as fruits and vegetables), and another might represent specialty item shopping (such as coffee or cheese).

This type of information is frequently used by merchants to help understand buying habits and suggestive or upselling opportunities. If you've ever wondered how Amazon determines how items show up as suggested for you to buy or why you get certain coupons in the mail, clustering machine learning models were very likely involved at some point.

Evaluation metrics

Since there are no labels to compare against, evaluating the performance of clustering is less straightforward than supervised learning. However, metrics such as **silhouette score** (or **silhouette coefficient**), the **Davies-Bouldin index**, and the **Calinski-Harabasz index** can be used to assess the quality of clustering by measuring the distance between clusters and the density of the clusters themselves.

Silhouette score

The silhouette score or silhouette coefficient measures how well each data point fits within its final assigned cluster. The score ranges from -1 to 1, where values closer to 1 indicate better-defined, less-overlapping clusters.

- A score close to 1 indicates that the clusters are well apart from each other and clearly defined
- A score of 0 indicates that the clusters are overlapping
- A score close to -1 indicates that the clusters are assigned inappropriately

In this case, this model's silhouette score is 0.128, which suggests that the clusters are overlapping or might not be distinctly separated. That can be expected with this type of data (a grocery shopping list), since shoppers use items at different rates and have different needs than each other, leading them to complex purchase decisions that might result in them buying the same things but for different reasons.

Davies-Bouldin index

The **Davies-Bouldin index** is used to measure the quality of clustering, where lower scores indicate better clustering.

The Davies-Bouldin index score for our grocery basket K-means clustering model is approximately 1.65. The score essentially evaluates the average similarity between each cluster and its most similar cluster, where similarity is a measure that combines the compactness (how close the points in a cluster are to each other) and the separation (how far apart different clusters are from each other) of the clusters.

A lower Davies-Bouldin index indicates that the clusters are compact (i.e., the points within each cluster are close to each other) and well-separated (i.e., the clusters are far apart from each other). Conversely, a higher score suggests less distinct clusters.

Generally, scores closer to 0 are more desirable.

Calinski-Barabasz index

The **Calinski-Harabasz index**, also known as the Variance Ratio Criterion, does not have a fixed range such as some other metrics (such as the silhouette score, which goes from -1 to 1). Instead, its value depends on the dataset's characteristics, including the number of samples, dimensions, and the inherent cluster structure. The Calinski-Harabasz index score for this model is 3.10.

A higher Calinski-Harabasz index score indicates that the clusters are dense (meaning points within a cluster are close to each other) and well-separated (meaning clusters are far apart from each other). This is interpreted as a model with a better-defined cluster structure. Unlike metrics such as accuracy, which ranges from 0 to 1, or the silhouette score, which has a theoretical range from -1 to 1, the Calinski-Harabasz index does not have a maximum value and is not bounded in a fixed range. Its absolute value is less informative without context.

The index is most useful when it's being used to compare different clustering models or configurations on the same dataset. For example, comparing the scores obtained from clustering the same data with different numbers of clusters (K) can help in choosing the best K by selecting the one with the highest Calinski-Harabasz score. In this example, we told the model to group the grocery baskets into three clusters. To effectively use the Calinski-Harabasz score, it would be useful to re-run the model breaking the baskets into two, four, or five clusters.

For example, after rerunning the K-means algorithm with parameters for two, four, and five clusters, the following scores were achieved:

- Two clusters: 2.997
- Four clusters: 2.73
- Five clusters: 2.504

In practice, because there is no fixed "good" threshold, the best approach is to use the Calinski-Harabasz index to compare the effectiveness of different clustering solutions on the same data and choose the one with the highest score. However, this score should be used alongside other metrics such as the silhouette score and the Davies-Bouldin index for a more comprehensive evaluation.

Applications

Clustering has a lot of real-world applications, from social sciences to marketing and threat modeling. Example applications include the following:

- **Market segmentation**: Grouping customers based on purchasing behavior, interests, or demographic profiles.
- **Anomaly detection**: Identifying unusual data points by finding which ones do not fit into any cluster.
- **Data organization**: Organizing large volumes of data into manageable and meaningful groups.
- **Pattern discovery**: Finding hidden patterns or intrinsic structures in data, such as grouping genes with similar expression patterns in bioinformatics.
- **Customer behavior analysis**: Understanding different customer groups and their purchasing patterns can help in optimizing product placements, store layouts, and inventory management.
- **Recommendation systems**: Clustering can help identify groups of similar items or users, which can then be used to recommend items to users based on the preferences of others in their group.
- **Social network analysis**: Clustering can help identify communities or groups within large networks of individuals based on their interactions or shared interests.

These applications show how versatile and powerful clustering can be in extracting meaningful patterns from vast amounts of data across different fields.

Identify features of deep learning techniques

Deep learning is an advanced subset of machine learning that mimics the human brain's way of learning through an artificial neural network structure. These networks consist of multiple layers of neurons that process data in a hierarchical manner, which is why the models are called **deep neural networks (DNNs)**. Deep learning automates feature extraction from large volumes of unstructured data, such as images and text, significantly enhancing machine learning tasks' accuracy and efficiency.

Unlike traditional machine learning, which relies on manual feature extraction, deep learning models learn to identify and differentiate data features automatically. This learning process requires significant computational power and data, utilizing backpropagation and optimization algorithms such as stochastic gradient descent to adjust neuron connections and minimize prediction errors.

Deep learning applications include regression, classification, natural language processing, and computer vision, revolutionizing fields such as autonomous driving, virtual assistants, facial recognition, and recommendation systems. The training process involves fitting data to predict outcomes based on features, iteratively adjusting the model to improve accuracy. This technology represents a significant advancement in machines' abilities to perform complex tasks by learning from data.

Just like other machine learning techniques discussed in this chapter, deep learning involves fitting training data to a function that can predict a label (y) based on the value of one or more features (x). The function ($f(x)$) is the outer layer of a nested function in which each layer of the neural network encapsulates functions that operate on x and the weight (w) values associated with them. The algorithm used to train the model involves iteratively feeding the feature values (x) in the training data forward through the layers to calculate output values for $\hat{y}$, validating the model to evaluate how far off the calculated $\hat{y}$ values are from the known y values (which quantifies the level of error, or loss, in the model), and then modifying the weights (w) to reduce the loss. The trained model includes the final weight values that result in the most accurate predictions.

So how does deep learning work? The foundation of deep learning is a structure called the **neural network**.

Neural networks refer to computational systems designed to mimic the human brain and nervous system's structure and function. Similar to the brain's neurons, artificial neural networks consist of units called neurons or nodes, interconnected with one another. These connections are characterized by weights and biases, activating subsequent nodes once input values surpass predefined thresholds. Visualize a neural network as a series of nodes organized in layers, where each node connects to several others in the neighboring layer, with the output of each node affecting the inputs of nodes in the next layer, kind of like a 3D flowchart where each condition and action can connect to other conditions and actions. *Figure 3.10* depicts an example of a simple neural network design:

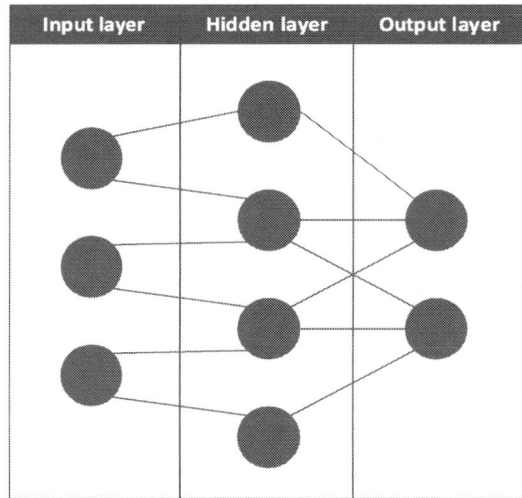

Figure 3.10 – Example of a simple neural network

Each input layer node is connected to two nodes in the hidden layer and the resultant data is connected to the output layer. The input layer of a neural network processes raw data and passes it to the nodes of hidden layers, which classify the data points according to the target criteria. As data progresses through successive hidden layers, the target value's focus becomes more refined, leading to more precise assumptions.

A **loss function** is used to compare the predicted $\hat{y}$ values against the known values. The function compiles those differences, resulting in the aggregate variance for multiple cases. This total variance is summarized as the **loss**. An optimization function may be employed to evaluate the weight of the various losses and determine how to adjust to minimize the loss. These changes are **backpropagated** throughout the neural network to replace the original values and the model re-learns based on the updated values. Each iteration of this process is known as an **epoch**; epochs are repeated until the loss and predictions fall within an acceptable threshold.

Finally, the output layer utilizes the information from the hidden layers to determine the most likely label.

When you hear people talk about **deep learning**, it's really about expanding the concept of neural networks with more hidden layers (representing more dimensions of data classification), resulting in more precise predictions.

Example

An example of deep learning in action is an image identification scenario where the goal is to predict animal types in images. In this case, a deep learning model, typically a **Convolutional Neural Network (CNN)**, would be trained on a large dataset of animal images. Each image in the dataset is labeled with the type of animal it contains (e.g., dog, cat, tiger, etc.).

During training, the CNN learns to recognize patterns and features in the images, such as shapes, textures, and colors, that distinguish one animal from another. The network consists of various layers, including input, hidden, and output layers. The input layer receives the raw image data, while the hidden layers process the data through a series of filters, identifying increasingly complex features at each layer. The output layer then uses the information extracted by the hidden layers to classify the image according to the type of animal it most likely represents.

Once the model is trained, it can be used to predict the type of animal in new, unseen images by processing the images through the same network and producing a prediction based on the features it has learned to recognize.

Applications

This ability to automatically and accurately classify images makes deep learning a powerful tool for tasks such as wildlife monitoring, pet identification, and even medical image analysis.

Deep learning has many of the same applications as clustering (as its goals are very similar—the identification and classification or grouping of previously unlabeled data). As such, real-world applications include everything that clustering can do, as well as many others:

- **Image recognition and computer vision**: Deep learning models, especially CNNs, are widely used in image recognition tasks due to the way they are structured, mimicking human visual perception. They can identify faces, objects, scenes, and actions in images and videos. This technology underpins various applications, including security surveillance, medical imaging diagnosis, and autonomous vehicles.

- **Natural Language Processing (NLP)**: Deep learning has significantly advanced the capabilities of NLP, enabling applications such as language translation, sentiment analysis, and chatbots. Models such as transformers and **Recurrent Neural Networks (RNNs)** have been pivotal in these advancements.

- **Speech recognition and generation**: Deep learning models are at the heart of voice-activated systems such as virtual assistants (e.g., Siri, Alexa), speech-to-text transcription services, and voice-enabled customer service systems.

- **Recommendation systems**: Deep learning is used to power recommendation engines on platforms such as Netflix, YouTube, and Amazon, enhancing user experience by personalizing content, products, and services based on individual preferences and past behavior.

- **Autonomous vehicles**: Deep learning models process and interpret the complex visual environment required for autonomous navigation, including recognizing traffic signs, signals, pedestrians, and other vehicles.

- **Fraud detection**: Financial institutions use deep learning to detect unusual patterns and prevent fraudulent activities in real-time, significantly reducing the risk of financial losses for both financial institutions and consumers.

- **Drug discovery and genomics**: In the field of biotechnology, deep learning aids in the discovery of new drugs and the understanding of genetic sequences, contributing to personalized medicine and the treatment of complex diseases.

- **Content generation**: Deep learning techniques are used to create realistic images, videos, text, and voice, enabling applications such as virtual reality, game development, and the creation of art and music.

- **Sentiment analysis**: Companies use deep learning to analyze customer feedback, social media comments, and reviews to gauge public sentiment, improve products, and tailor services.

These applications demonstrate the versatility and transformative potential of deep learning across different domains, driving innovation and improving efficiency, accuracy, and user experience.

Summary

In this chapter, you learned about many different types of machine learning scenarios such as regression, classification, and deep learning. You learned about both supervised and unsupervised learning, and where each of those is appropriate.

Machine learning is helpful in a variety of real-world scenarios, from weather forecasting to medical imaging analysis. You learned about applications for each type of machine learning technology and even how to compute several metrics to determine how accurate trained models are.

In the next chapter, we'll start talking about core machine learning concepts.

Exam Readiness Drill – Chapter Review Questions

Apart from a solid understanding of key concepts, being able to think quickly under time pressure is a skill that will help you ace your certification exam. That is why working on these skills early on in your learning journey is key.

Chapter review questions are designed to improve your test-taking skills progressively with each chapter you learn and review your understanding of key concepts in the chapter at the same time. You'll find these at the end of each chapter.

> **Before You Proceed**
>
> If you don't have a Packt Library subscription or you haven't purchased this book from the Packt store, you will need to unlock the online resources to access the exam readiness drills. Unlocking is free and needs to be done only once. To learn how to do that, head over to the chapter titled *Chapter 12, Accessing the Online Resources*.

To open the Chapter Review Questions for this chapter, perform the following steps:

1. Click the link – `https://packt.link/AI-900_CH03`.

    Alternatively, you can scan the following QR code (*Figure 3.11*):

Figure 3.11 – QR code that opens Chapter Review Questions for logged-in users

2. Once you log in, you'll see a page similar to the one shown in *Figure 3.12*:

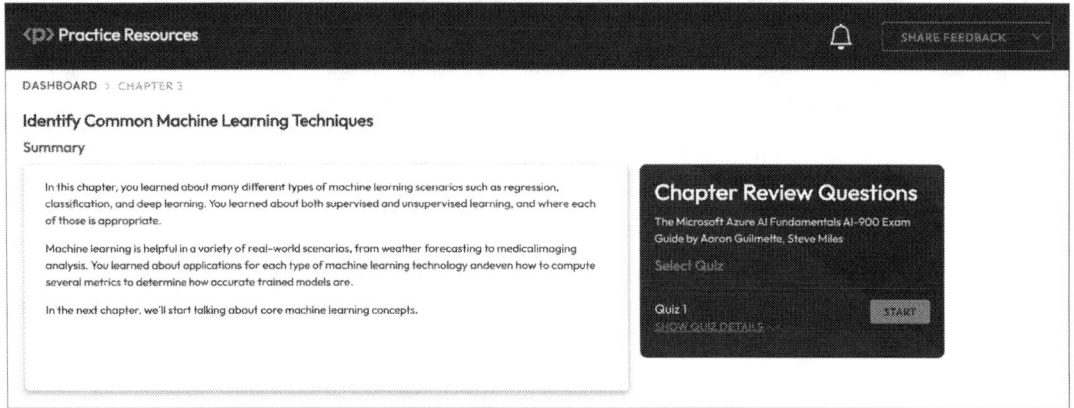

Figure 3.12 – Chapter Review Questions for Chapter 3

3. Once ready, start the following practice drills, re-attempting the quiz multiple times.

Exam Readiness Drill

For the first three attempts, don't worry about the time limit.

ATTEMPT 1

The first time, aim for at least **40%**. Look at the answers you got wrong and read the relevant sections in the chapter again to fix your learning gaps.

ATTEMPT 2

The second time, aim for at least **60%**. Look at the answers you got wrong and read the relevant sections in the chapter again to fix any remaining learning gaps.

ATTEMPT 3

The third time, aim for at least **75%**. Once you score 75% or more, you start working on your timing.

> **Tip**
> You may take more than **three** attempts to reach 75%. That's okay. Just review the relevant sections in the chapter till you get there.

Working On Timing

Your aim is to keep the score the same while trying to answer these questions as quickly as possible. Here's an example of how your next attempts should look like:

Attempt	Score	Time Taken
Attempt 5	77%	21 mins 30 seconds
Attempt 6	78%	18 mins 34 seconds
Attempt 7	76%	14 mins 44 seconds

Table 3.10 – Sample timing practice drills on the online platform

> **Note**
> The time limits shown in the above table are just examples. Set your own time limits with each attempt based on the time limit of the quiz on the website.

With each new attempt, your score should stay above **75%** while your "time taken" to complete should "decrease". Repeat as many attempts as you want till you feel confident dealing with the time pressure.

4
Describe Core Machine Learning Concepts

In the previous chapters, you were introduced to some basic **machine learning** (**ML**) concepts, including various models and scenarios where a particular type of model might be useful. In this chapter, we're going to explore concepts surrounding the actual data used in ML.

The objectives and skills we'll cover in this chapter include the following:

- Identify features and labels in a dataset for machine learning
- Describe how training and validation datasets are used in machine learning

By the end of this chapter, you should be able to clearly articulate the terminology surrounding ML.

Identify features and labels in a dataset for machine learning

As you learned in *Chapter 3, Identify Common Machine Learning Techniques*, **features** and **labels** are two fundamental concepts that define the data you work with when training ML models.

Features are individual measurable properties or characteristics of whatever is being observed. In ML models, features are used as input variables. These are the data points that you use to make predictions. For example, if you're trying to predict the price of a house, the features might include the number of bedrooms, the size of the house in square feet, the neighborhood it's in, how close it is to a fire station, or what the local property tax rates are. Features are represented by independent variables in your dataset that you believe will help you make accurate predictions about your target variable.

Labels, on the other hand, are the output you're trying to predict or classify.

In **supervised learning** (**SL**), each training example includes a label. Continuing with the house pricing example, the label would be the actual selling price of the house.

In classification tasks, labels are the categories assigned to data points. For instance, in an ML model trained to identify whether an email is spam or not, the labels might be "spam" and "not spam."

In this section, we'll dive a little deeper into working with features and labels in your datasets.

Identifying features in a dataset

Identifying features in an ML dataset involves understanding variables that can be used to predict the outcome (target variable). There are many things you can do to narrow down what's important for your ML model.

Let's go through them in this section.

Understanding the problem domain

Begin by understanding the domain or context of the problem. This involves researching the subject area to understand what factors might influence the outcome. For example, if you are working on a project to predict house prices, potential features could include the size of the house, the number of bedrooms, the number of bathrooms, the year it was built, the location, distance to fire stations, number of public libraries in the area, and statistics on the local school system.

When working through this step, it would likely be helpful to speak with domain experts to understand important variables. You could also look for existing literature, research, or studies to identify common predictors or variables used in similar problems.

Collecting data

Gather your data from relevant sources. This could include databases, reports, files, external APIs connected to industry data sources, or direct measurements. The data you collect will consist of various attributes or variables. You should work to ensure that the data collected is relevant to the problem domain and includes variables identified in your research of the subject matter.

For example, if you're working on a model that's going to predict housing prices, you'd likely look at data sources such as recent sale prices of houses in a particular zip code. Since you'd identified other features such as school system ratings and the distances to fire stations and libraries, you'd need to get that data as well—which would likely be from different data sources. You'd need to plot the distance from each house to the nearest library and fire station and add the dataset that you'll be training a model with.

Exploring the data

Perform **exploratory data analysis (EDA)** to get a feel for the data. This can include summarizing the statistics of the data, visualizing distributions and relationships between variables, and identifying any patterns or anomalies. Tools such as histograms, scatter plots, and correlation matrices can be useful here. You should also use statistical summaries (such as mean, median, mode, and standard deviation) to understand the distribution of each variable and identify areas where you have outliers.

Here's an example of a scatter plot:

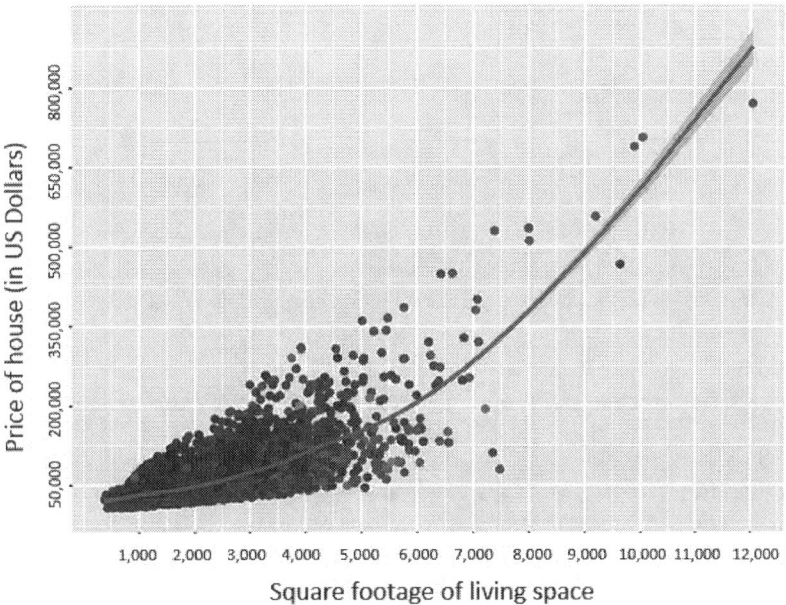

Figure 4.1 – Scatter plot showing the relationship between housing price and square footage

Selecting relevant variables

Not all variables in your dataset may be relevant or necessary for predicting the outcome. Select variables that are likely to influence the target variable based on your domain knowledge and initial data exploration. Variables that show a correlation with the target variable are often good candidates for features.

When identifying variables, it's important to consider the practical significance of variables in addition to their statistical significance. For example, going back to the housing example, you may have learned that a house's proximity to a library may not have a very big impact. During the EDA, you also may discover other variables that may seem important, such as proximity to a shopping center or the number of closets and storage areas.

After reviewing your preliminary data, you may discover that you have missing attributes or values or that some data may be irrelevant to the problem context. Consider discarding that data since it may reduce the effectiveness of your model. Continue iterating until you settle in on relevant features.

Feature engineering

This involves creating new features from existing ones through various techniques such as binning, aggregation, and combination of attributes. For example, from a dataset containing dates, you might extract features such as the day of the week, the month, or the year. Or, you may decide to collapse or combine multiple date ranges into fewer features.

In the house pricing example, you may decide to aggregate data by month or week instead of having individual house prices by day. This may reduce some noise and help focus on trends more easily.

Advanced techniques, such as polynomial features, can help capture non-linear relationships. In a house, a non-linear example might be the relationship between the number of bathrooms and closets. One method of creating a polynomial feature would be by multiplying two unrelated features together. In this example, you could multiply the number of bathrooms and closets: a house that has 3 bathrooms and 7 closets could have a new feature with a value of 21.

Feature engineering can also involve transforming variables, such as scaling or normalizing, to make them more suitable for ML models. For example, you may decide to round housing prices to the nearest $25,000 or group houses by the number of bedrooms, such as 0-2, 3-4, 5-6, and 7+. Each of these techniques can be used to help streamline the data and help produce a clearer set of predictions.

Handling missing values

Decide how to handle missing data in your potential features. You might fill in missing values with the mean or median (imputation), discard them, or use a model to predict and fill them. Be sure to consider the reasons for missing data to determine if it's random or not.

Removing irrelevant or redundant features

Eliminate features that are irrelevant to the outcome or that duplicate information contained in other features. Redundant or irrelevant features can introduce noise and lead to overfitting. As you develop the model, you may discover that you need to remove features to help refine the model to produce better results.

Consulting with experts

If possible, consult with domain experts to validate your selection of features and data sources. They might provide insights into which variables are most influential or suggest additional variables that you hadn't considered, as well as indicate any known biases for your data source selections.

Using feature selection techniques

There are automated feature selection techniques such as **forward selection**, **backward elimination**, and **recursive feature elimination** that can help identify the most important features based on statistical tests or model performance:

- **Forward selection**: Forward selection is a feature selection technique used to build a model by iteratively adding one feature at a time, starting with the most significant or promising feature. The process continues until a stopping criterion is met, such as reaching a predetermined number of features or until the addition of new features no longer improves the model's performance significantly. For example, with our house pricing example, this might mean starting with overall square footage as the most promising feature that has an impact on the price of a house, and then in the next iteration, add the number of bedrooms.

- **Backward elimination**: This is simply the opposite process of forward selection. Instead of adding features until the model doesn't change, you start with all of the features to train a model and take out features until the stopping criterion is met—such as the number of features remaining or until the removal of features no longer improves the model.

- **Recursive feature elimination**: Similar to backward elimination, recursive feature elimination is a process that starts with a full set of features and then removes them. Whereas backward elimination simply removes the least significant features, recursive feature elimination removes features based on their importance and interaction with other features.

You'll want to temper any automated feature selection tools with domain knowledge, expert insight, and data understanding to ensure you're choosing the most appropriate set of features.

Remember—model development is an iterative process. As you build and develop your models, you might discover that some features are more important than others or that some can be removed without decreasing model performance (in regard to accuracy).

Identifying labels in a dataset

Identifying labels in an ML dataset involves understanding the outcome or target variable that your model aims to predict. Here's how you can identify labels in a dataset.

Defining the objective

Start by clearly defining the objective of your ML project. Are you trying to predict a continuous value (regression), classify data into categories (classification), or identify groups of similar instances (clustering)? Your objective will guide what your label should be.

Understanding the data

Examine your dataset and understand each variable. In SL, the label is the variable that is being predicted, which could be the outcome of an event, the classification category, or the future value of a series.

Identifying the target variable

In most datasets used for SL, there is usually a specific column that serves as the target variable (label). This could be a column indicating "Yes" or "No" for a binary classification problem, a numerical value for a regression problem, or category labels for a multiclass classification problem.

Consulting domain experts

If it's not clear which variable should be used as the label, consult with domain experts or stakeholders of your ML project. They can provide insights into what predictions would be most valuable based on the dataset, business outcomes, and research objectives.

Exploring the data

Use EDA to better understand potential labels. For instance, if you're working with a dataset where the objective is to predict whether an email is spam or not, the label could be a column indicating "spam" or "not spam." Look for a column or other output with categorical or binary data that fits the problem you are trying to solve.

Checking data documentation

If your dataset comes with documentation or a **data dictionary**, review this material to understand the role of each variable. Often, the documentation will explicitly state which column is the target variable (label) for prediction. If the documentation doesn't identify the label, it may provide insights about existing fields or column names to help you determine a label.

Look for pre-labeled data; in some cases, especially in SL tasks, datasets are already labeled. This means that for each record, there is an accompanying label that has been previously determined. This is common in datasets used for training models, where the goal is to learn the relationship between input features and labels.

Considering the problem type

The nature of your label depends on the type of problem you are trying to use ML to solve.

For classification, labels are categorical and represent different classes (for example, "spam" or "not spam" for binary classification dealing with whether an email is junk mail or not; "cat," "dog," and "bird" for multiclass classification identifying animals from pictures).

For regression, labels are continuous values (such as house prices or temperatures).

For clustering (an **unsupervised learning** (UL) task), labels are not provided, and the goal is to discover them through the grouping of similar data points.

Cleaning the data

Ensure your label data is clean and consistent. This might involve correcting mislabeling, handling missing values, and ensuring labels are in a format that can be used for modeling (for example, converting strings to numerical categories).

As you develop your model, you may need to revisit and re-evaluate your choice of labels (just as you may need to revisit your choice of features). The effectiveness of your model in predicting these labels will help you understand if you have identified the correct labels or if adjustments are needed.

Describe how training and validation datasets are used in machine learning

In ML, **training** and **validation** sets are subsets of your overall dataset used during the model development phase. Their roles are distinct but complementary, aimed at creating a model that is able to make accurate predictions about new, unseen data.

You may recall seeing the concepts of training and validation sets in *Chapter 3, Identify Common Machine Learning Techniques* when we discussed dividing the dataset into sections—a subset that would be used to train the model, and a "held back" or "reserved" part of the data that we could use to test the predictions. These are the training and validation sets, respectively.

Training set

This is the data on which the ML model is trained. The model learns to make predictions or decisions based on this data. The training set is used to fit the parameters of the model, such as the weights in a **neural network** (**NN**) or the coefficients in linear regression.

The training set in ML is the actual dataset used to train the model. Training involves adjusting the model's parameters to minimize errors, typically through a process known as learning. The size and quality of the training set can significantly influence the performance of the ML model. A larger training set provides more examples from which the model can learn, potentially leading to better generalization when the model is used to make predictions on new data. However, the data must also be representative of the real-world scenario the model will be applied to, encompassing a broad range of examples and variations.

During the training phase, the model iteratively adjusts its parameters to reduce the difference between the predicted output and the actual output, as defined by a specific mathematical loss function. This process can vary depending on the type of model and learning algorithm. For instance, in SL, each example in the training set includes both the input features and the corresponding target label. The model uses these pairs to learn underlying patterns in the data. In UL, where there are no labels, the model tries to learn the underlying structure of the data based on the input features alone.

The effectiveness of the training process (in both SL and UL) is largely dependent on the quality of the training data, the volume of data in the training set, the relevance of the features selected, and the suitability of the model for the problem at hand. If possible, training on actual data (as opposed to synthetic data) is preferred, as it helps the model learn about natural outliers and variances. Sometimes, however, due to privacy or other responsible **artificial intelligence** (**AI**) development principles, actual data may not be available.

> Generating your own training data
>
> You may also want to consider asking a **generative AI** (**GenAI**) model to create training data for you. This may be useful in helping you understand relationships between features or protecting privacy if a potential dataset contains personal information. However, training data generated by an AI model can also amplify any bias in the data that was used to train the generative model, leading to skewed or unrealistic training data. In either case, when using GenAI, you'll need to take precautions to ensure that the data is representative of what you're trying to achieve.

Typically, the training set constitutes a larger portion of the entire dataset, often ranging from 60% to 80%. The aim is to provide the model with a diverse and comprehensive set of examples that mirror the real-world scenarios in which it will be applied.

If you're asking yourself, "How do I know if the model is trained well enough?" or "How will I know when I'm done training?" that's where validation sets come in.

Validation set

This subset of the dataset is used to provide an unbiased evaluation of a model fit on the training dataset while tuning the model's **hyperparameters** (settings or configurations that are not learned from the data) that the model is unable to adjust automatically. The validation set acts as a proxy for the test set since it is not used for training the model and hence can help in estimating how well the model has generalized to unseen data. Typically, the validation set might be about 20% to 30% of the entire dataset.

It is crucial to avoid **overfitting** (sometimes referred to as **overtraining**), a situation where the model performs well on the training data but poorly on new, unseen data.

> What's a hyperparameter?
>
> An ML model hyperparameter is a configuration setting that is external to the model and influences its learning process. Unlike model parameters, which are learned from the training data, hyperparameters are predefined by the user and affect aspects such as model complexity, regularization, and optimization. Examples include the learning rate in gradient descent, the depth of a decision tree, or the number of hidden layers in an NN. Hyperparameter tuning is crucial for optimizing model performance. Don't worry, though—from the perspective of the *AI-900* exam, the important concept is that hyperparameters are external to the model.

Using a validation set helps detect issues such as **overfitting**. Overfitting happens when a model learns noise or random fluctuations in the training data instead of actual underlying patterns. By evaluating the model on the validation set, you can identify when overfitting is occurring and take steps to mitigate it, such as simplifying the model, applying regularization techniques, or obtaining more training data.

Additionally, the validation set allows for the comparison of different models and configurations in a controlled manner. After the model has been trained on the training set, its performance on the validation set provides an unbiased evaluation. Only after the model has been optimized and selected based on its performance on the validation set should it be tested on the test set to assess its generalization capabilities to new, unseen data. This approach ensures that the final evaluation of the model is based on data that has not been used during the training or validation phases, providing a more accurate measure of its predictive performance and generalization ability.

The process usually involves training the model on the training set and then evaluating its performance on the validation set. Based on this evaluation, adjustments can be made to the model's configuration. Once the model performs satisfactorily on the validation set, it can then be tested on a separate test set to further evaluate its performance in a completely unseen data scenario. This practice helps ensure that the model is not just memorizing the training data but actually learning patterns that are generalizable.

Summary

This chapter expanded on concepts relating to data in regard to ML. You learned about techniques for identifying features and labels in datasets as well as techniques for ensuring data is suitable for learning. You learned about the concepts and purposes of both the training set and validation set as well.

In the next chapter, we'll dive a little deeper into Azure Machine Learning concepts and capabilities.

Exam Readiness Drill – Chapter Review Questions

Apart from a solid understanding of key concepts, being able to think quickly under time pressure is a skill that will help you ace your certification exam. That is why working on these skills early on in your learning journey is key.

Chapter review questions are designed to improve your test-taking skills progressively with each chapter you learn and review your understanding of key concepts in the chapter at the same time. You'll find these at the end of each chapter.

> **Before you proceed**
>
> If you don't have a Packt Library subscription or you haven't purchased this book from the Packt store, you will need to unlock the online resources to access the exam readiness drills. Unlocking is free and needs to be done only once. To learn how to do that, head over to the chapter titled *Chapter 12, Accessing the Online Resources*.

To open the Chapter Review Questions for this chapter, perform the following steps:

1. Click the link – `https://packt.link/AI-900_CH04`.

   Alternatively, you can scan the following QR code (*Figure 4.2*):

   Figure 4.2 – QR code that opens Chapter Review Questions for logged-in users

2. Once you log in, you'll see a page similar to the one shown in *Figure 4.3*:

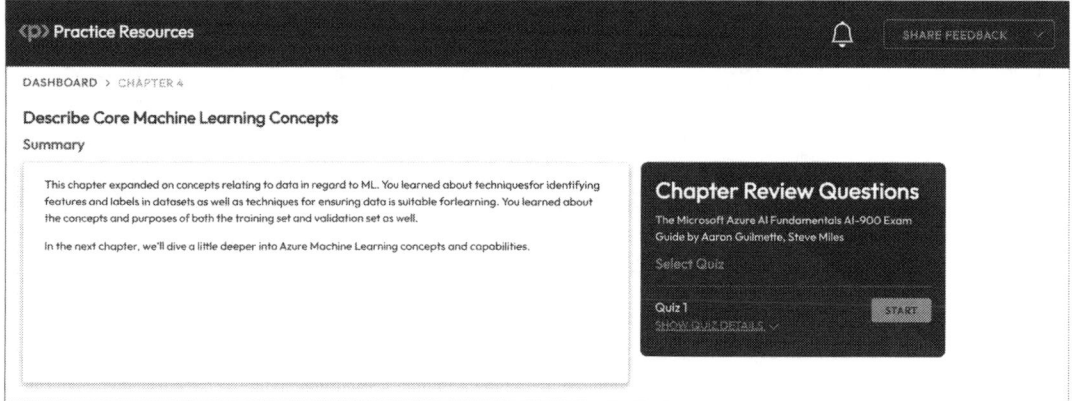

Figure 4.3 – Chapter Review Questions for Chapter 4

3. Once ready, start the following practice drills, re-attempting the quiz multiple times.

Exam Readiness Drill

For the first three attempts, don't worry about the time limit.

ATTEMPT 1

The first time, aim for at least **40%**. Look at the answers you got wrong and read the relevant sections in the chapter again to fix your learning gaps.

ATTEMPT 2

The second time, aim for at least **60%**. Look at the answers you got wrong and read the relevant sections in the chapter again to fix any remaining learning gaps.

ATTEMPT 3

The third time, aim for at least **75%**. Once you score 75% or more, you start working on your timing.

> Tip
>
> You may take more than **three** attempts to reach 75%. That's okay. Just review the relevant sections in the chapter till you get there.

Working On Timing

Your aim is to keep the score the same while trying to answer these questions as quickly as possible. Here's an example of how your next attempts should look like:

Attempt	Score	Time Taken
Attempt 5	77%	21 mins 30 seconds
Attempt 6	78%	18 mins 34 seconds
Attempt 7	76%	14 mins 44 seconds

Table 4.1 – Sample timing practice drills on the online platform

> Note
>
> The time limits shown in the above table are just examples. Set your own time limits with each attempt based on the time limit of the quiz on the website.

With each new attempt, your score should stay above **75%** while your "time taken" to complete should "decrease". Repeat as many attempts as you want till you feel confident dealing with the time pressure.

5
Describe Azure Machine Learning Capabilities

So far, we've talked a lot about foundational concepts for machine learning, including scenarios, models, algorithms, and training data. You've seen a few simple examples of machine learning. You may have even dusted off your college statistics course knowledge to work through those examples yourself.

Azure Machine Learning (sometimes stylized as **Azure ML** or **AzureML**) is the group of Microsoft Azure services that puts all of those concepts to work. Azure ML is comprised of a suite of tools that are used to manage the entire machine learning life cycle. Azure ML is used by a variety of engineers, data scientists, and other professionals to train, build, and deploy models and machine learning-integrated workflows.

The objectives and skills we'll cover in this chapter are as follows:

- What is Azure ML?
- Describe capabilities of **automated machine learning** (AutoML)
- Describe data and compute services for data science and machine learning
- Describe model management and deployment capabilities in Azure ML
- Build a machine learning model in Azure ML

By the end of this chapter, you should be able to describe the features, capabilities, and supporting services for Azure ML.

Let's get started!

What is Azure ML?

Before we dive into the particulars of machine learning on the Azure platform, let's step back a minute and talk about some of the features, capabilities, and goals of Azure ML.

Azure ML enhances the capabilities and efficiency of machine learning workloads through a comprehensive range of tools and features:

- **Centralized data management**: Azure ML offers a unified repository for storing and managing datasets, facilitating easy access and reuse across various machine learning projects. This centralized storage supports efficient data handling for both model training and evaluation, streamlining the data preparation process.

- **Scalable compute resources**: Azure ML provides on-demand compute resources tailored for machine learning tasks. Users can leverage these resources to run extensive machine learning jobs, including model training and batch inferencing, without the need for upfront hardware investments. This flexibility allows for cost-effective scaling according to the complexity and size of the tasks.

- **Automated machine learning** (**AutoML**): AutoML simplifies the process of applying machine learning by automatically testing multiple training jobs with various algorithms and hyperparameters. This feature helps users quickly identify the most effective model for their specific dataset, significantly reducing the time and expertise required for model selection and tuning.

- **Orchestrated pipelines and visual tools**: Azure ML includes intuitive visual tools that allow users to create and manage orchestrated workflows, known as **pipelines**. These pipelines automate and streamline the end-to-end machine learning processes, from data preprocessing and model training to deployment and inferencing, ensuring reproducibility and efficiency.

- **Framework integration**: The platform integrates seamlessly with popular machine learning frameworks and tools such as **MLflow**, **TensorFlow**, **PyTorch**, and **scikit-learn**. This compatibility enables data scientists and developers to manage the life cycle of their machine learning models, from training and evaluation to deployment and monitoring, within a familiar environment using familiar tooling, all while leveraging existing code and libraries.

- **Responsible AI practices**: Azure ML is committed to responsible AI by providing built-in tools and features for monitoring and evaluating AI ethics considerations. This includes visualizing model performance, understanding model predictions through explainability features, and assessing model fairness to ensure that AI systems are transparent, fair, and accountable.

- **Tooling and capabilities**: Azure ML provides several tools that make machine learning accessible to those with all levels of experience. Data scientists and engineers can take advantage of code-first approaches through Python, while those with less experience with coding and development can use the web-based **Azure Machine Learning Studio** to manage machine learning assets.

Together, these features make Azure ML a comprehensive and user-friendly platform that addresses the needs of both novice and experienced machine learning practitioners, promoting efficient development, deployment, and maintenance of machine learning models at scale.

In the next section, we'll begin focusing on the specific features of AutoML in Azure.

Describe capabilities of AutoML

AutoML is a service that automates the process of applying machine learning to solve problems. It significantly reduces the complexity and time needed to produce a model by automating various steps of the machine learning process, including data **preprocessing**, feature selection, algorithm selection, and hyperparameter tuning.

With AutoML, users can quickly create high-quality machine learning models while maintaining full control and transparency. The service is designed to accommodate both novices and experts in machine learning. For beginners, it simplifies the process by abstracting away many of the complexities involved in building and tuning machine learning models. For experts, it provides a fast way to experiment with different models and parameters, saving time that can be used to focus on other aspects of their projects.

> **What's preprocessing?**
>
> Preprocessing is the idea of preparing the data before actually using it in machine learning models. This can involve several normalization processes and content preparation, such as converting text into tokens (chunks) for natural language processing, or using some of the techniques you learned in the previous chapter surrounding feature selection and dimensionality reduction.

The process with AutoML involves providing a dataset and specifying the target metric or outcome you are interested in. The service then automatically preprocesses the data, selects appropriate machine learning algorithms, and tunes their hyperparameters to find the best possible model based on the provided data and settings. Throughout this process, AutoML keeps track of all the **experiments**, providing detailed reports and metrics that allow users to understand how different models perform and why certain models are chosen.

> **What's an experiment?**
>
> Experiments in Azure ML and AutoML refer to the process of running one or more trials to train and validate machine learning models. An experiment is a type of container object, grouping all the assets related to a particular model. They're used to systematically test, track, and compare the results of different runs to determine the most effective configurations. An experiment typically contains the following components:
> - Data
> - Algorithms and models
> - Parameters and settings
> - Runs
> - Metrics and outputs
> - Tracking and comparison

Additionally, AutoML integrates with other Azure services, enabling models to be deployed seamlessly in production environments, model performance monitoring, and the ability to retain models with new data. This integration supports a comprehensive machine learning life cycle, from data preparation to model deployment and management. *Figure 5.1* depicts a high-level overview of the AutoML process:

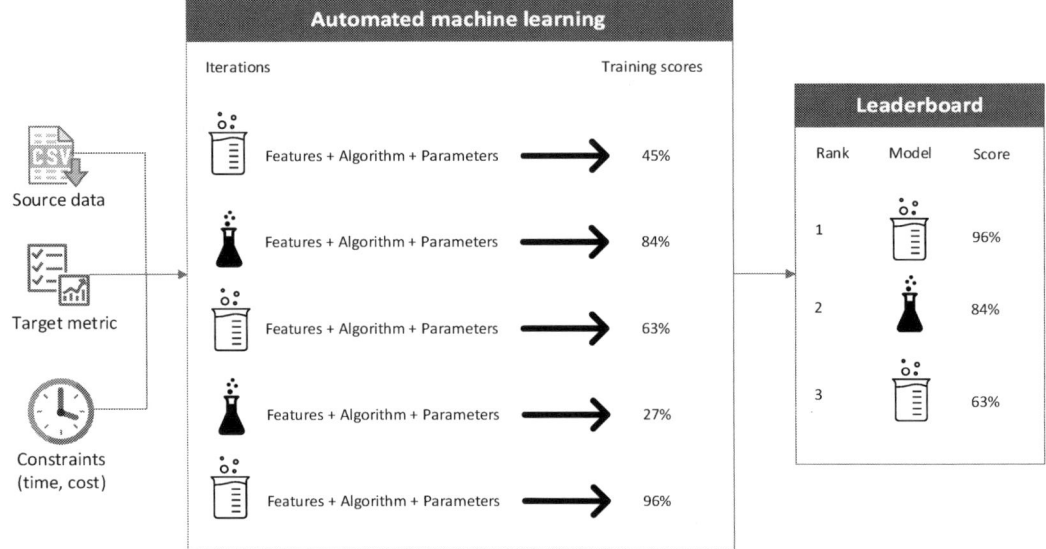

Figure 5.1 – Overview of the AutoML process

AutoML also allows you to create a Responsible AI dashboard so that you can track your adherence to Microsoft's principles of responsible AI (which you learned about in *Chapter 2, Identify the Guiding Principles for Responsible AI*).

AutoML use cases

AutoML is useful in a variety of scenarios and can help even novices in data science create and manage models and data pipelines. The goal of AutoML is to simplify the entire machine learning experience, helping data scientists and engineers focus more on the outcomes instead of the tooling. This section describes, at a high level, the types of models and use cases where AutoML is applicable.

Classification

Classification is a supervised learning approach that's used in machine learning where models are trained on labeled data and then apply the learned patterns to new, unseen data. Azure ML supports classification tasks and offers specialized features such as deep neural network text **featurizers** to enhance model performance. The objective of classification models is to accurately predict the category or class of new data instances, based on the knowledge gained from the training dataset. Typical applications of classification models include fraud detection, handwriting recognition, and object detection.

> **What's a featurizer?**
>
> A featurizer is a component or technique that's used to transform raw data into something the machine learning model can work with. Featurizers extract the features (hence the name) from the content, representing it in a way that it's compatible with the training process. Featurizers can also perform dimensionality reduction to help simplify or reduce the complexity of the model, speeding up the performance and efficiency of the model. Featurizers can also help normalize data or perform exception handling for missing data elements.

Regression

Regression, like classification, is a type of supervised learning task that's supported by Azure ML and tailored specifically for predicting numerical outcomes. Unlike classification, which predicts categorical outcomes, regression models forecast continuous numerical values based on independent variables.

Regression aims to determine the relationship between these variables, such as predicting an automobile's price from features like gas mileage and safety ratings. Azure ML provides specialized featurization for regression problems and supports a range of algorithms for these tasks through AutoML.

Time series forecasting

AutoML in Azure ML can be leveraged to generate high-quality time series forecasts for various business needs, such as predicting revenue, inventory levels, sales, or customer demand. This process treats time series forecasting as a multivariate regression problem, where past values are used alongside other predictors to enhance forecasting accuracy.

Unlike traditional methods, this approach can incorporate multiple contextual variables to understand their interrelationships. AutoML learns a comprehensive model that can apply to all items and prediction horizons in the dataset, making it possible to generalize predictions to new, unseen series with the benefit of a larger data pool for model training.

Computer vision

Azure ML provides support for computer vision tasks, enabling the creation of models for image classification and object detection. This allows seamless integration with Azure's data labeling features, the use of labeled data for model generation, and optimization of model performance through algorithm selection and hyperparameter tuning. Users can download or deploy these models as web services, and scale operations effectively using Azure ML's **machine learning operations** (**MLOps**) and ML Pipelines capabilities.

Natural language processing (NLP)

Support for NLP in Azure ML provides a comprehensive and user-friendly framework for developing, training, and deploying models tailored for text data. This includes tasks such as text classification and named entity recognition.

Azure ML supports the entire life cycle of NLP model training, from data preparation to model deployment. It utilizes state-of-the-art deep neural network approaches, including the latest pre-trained models, such as **Bidirectional Encoder Representations from Transformers** (**BERT**), which are renowned for their effectiveness in understanding the nuances of human language.

Training, validation, and test scenarios

AutoML in Azure allows you to provide training data for machine learning model training and lets you specify the type of model validation to be used. It performs model validation as part of the training process, tuning the model's hyperparameters with validation data to best fit the training data.

However, using the same validation data for each iteration introduces a risk of model evaluation bias as the model may *overfit* the validation data. To mitigate this, AutoML enables the use of separate test data to evaluate the final model it recommends at the experiment's conclusion. Providing test data in your AutoML experiment configuration ensures that the recommended model is tested objectively, helping to confirm the absence of bias in the final model and its ability to generalize well with previously unseen data.

Feature engineering

Feature engineering involves creating new features (or variables) from existing data based on domain knowledge to improve a machine learning algorithm's performance. In Azure ML, this includes applying scaling and normalization techniques, collectively known as **featurization**.

In AutoML experiments, featurization processes such as feature normalization, handling missing data, and converting text into numeric values are automated but can be tailored to fit specific data needs. This not only aids in enhancing model learning but also helps in addressing issues such as overfitting and data imbalance. The featurization steps that are incorporated during model training are automatically applied to new input data during predictions, ensuring consistency and accuracy in results.

Ensemble models

What about scenarios where more than one model might help predict more accurately?

AutoML incorporates **ensemble** models by default to enhance predictive performance and machine learning outcomes. Ensemble learning combines several models to form a single prediction, contrasting with approaches that rely on individual models. In AutoML, the final stages of a job often include ensemble iterations.

The process utilizes two main methods for ensemble learning:

- **Voting**: This method uses the weighted average of predicted probabilities (in classification tasks) or target values (in regression tasks) from different models to make predictions.

- **Stacking**: This approach involves combining various models and using a meta-model to make predictions based on the outputs from the initial models. For classification, LogisticRegression serves as the default meta-model, while ElasticNet is used for regression and forecasting.

> **Mix-and-match, but not that way**
>
> In AutoML, ensemble models are specific to either classification or regression tasks but are not mixed within the same ensemble. This means that an ensemble for a classification task will combine multiple classification models, whereas an ensemble for a regression task will combine multiple regression models.
>
> The ensemble methods that are used, such as voting for classification and stacking for both classification and regression, are tailored to handle models of the same type (all classifiers or all regressors). The logic behind this approach is that combining models of the same type ensures that the predictions being averaged (in the case of voting) or used as input for a meta-model (in the case of stacking) are compatible and meaningful when aggregated.
>
> Another reason an ensemble model would not mix and match between different types of models is due to the differing types of output (categorical versus continuous), which serve different purposes. The metrics and outputs of the classifier and regressor models are different, resulting in compatible datasets to be able to do a comparison. To paraphrase, they're apples and oranges.

AutoML employs the **Caruana ensemble selection algorithm**, initiating the ensemble with up to five of the top-performing models, provided they are all within a 5% performance threshold of the leading model to ensure quality. With each iteration, a new model is tested within the existing ensemble, and if it improves the collective performance, it is included in the ensemble, enhancing the overall predictive strength.

> **What is the Caruana ensemble selection algorithm?**
>
> The Caruana ensemble selection algorithm refers to a method developed by Rich Caruana and his colleagues for creating ensemble machine learning models. This method is particularly known for its application in ensemble learning to improve the predictive performance of models by combining the strengths of various individual models. For more information on the Carauna ensemble selection algorithm, see `http://www.niculescu-mizil.org/papers/shotgun.icml04.revised.rev2.pdf`.

Let's shift gears and look at the services that support machine learning in Azure.

Describe data and compute services for data science and machine learning

When working with machine learning in Azure, it's important to be familiar with the types of resources, connections, and elements that you can work with. Let's look at each of the main types of services and resources associated with machine learning workloads.

Compute

In Azure ML, **compute** refers to the computing resources or power that are allocated for running machine learning jobs (such as training models or running experiments) or hosting service endpoints. This can range from **serverless computing** (such as functions that require a minimal amount of compute resources to execute a command) to fully deployed server clusters.

Azure ML supports various types of compute resources to cater to different needs and scenarios. Let's take a look.

Compute cluster

This is a scalable, managed compute infrastructure that allows users to easily set up a cluster of virtual machines equipped with CPU or GPU processing capabilities. Compute clusters are ideal for running large-scale machine learning experiments and training jobs in the cloud. They provide flexibility in choosing the size and number of nodes, enabling users to scale resources according to the workload's requirements.

Serverless compute

For scenarios where managing a compute cluster may be unnecessary or too resource-intensive, Azure ML offers serverless compute options. These options allow users to execute machine learning tasks without having to worry about the underlying infrastructure since Azure ML manages the compute life cycle, scaling, and provisioning automatically.

Compute instance

This is a managed cloud-based development environment that's fully equipped with popular data science and machine learning tools and frameworks. Compute instances serve as personal, customizable virtual machines that can be used for developing, training, and testing machine learning models. They are similar to traditional virtual machines but are optimized for machine learning and data science workflows.

Kubernetes cluster

For deploying and managing machine learning models in production environments, Azure ML supports integration with **Azure Kubernetes Service (AKS)**. Users can deploy their trained models to AKS clusters directly from the Azure ML workspace. This setup is ideal for high-scale, production-grade machine learning model deployments, providing advanced management features and scalability.

Attached compute

Azure ML also offers the flexibility to attach external compute resources to the Azure ML workspace. This means users can leverage their existing infrastructure – such as on-premises data centers or other cloud environments – for training and **inference** purposes. Attached compute resources can be used seamlessly within Azure ML workflows, providing a bridge between Azure ML services and external environments.

By offering a range of compute options, Azure ML ensures that users can select the most appropriate computing resources for their specific machine learning tasks, whether it's for model development, training, or deployment, thereby optimizing performance and cost-efficiency.

Data

Data is one of the most critical factors in developing machine learning models.

In Azure ML, managing and utilizing data efficiently is a crucial aspect of configuring and managing machine learning workloads. Azure ML accommodates a wide variety of data types and sources, making it versatile for various data science and machine learning projects. You can work with the following data types and sources in Azure ML:

- **Uniform Resource Identifiers(URIs)**: These are references to data locations, either in local storage or cloud-based storage systems. Azure ML supports two primary URI types for data management:

    - **uri_folder**: This represents a directory or a collection of files stored in a particular location. It's ideal for scenarios where your data is split across multiple files or when you want to process an entire directory of data in your machine learning jobs.

    - **uri_file**: This specifies a single file, which is useful for tasks that require processing or analyzing one data file at a time. Both the `uri_folder` and `uri_file` types facilitate easy access to data by allowing Azure ML workloads to mount or download content directly onto the compute nodes executing the job.

- **Tables (tabular data abstraction)**: **mltable** is Azure ML's abstraction for tabular data, offering a structured format that's conducive to many types of machine learning algorithms. The mltable format supports a rich set of operations, including filtering, transformation, and aggregation, making it a powerful tool for preprocessing and feature engineering in machine learning pipelines.
- **Primitives**: These are basic data types that form the building blocks for more complex data structures. Azure ML supports several primitive types, including the following:
    - **string**: Text data, which is useful for labels, categories, and any form of text analysis or manipulation.
    - **boolean**: A true or false value, often used for binary classification tasks or flagging records and frequently represented by a 0 (false) and 1 (true)
    - **number**: Numeric data, which can be integers or floating-point numbers, which is crucial for most analytical and statistical operations in machine learning

For most data handling scenarios within Azure ML, URIs (uri_folder and uri_file) are commonly used to pinpoint the exact location of data within storage solutions. This approach simplifies the process of integrating data into machine learning workflows as you can easily map data locations to the filesystem of compute resources. Whether the data needs to be mounted as a drive or downloaded directly onto the compute node, Azure ML provides flexible options to ensure that your data is readily accessible for processing, training, and inference tasks.

By supporting a diverse range of data types and sources, Azure ML ensures that users can efficiently manage and utilize their data, regardless of its format or storage location, facilitating seamless integration into machine learning workflows.

Datastore

While the term data refers to content (both its values and format), datastore refers to the locations of that data.

In Azure ML, datastores play a vital role in managing and accessing data efficiently. A datastore in Azure ML is essentially a secure mechanism for storing connection information to your data storage services hosted on Azure. This setup ensures that sensitive data such as connection strings or access keys are not hard-coded into your scripts, enhancing security and simplifying data access management.

When working with Azure ML, you can **register** (or connect) a new datastore or manage existing ones to streamline the connection to various Azure storage services. This registration process encapsulates the authentication details, allowing your machine learning scripts and workflows to access data seamlessly without repeatedly providing security credentials.

> **Note**
> Credentials can also be stored in Azure Key Vault.

The Azure ML's **command-line interface (CLI)** v2 and **software development kit (SDK)** v2 extend support to various types of cloud-based storage services, enabling broad compatibility with different data storage needs. The following services are supported:

- **Azure Blob Storage container**: Ideal for storing large amounts of unstructured data, such as images, text files, or binary data, which can be used in machine learning experiments and model training.

- **Azure Files Share**: Offers shared storage for legacy applications using the standard **server message block (SMB)** protocol. This is suitable for scenarios where files need to be accessed and shared across multiple virtual machines or services.

- **Azure Data Lake Storage (ADLS)**: Designed for big data analytics, it provides a scalable and secure storage solution for large datasets. ADLS is optimized for performance in analytical scenarios and supports fine-grained security control.

- **Azure Data Lake Storage Gen2**: This service combines the features of Azure Blob Storage and ADLS, offering a highly scalable and cost-effective storage solution that supports both analytics and hierarchical filesystem capabilities.

By leveraging these datastores, Azure ML users can efficiently manage their data's life cycle, from ingestion and storage to training and model deployment, ensuring that the right data is accessible at the right time for machine learning workflows. This integration simplifies the process of connecting to different Azure storage services, enabling data scientists and ML practitioners to focus more on developing and refining their models rather than managing data connections.

Environments

In Azure ML, environments are a fundamental concept as they act as containers for the software dependencies, libraries, and runtime context needed to run machine learning models and scripts. These environments ensure that your machine learning workflows are reproducible, scalable, and portable across different compute targets, from local development machines to cloud-based compute resources.

There are two core types of environments: **curated** and **custom**. Curated environments are defined, managed, and updated by Microsoft and include popular machine learning frameworks and tooling. Custom environments, on the other hand, are built by the user. To create an environment, you would typically use the following features:

- A Docker image
- A Docker image with conda YAML package management for customization
- A Docker build context

Users might choose a custom environment if they have specific package dependencies or specific versions of libraries or if there are certain regulatory requirements that they need to comply with.

Azure ML environments can be versioned and managed centrally, allowing data scientists and developers to share, replicate, and deploy machine learning models consistently. Once defined, an environment can be reused across multiple experiments, pipelines, and deployments, minimizing the "it works on my machine" problem by ensuring that the runtime context is the same regardless of where the code is executed.

Environments can be created and managed through the Azure Machine Learning Studio UI, CLI, or SDK, providing flexibility in how you define and manipulate your machine learning contexts. Additionally, Azure ML provides a repository of pre-built environments for common machine learning tasks and frameworks, allowing you to quickly start your projects without having to manually configure every aspect of the environment.

Model

Models, in the context of Azure ML operations, are the output of the machine learning training process. Models are binary files that represent a machine learning model and its associated metadata.

Workspaces

In Azure ML, a workspace acts as the primary organizational resource or container, serving as a centralized hub for all machine learning activities and artifacts. It is designed to streamline the process of developing, training, and deploying machine learning models by providing a unified environment where data scientists and developers can manage their projects, experiments, and resources.

The workspace encompasses a wide range of elements that are essential for machine learning workflows:

- **Job history**: This element maintains comprehensive records of all machine learning jobs that are executed within the workspace, capturing details such as execution logs, performance metrics, outputs, and even snapshots of the scripts used. This historical data facilitates an analysis and comparison of different runs over time.

- **Resource management**: The workspace organizes and provides easy access to various Azure resources that are utilized in machine learning projects, such as datastores for data storage and compute resources for processing and model training. This centralized management simplifies the task of configuring and scaling resources according to project needs.

- **Asset storage**: Beyond just managing resources, the workspace stores all the machine learning assets that are created during the model development life cycle. This includes trained models ready for deployment, custom environments specifying the runtime context and dependencies, reusable components for building pipelines, and data assets such as datasets and data transformations.

- **Collaboration and versioning**: By serving as a shared environment, the workspace enables team collaboration, allowing multiple users to work on projects, share assets, and contribute to experiments. It supports versioning of assets such as models and environments, ensuring that teams can manage changes and maintain consistency across different stages of the project.
- **Integration with Azure services**: Workspaces are deeply integrated with other Azure services, enabling seamless deployment of models as web services, implementation of MLOps practices with Azure Pipelines, and monitoring of deployed models with Azure Application Insights.

Azure ML workspaces are accessible through the Azure portal, SDK, and CLI, offering flexibility in how users interact with their machine learning resources and assets. By encapsulating all aspects of machine learning projects within a single workspace, Azure ML significantly reduces the complexity of managing machine learning life cycles and enables data scientists to focus more on model development and less on infrastructure management.

Subscription

The subscription is a financial component that establishes the relationship between the Azure customer (you) and Microsoft.

Storage account

A storage account is a resource that gives you access to a variety of storage objects, such as blobs, files, queues, and tables. A storage account has a unique namespace and can be accessed over HTTP or HTTPS.

Key Vault

Azure Key Vault is a secure store for authentication data (such as usernames and passwords, commonly referred to as **secrets**). Training jobs might require a secret to access the data, compute, or other services.

Application Insights

Application Insights can be used to provide logging and monitoring for your model. This integration allows you to do the following:

- **Monitor your machine learning models**: Once your machine learning model is deployed as a web service, Application Insights can be used to monitor its performance, availability, and usage. This includes tracking how often the model is called, response times, success rates, and any failures or exceptions that occur.
- **Log custom events and metrics**: You can log custom events, traces, and metrics from your machine learning models to Application Insights. This can include detailed information about the data being processed, predictions being made, and any other metrics relevant to your model's performance and usage.

- **Analyze and visualize telemetry data**: Application Insights provides tools for analyzing and visualizing the telemetry data that's been collected from your machine learning services. This can help you understand how your models are being used, identify trends or anomalies in their performance, and troubleshoot issues.
- **Set up alerts**: You can configure alerts in Application Insights based on metrics or events related to your machine learning service. This can help you respond quickly to potential issues, such as a drop in prediction accuracy or an increase in response times.
- **Diagnose issues with Live Metrics Stream**: Application Insights' Live Metrics Stream provides real-time visibility into the performance and health of your machine learning services, allowing you to diagnose issues as they happen.

Container Registry

Azure Container Registry is a managed, private Docker registry service based on the open source Docker Registry 2.0. It is used to store and manage container images that are used in Azure ML for various purposes, such as training and deploying models.

With that, let's start examining some of the overall model management and deployment features in Azure ML.

Describe model management and deployment capabilities in Azure ML

As you've already seen throughout this chapter, Azure ML has a lot of capabilities –ranging from developing to deploying both simple and complex machine learning models.

In this section, we'll look at three different (yet connected) areas of model management in Azure ML:

- Model management
- Model deployment capabilities
- Machine learning operations

Let's look at each of them.

Model management and deployment capabilities

Azure ML offers robust model deployment capabilities, allowing data scientists and developers to operationalize their machine learning models efficiently and at scale. These capabilities span various deployment targets, including cloud, on-premises, and edge environments, and provide the flexibility to meet a wide range of operational requirements.

Over the next few pages, we'll look at the key deployment capabilities of Azure ML.

Deployment targets

Depending on the size of your models and how comfortable you are with different types of infrastructure, you can deploy Azure ML models to a variety of targets, including the following:

- **Azure Kubernetes Service (AKS)**: Ideal for high-scale production deployments, AKS provides a managed Kubernetes environment that supports advanced scenarios such as autoscaling, A/B testing, and high availability. If your deployment involves complex workflows or requires integration with other microservices or backend systems, AKS provides the necessary infrastructure and tools for managing such deployments. Choose AKS when you need to deploy large-scale, production-grade machine learning models that require auto-scaling and high availability.

- **Azure Container Instances (ACI)**: Best suited for low-scale CPU-based workloads and development/testing scenarios, ACI offers a cost-effective and simple deployment option without the need for Kubernetes expertise. Choose ACI for quick prototyping, testing, and development of machine learning models without the overhead of managing a Kubernetes cluster.

- **Azure Machine Learning Compute Instances**: This is useful for batch-scoring scenarios or when you need to run predictions on a schedule or on-demand without a web service. Choose Azure Machine Learning Compute Instances for development, experimentation, and interactive exploration of datasets and models using Jupyter Notebooks.

- **Edge devices**: For scenarios requiring low-latency predictions or where data privacy is a concern, models can be deployed to edge devices using Azure IoT Edge. This allows for local model inference, reducing the need to send data back to the cloud for processing. Choose an edge device deployment in scenarios where real-time inference is required, or where network connectivity is limited or unreliable.

Model packaging

Azure ML packages models as **Docker containers**, which can be deployed anywhere that Docker containers are supported. A container holds all of the code and support tooling necessary to support the model. This approach ensures consistency across different environments and simplifies the deployment process, such as moving from development to production.

Model management and versioning

Azure ML provides a central repository for storing and managing trained models. You can version models, track their metadata, and manage their life cycle from training to retirement.

Monitoring and diagnostics

Once deployed, Azure ML offers tools for monitoring the health and performance of your models in production. This includes data drift monitoring, application insights integration for telemetry, and logging capabilities to help diagnose issues.

Security and compliance

Azure ML deployments can be secured using standard Azure security controls, including network isolation with virtual networks, encryption in transit and at rest, and authentication and authorization controls. Compliance with industry standards and regulations is also supported through **Azure Policy** (**AzPolicy**).

> **Further reading**
>
> For more information on using AzPolicy with Azure ML, go to `https://learn.microsoft.com/en-us/azure/machine-learning/security-controls-policy`.

Scalability and performance

Depending on the deployment target, Azure ML supports autoscaling to automatically adjust resources based on the load, ensuring that your deployments can handle varying levels of demand efficiently.

Integration with MLOps practices

The deployment capabilities are designed to integrate seamlessly with **machine learning operations** (**MLOps**) practices, supporting **continuous integration and delivery** (**CI/CD**) pipelines for machine learning models. This allows for automated model training, validation, deployment, and monitoring within a robust DevOps framework.

By leveraging these deployment capabilities, organizations can streamline the process of bringing machine learning models into production, ensuring they are scalable, secure, and maintainable over time.

MLOps

MLOps is a set of operational principles, based on DevOps, that include the concepts of CI/CD and are designed to operationalize the life cycle of machine learning tasks.

Azure MLOps represents a comprehensive approach to integrating machine learning models into production environments seamlessly and efficiently. As machine learning technologies advance, creating models that deliver precise forecasts has become more accessible. However, transitioning these models from development to production poses unique challenges that require a structured approach, combining people, processes, and technology to operationalize machine learning within an enterprise effectively.

Consider a situation where you have developed a machine learning model that surpasses all expectations in terms of accuracy and has garnered the admiration of your organization's stakeholders. The next step is deploying this model into a live environment, which might present unforeseen complexities. Before deployment, the organization must establish a framework involving the necessary governance, personnel, workflows, and tooling to leverage the machine learning model effectively in production settings.

As the landscape evolves, there might be occasions where an updated model outperforms the existing one in production. Introducing a new model into a live environment raises critical considerations:

- Ensuring the transition to the new model does not disrupt ongoing business operations that depend on the current system.

- In light of regulatory demands, there may be a need to justify the predictions made by the new model or to reproduce the model entirely should it generate unexpected or biased outcomes due to new data.

- Given the dynamic nature of data, it's essential to periodically retrain the model to sustain its accuracy. This necessitates designating an individual or team responsible for data management, monitoring model performance, retraining efforts, and addressing any model failures.

While some aspects of MLOps align with traditional DevOps practices – such as implementing unit and integration tests and utilizing version control – other elements are uniquely tailored to machine learning:

- Facilitating continuous experimentation and benchmarking against existing models

- Monitoring for shifts in incoming data to identify data drift

- Automating model retraining processes and establishing rollback mechanisms for rapid recovery from setbacks

- Developing and maintaining scalable data pipelines for both training models and executing predictions

The essence of MLOps is to bridge the divide between the developmental phase and operational deployment, thereby accelerating the delivery of value to end users. This transition demands a reevaluation of conventional development and deployment strategies to better align with the agile nature of machine learning applications.

Monitoring models as part of MLOps helps detect **drift** (the change in data over time that causes deviations in the model). Drift is overcome through the process of **adaptation** – periodically retraining the model based on updated data.

It's important to recognize that MLOps requirements can vary significantly between organizations. The architecture that's designed for MLOps in a large, global corporation is likely to differ considerably from the setup in a smaller, emerging company. Organizations typically start with modest initiatives and expand their MLOps capabilities as their experience, portfolio of models, and operational maturity increase.

In the next section, you'll put some of the things you've used into practice by creating a machine learning model of your own.

Build a machine learning model in Azure ML

In *Chapter 3*, *Identify Common Machine Learning Techniques*, you learned about some of the core ideas behind how machine learning works (including model names, sample algorithms, and the basics of validation).

In this section, we're going to have a break from the theory and create a machine learning model in Azure ML!

> **Prerequisites**
>
> To complete this exercise, you will need an Azure subscription (either trial or paid) so that you can configure and access Azure resources. You can sign up for Azure credit at `https://azure.microsoft.com/en-us/pricing/offers/ms-azr-0044p/`.

Creating a machine learning workspace

Once you have enabled Azure services in your environment, follow these steps to configure the services and set up a model:

1. Navigate to the Azure portal (`https://portal.azure.com`) and sign in.
2. Under **Azure services**, click **Create a resource**.
3. Filter using the text `machine learning`, select **Create** under **Azure Machine Learning**, and then select **Azure Machine Learning**, as shown in *Figure 5.2*:

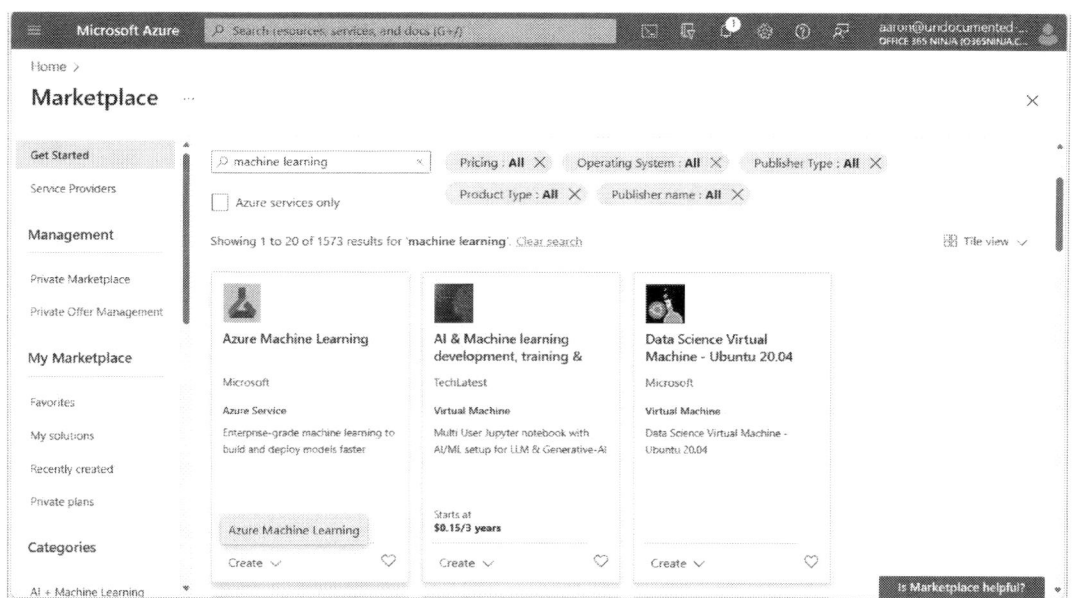

Figure 5.2 – Creating an Azure ML resource

4. On the **Create a machine learning workspace** page, select a **Subscription** option. Also, select an existing **Resource group** (or **Create** a new one).

5. Under **Workspace details**, enter a **Name** value for the workspace and select a **Region** option. You can leave the rest of the settings as-is. See *Figure 5.3*:

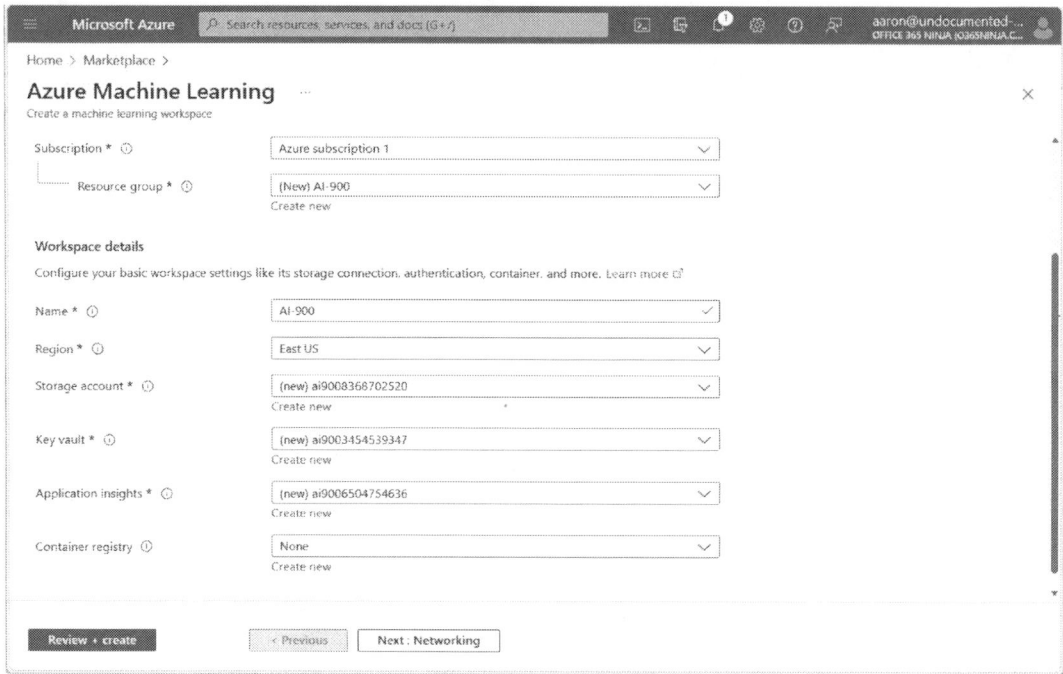

Figure 5.3 – Creating a machine learning workspace

6. Click **Review + create** and then click **Create**.
7. Click **Go to resource** (or open a new browser tab and navigate to https://ml.azure.com to launch Azure Machine Learning Studio), then select the new workspace name you deployed).

Now that you've created a workspace, it's time to start working with AutoML!

Using AutoML to train a model

In this section, you'll start working inside Azure Machine Learning Studio to train a model.

> **Sample datasets**
>
> You can find sample datasets suitable for Azure ML all over the internet. Kaggle (https://www.kaggle.com) contains nearly 300,000 datasets and is constantly being updated. Other popular sources for data include OpenML (https://openml.orgv), Carnegie Mellon University (https://guides.library.cmu.edu/machine-learning/datasets), and the UCI Machine Learning Repository (https://archive.ics.uci.edu/). Many datasets include information on what type of models or scenarios they are suitable for (such as binary classification or regression), so when choosing a dataset, you'll need to configure the parameters for your AutoML job accordingly.

In this example, we'll be using a dataset that predicts engine health based on several metrics captured from sensor readings, though you can use any dataset. You can download the dataset for this chapter from this book's GitHub repository: `https://github.com/PacktPublishing/Microsoft-Azure-AI-Fundamentals-AI-900-Exam-Guide`.

Let's get started:

> **Note**
> Microsoft also provides a sample dataset, available at `https://aka.ms/bike-rentals`, that can be used for this regression task.

1. From Azure Machine Learning Studio, under **Authoring**, select **Automated ML**:

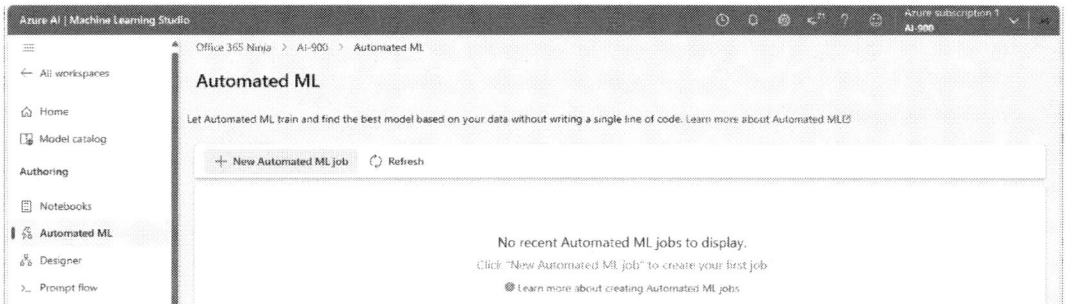

Figure 5.4 – Selecting Automated ML

2. Click **New Automated ML job**.
3. On the **Basic settings** page, enter **Job name** and **New experiment name** values (or accept the defaults). Click **Next**:

98   Describe Azure Machine Learning Capabilities

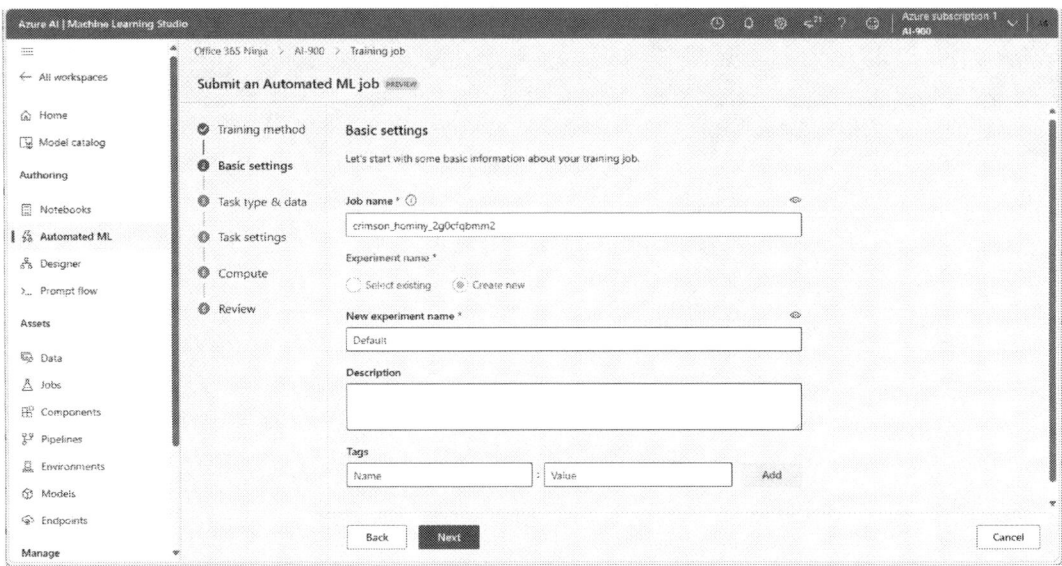

Figure 5.5 – Configuring the Basic settings page

4. If you are using the engine health dataset, set **Select task type** to **Classification**. If you are using the Microsoft-provided bike rental dataset, choose **Regression** as the task type.

5. Under **Select data**, click **Create**:

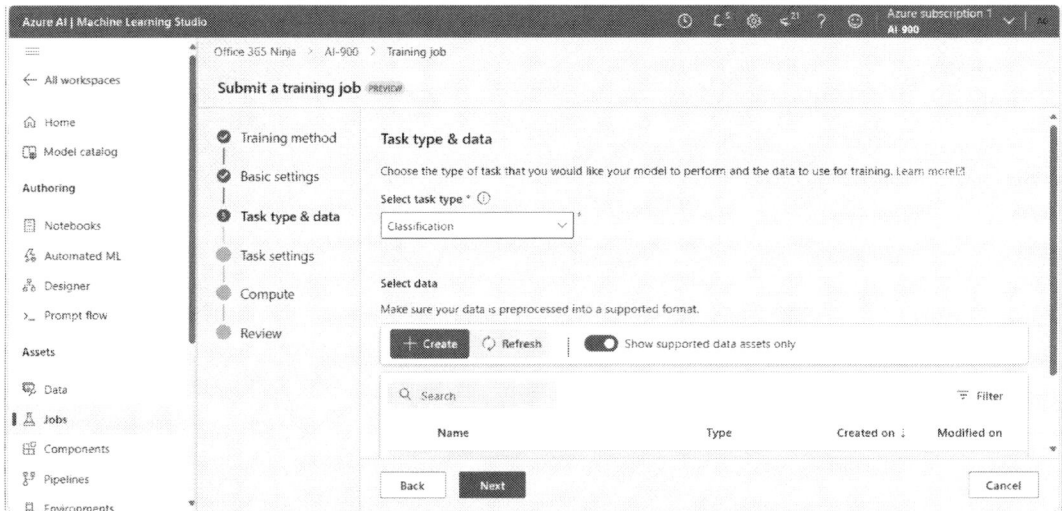

Figure 5.6 – Configuring the task's type and data

6. On the **Data type** page, enter **Name** and **Type** values. In this case, the source data is going to be a CSV file, so you can select **Tabular** for **Type** and click **Next**:

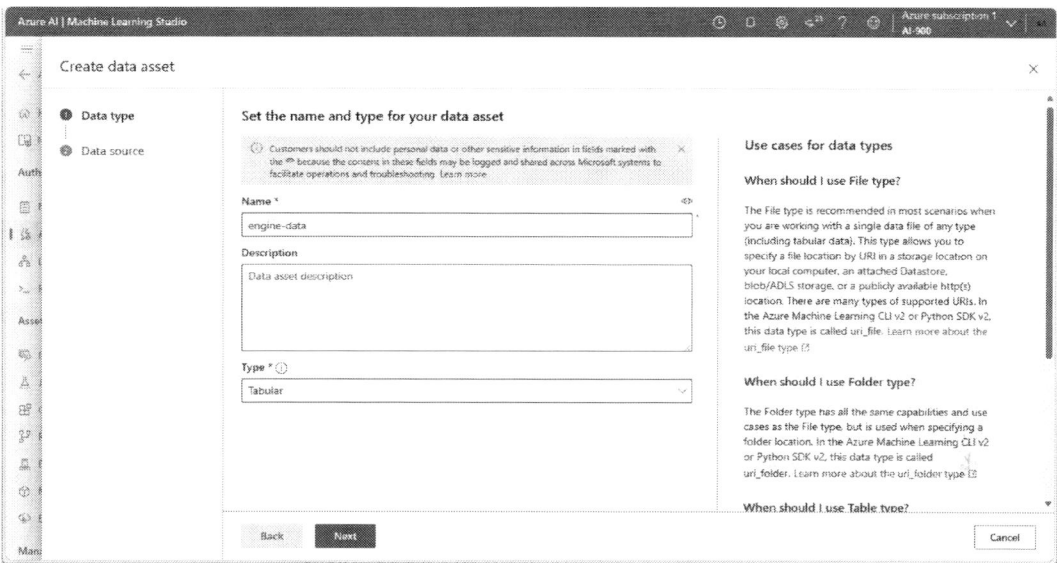

Figure 5.7 – Configuring the data asset

7. On the **Data source** page, select a source location. If you have downloaded a dataset to your local computer, you can select **From local files**. If you have an HTTP-enabled endpoint where your tabular data is stored, select **From web files**. After selecting the source for your dataset, click **Next**:

    A. If you selected **From web files** for the data source location, enter the URL where the data is stored.

    B. If you selected **From local files**, select **Azure Blob Storage** for **Datastore type** and click **Next**. See *Figure 5.8*:

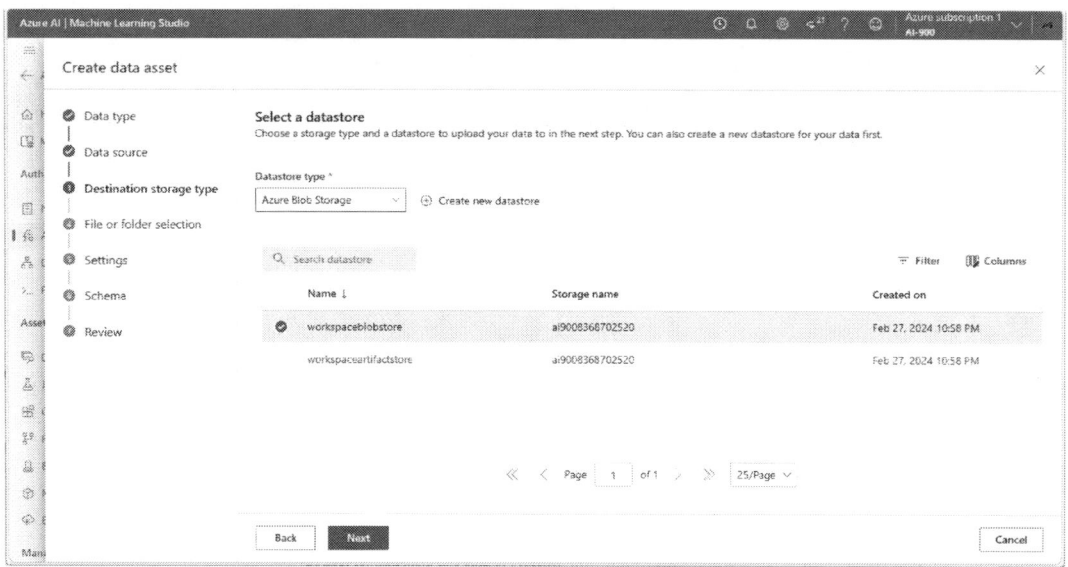

Figure 5.8 – Selecting a data store location

8. If you selected **From local files** for the data source, click **Upload files or folder** and browse to the location where your source data is located. Click **Next** when you're finished.

9. Once the data has been imported, you'll have a chance to review it. Azure ML will automatically detect the format of the data, so you'll want to ensure it's correct. Click **Next** to continue:

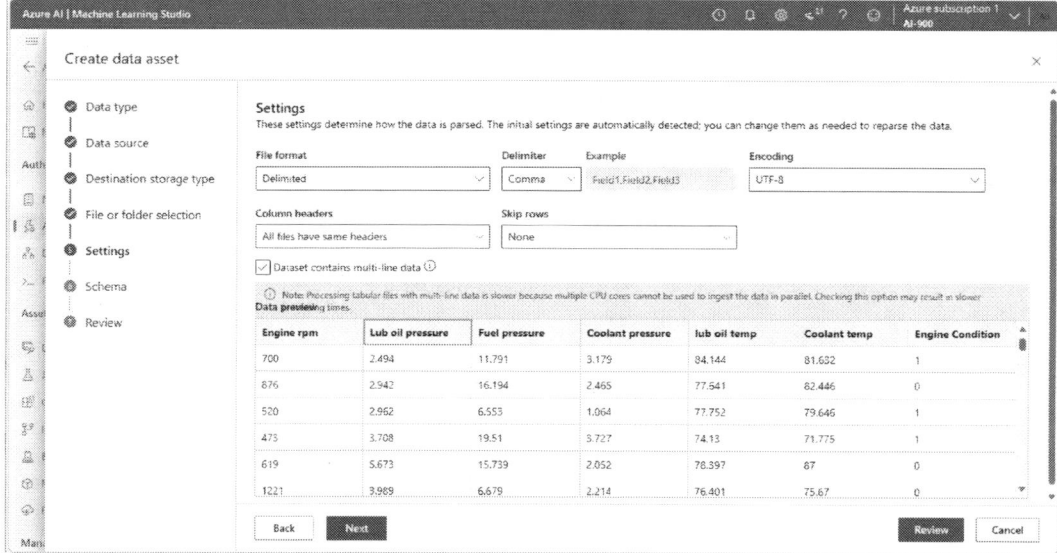

Figure 5.9 – Viewing the imported data

Build a machine learning model in Azure ML   101

10. On the **Schema** page, click **Next**.
11. On the **Review** page, click **Create**.
12. Once the dataset has been created, select the dataset and click **Next** to submit the AutoML job. See *Figure 5.10*:

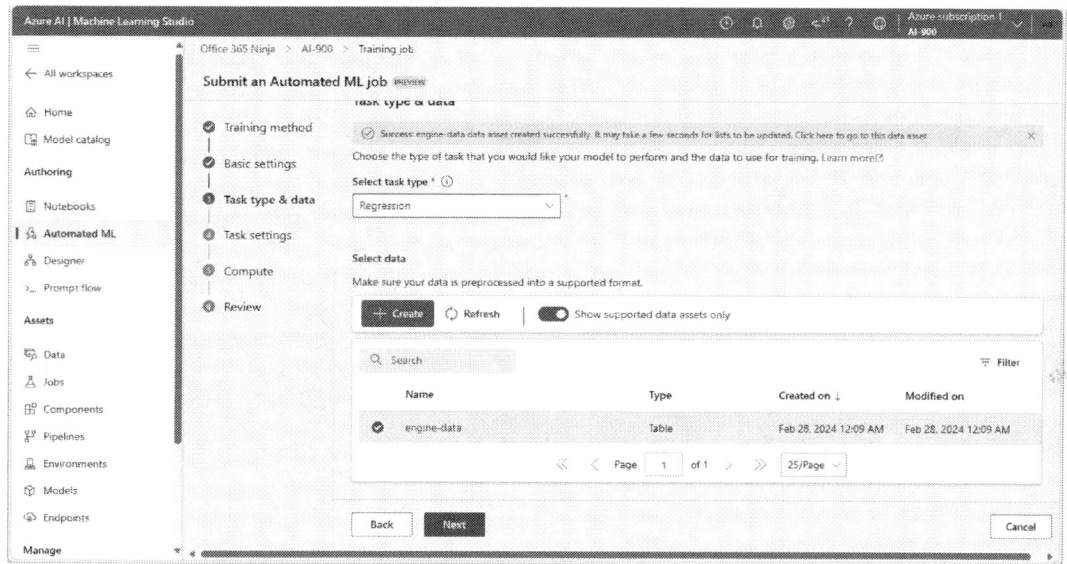

Figure 5.10 – Selecting the dataset

13. On the **Task settings** page, select a **Target column** value. This is the label that you are going to predict. For this example, select **Engine Condition**. If you are using the Microsoft-provided bike rental dataset, choose **Rentals**, as that is the value you are trying to predict:

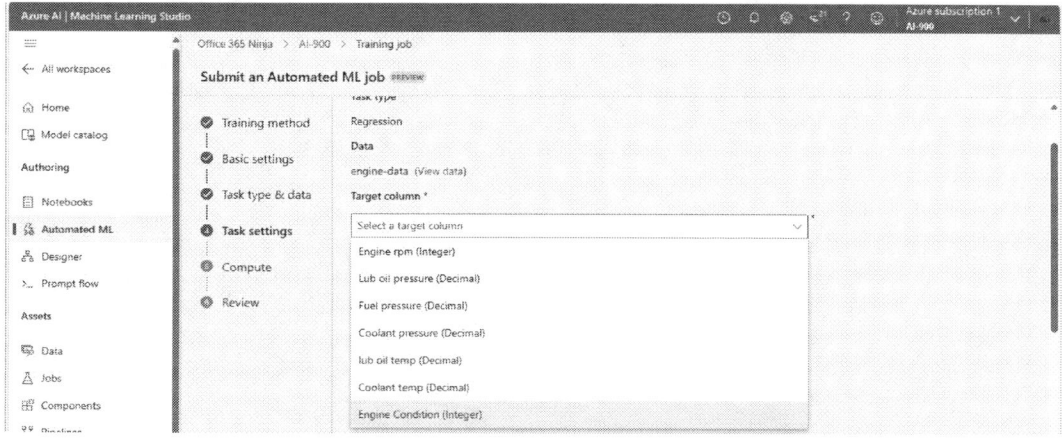

Figure 5.11 – Configuring a target column

14. Select **View additional configuration settings**. On the **Additional configuration** flyout, configure the following settings:

    A. If you're using the engine health dataset, under **Primary metric**, select **AUCWeighted**.

    B. If you're using the bike rental dataset, under **Primary metric**, select **NormalizedRootMeanSquaredError**.

15. Clear the **Use all supported models** checkbox and choose models that might best support your data type (you can leave the default selected, but it will take longer to go through each of the models). If your data source has recommended model types, select those:

    A. For the engine health model, select **LogisticRegresion**, **DecisionTree**, **RandomForest**, **KNN**, and **LightGBM**.

    B. For the Microsoft-provided bike rental model, select **RandomForest** and **LightGBM**:

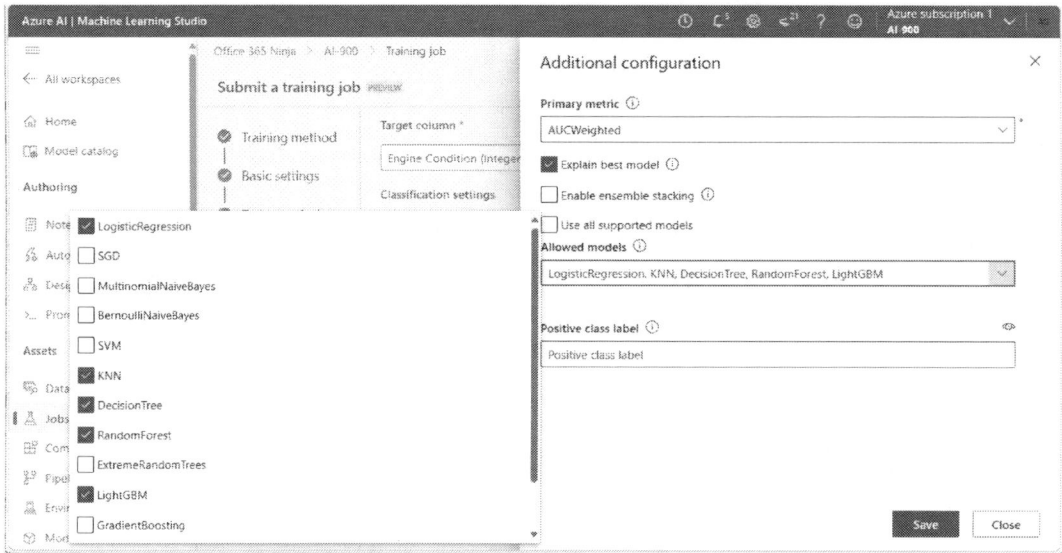

Figure 5.12 – Configuring additional job parameters

> **Further reading**
>
> For more information on which primary metric choices may work best for your model, check out `https://learn.microsoft.com/en-us/azure/machine-learning/how-to-configure-auto-train?view=azureml-api-2&tabs=python#supported-algorithms`.

16. Click **Save**.
17. Under **Limits**, configure the following values:

    Max trials: 3

    Max concurrent trials: 3

    Max nodes: 3

    Metric score threshold: 0.085

    Experiment timeout: 45 minutes

    Iteration timeout: 30 minutes

    Enable early termination: Selected

18. Under **Validate and test**, configure the following values:

    Validation type: Train-validation split

    Percentage validation of data: 10

    Test data: None

19. Click **Next**.
20. On the **Compute** page, configure the following values:

    Select compute type: Serverless

    Virtual machine type: CPU

    Virtual machine tier: Dedicated

    Virtual machine size: Standard_DS3_v2 is recommended, though you can use any

    Number of instances: 1

21. Click **Next**:

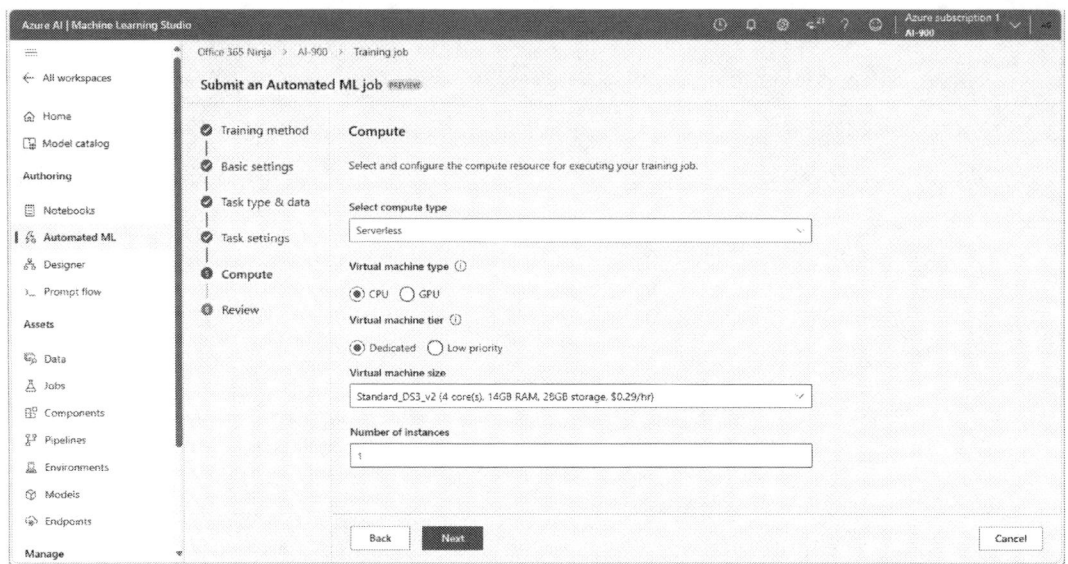

Figure 5.13 – Configuring compute settings

22. On the **Review** page, click **Submit training job**.

The job will be submitted and started automatically. After the job has been submitted, you can refresh the **Jobs** page to see its current status, as shown in *Figure 5.14*:

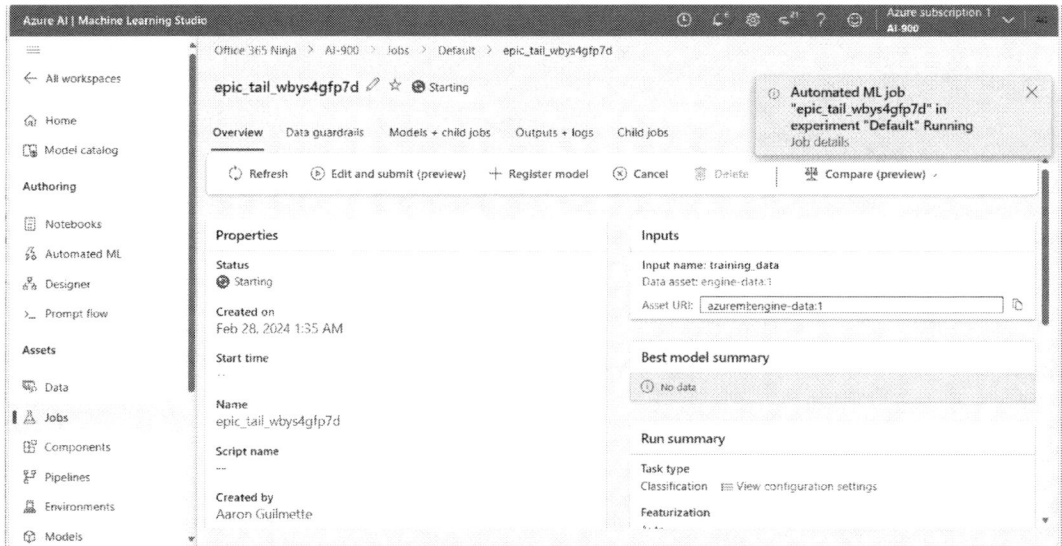

Figure 5.14 – AutoML job status

Reviewing and selecting the best model

Once model training has been completed, scroll down on the **Overview** tab to view the **Best model summary** area. See *Figure 5.15*:

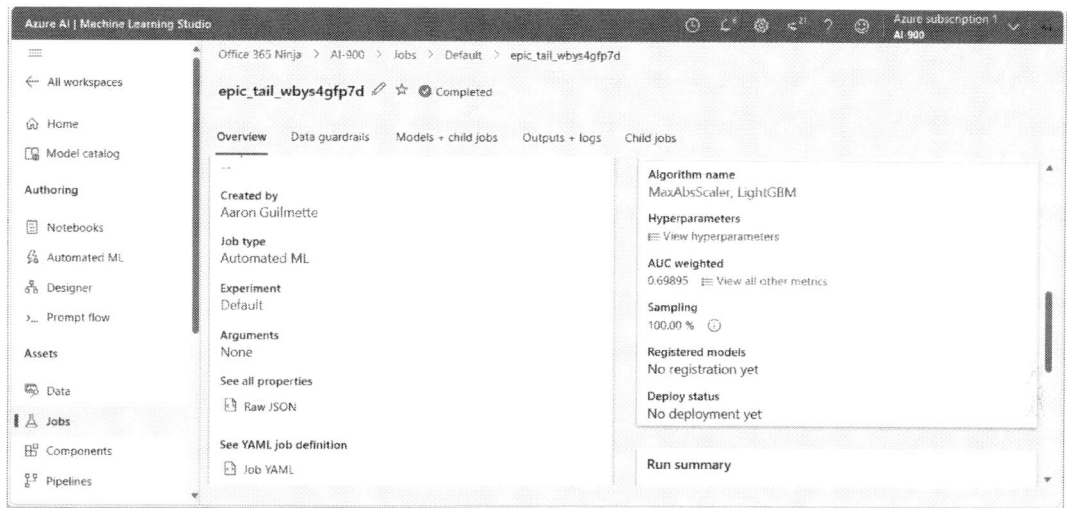

Figure 5.15 – Reviewing the training information

Select the value for **Algorithm name** and then select the **Metrics** tab to review the details of the model's performance:

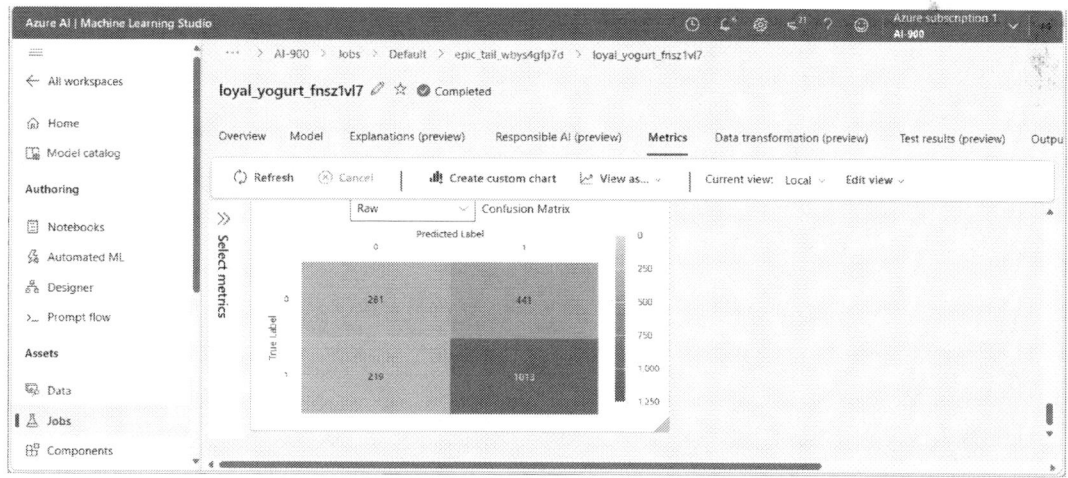

Figure 5.16 – Reviewing the model metrics

Deploying and testing the model

With the model trained and the best algorithm selected, you can deploy it. To do so, follow these steps:

1. Inside Azure Machine Learning Studio, navigate to the **Model** tab for the best model trained.
2. Click **Deploy** and select **Web service**:

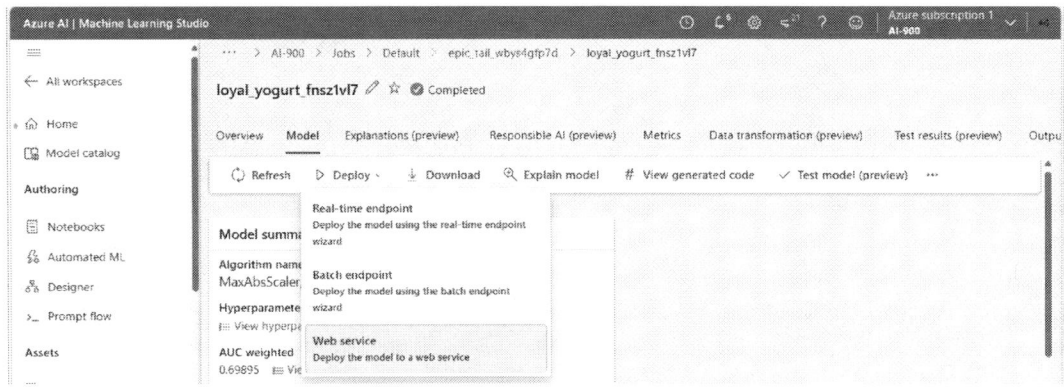

Figure 5.17 – Deploying a model

3. On the **Deploy a model** flyout, enter **Name** and **Description** values.
4. Under **Compute** type, select **Azure Container Instance**.
5. Scroll to the bottom of the flyout and click **Deploy**.

The model will deploy as a web service. It may take 5-10 minutes, depending on the size of the dataset and model type.

Testing the deployed model service

Once the model has been deployed, you can manually submit test data to see what its predictions might be. To submit a test, follow these steps:

1. Inside the workspace you have configured, select **Endpoints**.
2. Under **Real-time endpoints**, select the endpoint that you provisioned as a web service.
3. Select the **Test** tab.
4. Select the **Form editor** radio button to enter data values in the web form or select the **JSON editor** radio button to update test values in a pre-configured JSON array. Depending on your dataset and model type, you may only see the JSON editor.
5. Fill out test inputs for each of the displayed features.

A. **Engine health model**: Specify values for **Engine RPM**, **Lub oil pressure**, **Fuel pressure**, **Coolant pressure**, **Lub oil temp**, and **Coolant temp**. Click **Test** and review the values under **Test result**. **Results** that display *int 1* mean that the engine is likely healthy, while **Results** that display *int 0* indicate the engine is likely unhealthy:

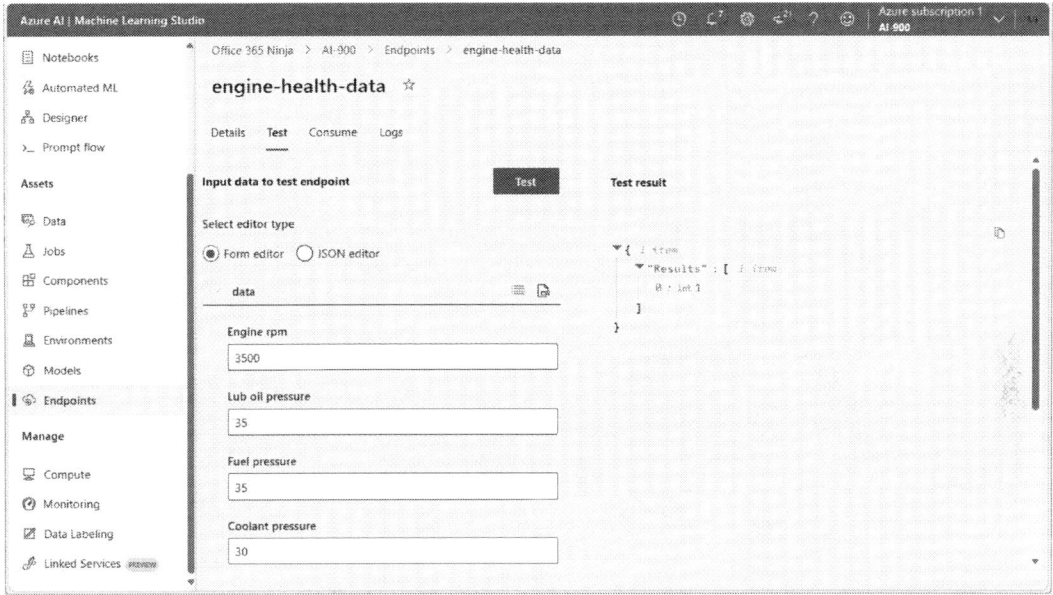

Figure 5.18 – Testing the classification model

B. **Bike rentals model**: Specify numeric values for **day**, **mnth**, **year**, **season**, **holiday**, **weekday**, **working day**, **weathersit**, **temp**, **atemp**, **hum**, and **windspeed**. Click **Test** and review the values under **Test result**. **Results** should show an integer that predicts the number of predicted bike rentals.

Congratulations! You've trained machine learning models to help predict outcomes based on training data! You can continue exploring other models and datasets to see what insights you can uncover.

Teardown

When you're done exploring Azure ML and AutoML, you can delete the configured resources in Azure to avoid incurring unwanted Azure service charges. To do so, follow these steps:

1. In Azure Machine Learning Studio, on the **Endpoints** tab, select any endpoints that you have published.
2. Click **Delete** and then confirm the deletion.
3. Click **Home**, and then click **Workspaces**.

4. Navigate to the Azure portal (https://portal.azure.com) and search for Resource groups.

5. Select the resource group you specified when you created the Azure ML workspace.

6. Click **Delete resource group**, enter the name of the resource group to confirm that you want to delete it, and then click **Delete**.

With that, of your resources will be deprovisioned.

Summary

In this chapter, you learned about the features and capabilities of Azure ML and AutoML. You learned about the data and compute services and components that are used to support Azure ML, such as compute clusters, models, workspaces, and storage accounts.

You also learned about the model management and deployment capabilities of Azure ML, as well as the concepts surrounding MLOps.

Finally, you learned how to deploy Azure ML models, train them with sample data, and then test against them.

In the next chapter, you'll begin exploring computer vision solutions.

Exam Readiness Drill – Chapter Review Questions

Apart from a solid understanding of key concepts, being able to think quickly under time pressure is a skill that will help you ace your certification exam. That is why working on these skills early on in your learning journey is key.

Chapter review questions are designed to improve your test-taking skills progressively with each chapter you learn and review your understanding of key concepts in the chapter at the same time. You'll find these at the end of each chapter.

> **Before you proceed**
>
> If you don't have a Packt Library subscription or you haven't purchased this book from the Packt store, you will need to unlock the online resources to access the exam readiness drills. Unlocking is free and needs to be done only once. To learn how to do that, head over to the chapter titled *Chapter 12, Accessing the Online Resources*.

To open the Chapter Review Questions for this chapter, perform the following steps:

1. Click the link – https://packt.link/AI-900_CH05.

    Alternatively, you can scan the following QR code (*Figure 5.19*):

Figure 5.19 – QR code that opens Chapter Review Questions for logged-in users

2. Once you log in, you'll see a page similar to the one shown in *Figure 5.20*:

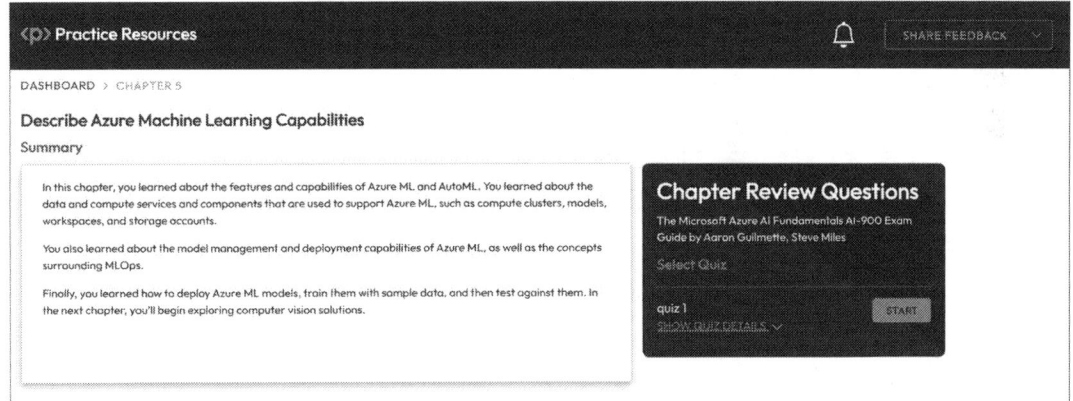

Figure 5.20 – Chapter Review Questions for Chapter 5

3. Once ready, start the following practice drills, re-attempting the quiz multiple times.

Exam Readiness Drill

For the first three attempts, don't worry about the time limit.

ATTEMPT 1

The first time, aim for at least **40%**. Look at the answers you got wrong and read the relevant sections in the chapter again to fix your learning gaps.

ATTEMPT 2

The second time, aim for at least **60%**. Look at the answers you got wrong and read the relevant sections in the chapter again to fix any remaining learning gaps.

ATTEMPT 3

The third time, aim for at least **75%**. Once you score 75% or more, you start working on your timing.

> **Tip**
> You may take more than **three** attempts to reach 75%. That's okay. Just review the relevant sections in the chapter till you get there.

Working On Timing

Your aim is to keep the score the same while trying to answer these questions as quickly as possible. Here's an example of how your next attempts should look like:

Attempt	Score	Time Taken
Attempt 5	77%	21 mins 30 seconds
Attempt 6	78%	18 mins 34 seconds
Attempt 7	76%	14 mins 44 seconds

Table 5.1 – Sample timing practice drills on the online platform

> **Note**
> The time limits shown in the above table are just examples. Set your own time limits with each attempt based on the time limit of the quiz on the website.

With each new attempt, your score should stay above **75%** while your "time taken" to complete should "decrease". Repeat as many attempts as you want till you feel confident dealing with the time pressure.

Part 3: Describe Features of Computer Vision Workloads on Azure

In this part, you'll begin exploring **computer vision**—the concepts and technologies that allow computers to look at images and identify objects and text.

This part includes the following chapters:

- *Chapter 6, Identify Common Types of Computer Vision Solutions*
- *Chapter 7, Identify Azure Tools and Services for Computer Vision Tasks*

6
Identify Common Types of Computer Vision Solutions

In *Chapter 5*, *Describe Azure Machine Learning Capabilities*, you learned to describe the capabilities of **automated machine learning** (**AutoML**), data and compute services for data science and **machine learning** (**ML**), as well as model management and deployment capabilities in Azure Machine Learning.

In this chapter, you will learn about the Azure solutions available to solve problems for the **artificial intelligence** (**AI**) area of **computer vision** (**CV**), which encompasses manipulating, analyzing, interpreting, and deriving information and understanding from the pixel values of digital sources such as images and videos.

This content requires some understanding of ML principles; if you have skipped straight to this chapter and are new to ML or just want to refresh on some existing knowledge, then you can refer to *Part 2 – Describe the Fundamental Principles of Machine Learning on Azure* as an ML primer before you continue with this chapter.

CV solutions can provide *pre-built* and *customizable* **ML models** that can be used by developers to enhance their applications, software, and services.

The objectives and skills we'll cover in this chapter include the following:

- Introduction to CV solutions
- Identify features of image classification solutions
- Identify features of object detection solutions
- Identify features of **optical character recognition** (**OCR**) solutions
- Identify features of facial detection and facial analysis solutions

By the end of this chapter, you should be aware of the features of solutions for detecting and analyzing images, objects, optical characters, and faces.

Introduction to CV solutions

The goal of **CV** solutions is to gain insights, meaning, and understanding from an image; that is, what information is the image telling me?

Image processing

CV's capabilities are built upon the concept of *interpretation, understanding,* and *manipulation* of an image through its **pixel values**; computers see an array of *numeric pixel values* when they look at an image.

This computer processing of images is illustrated in *Figure 6.1*, which shows how a slice of pepperoni pizza (*my personal favorite; no pineapple allowed*) would appear to a computer:

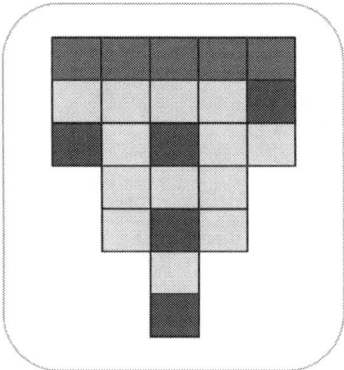

Figure 6.1 – How an image appears to a computer

Images are seen as **pixel arrays**, the array in *Figure 6.1* is made up of **7 rows** and **5 columns**; the *image resolution* is therefore expressed as **7 x 5**. Each pixel in the array for a color image is given a **numeric pixel value** that represents the **RGB channels** (*layers*); for grayscale images, the pixel values would be represented by differing shades of gray, each with a value of between *255* for *white* pixels and *0* for *black* pixels.

Pixel values are altered through the use of **filters** to carry out image processing operations for visual effect creation.

There are many filters, some of which are as follows:

- Blur
- Color inversion
- Edge detection
- Sharpen

Introduction to CV solutions   115

This image filter operation is carried out by **convolving** (*moving or passing*) the filter over an image, which provides a new array of values for the image that will manipulate (*change/alter*) the RGB layer pixel values. This provides a transformed image that is different from the original; this is a common use case seen in digital photo editing on your smartphone or image editing software.

You can see this illustrated in *Figure 6.2*:

Figure 6.2 – Image filter operation example

In this image, a simple filter has been applied to a portion of the image, which changes the affected pixels where the filter has been passed over.

CV ML

An ML model that has been trained on a vast volume of images allows us to extract information that can be actionable or provide meaning. This can be better understood from *Figure 6.3*, which shows a simple example that can provide *descriptive information* by returning associated **tags** from the image:

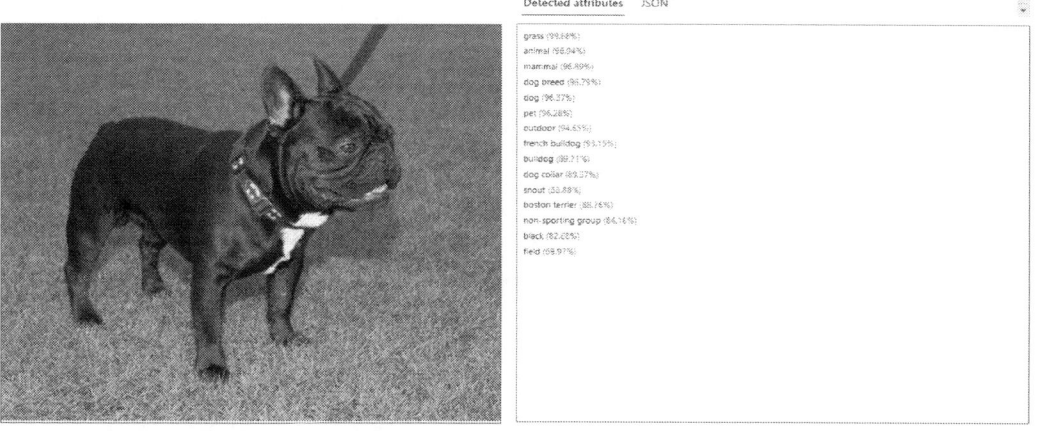

Figure 6.3 – Image analysis information provided using CV

116   Identify Common Types of Computer Vision Solutions

In *Figure 6.3*, the detected attributes can be seen in the JSON output, such as identifying the image as `dog` and the breed as `french bulldog`, and with confidence ratings.

The following is the corresponding API's JSON response for the object detection from *Figure 6.3*:

```
{ "aim-request-id": "3800844f-2eb1-4abf-9cb3-d8f055e247f0",
  "content-length": "867",
  "content-type": "application/json; charset=utf-8",
  "modelVersion": "2023-10-01",
  "metadata": {
    "width": 720,
    "height": 576
  },
  "tagsResult": {
    "values": [
      {
        "name": "grass",
        "confidence": 0.996832013130188
      },
      {
        "name": "animal",
        "confidence": 0.9693894386291504
      },
      {
        "name": "mammal",
        "confidence": 0.9689017534255981
      },
      {
        "name": "dog breed",
        "confidence": 0.9679374694824219
      },
      {
        "name": "dog",
        "confidence": 0.9637042880058289
      },
      {
        "name": "pet",
        "confidence": 0.9628428220748901
      },
      {
        "name": "outdoor",
        "confidence": 0.9465276002883911
      },
      {
```

```
      "name": "bulldog",
      "confidence": 0.8970986008644104
    },
    {
      "name": "dog collar",
      "confidence": 0.8937236070632935
    },
    {
      "name": "snout",
      "confidence": 0.888845682144165
    },
    {
      "name": "black",
      "confidence": 0.8267985582351685
    },
  ]
 }
}
```

Both *pre-trained* and *custom models* can be used for image analysis; the custom vision model would be used where you wish to train the model with your own image collection and not images from the dataset that was used with the pre-trained model.

The **foundation model** used for the tasks of CV is the **Microsoft Florence model**. It is pre-trained on vast amounts of captioned internet images in order to build models that can be used for image analysis tasks such as the following:

- **Image classification**: This is the capability of identifying an image category; can detect objects and people in a photo, and how many appear

- **Object detection**: This is the capability of identifying object location in an image, photo, or video; could detect location

- **Captioning**: This is the capability of generating human-readable descriptions for everything that appears in images such as a photo

- **Tagging**: This is the capability of generating a list of tags that can be associated with an image for its detected attributes

- **OCR**: This is the capability of extracting printed or handwritten text from **documents**, such as forms, invoices, expense receipts, and **images**, which could include vehicle number plates, street signs, product brand labels, names on movie posters, and so on

Figure 6.4 represents how the CV tasks listed previously use **adaptive models** built from the **Microsoft Florence foundation model**:

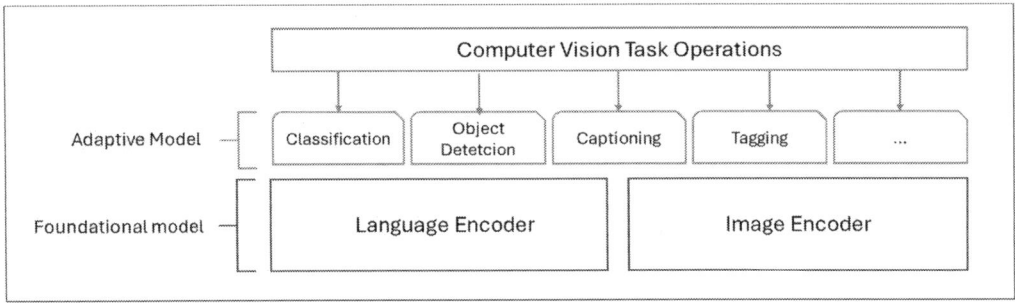

Figure 6.4 – Microsoft Florence multi-modal model for image data

This **multi-modal** foundational model of **Microsoft Florence** has included in it both a **language encoder**, which provides **text embeddings**, and an **image encoder**, which, based on `pixel values`, extracts features of the image.

You can learn more about **Project Florence** at this URL: `https://www.microsoft.com/en-us/research/project/projectflorence/`

In the first section of this chapter, you were introduced to the concept of CV. You then learned about the Microsoft Florence model and how it can be used as a foundation for CV tasks. In the following sections, you will learn to identify the features of CV solutions.

Identify features of image classification solutions

The CV capabilities of Azure Machine Learning can be used as a solution for image classification.

CV includes APIs that can interpret information and provide understanding from still and streaming images and allow further processing and analysisto take place.

Image classification refers to category prediction or classing of an image or sub-regions into groups based on predefined *classes* or *categories*; it addresses the question of "What is in this picture?".

An example of image classification can be seen in *Figure 6.5*:

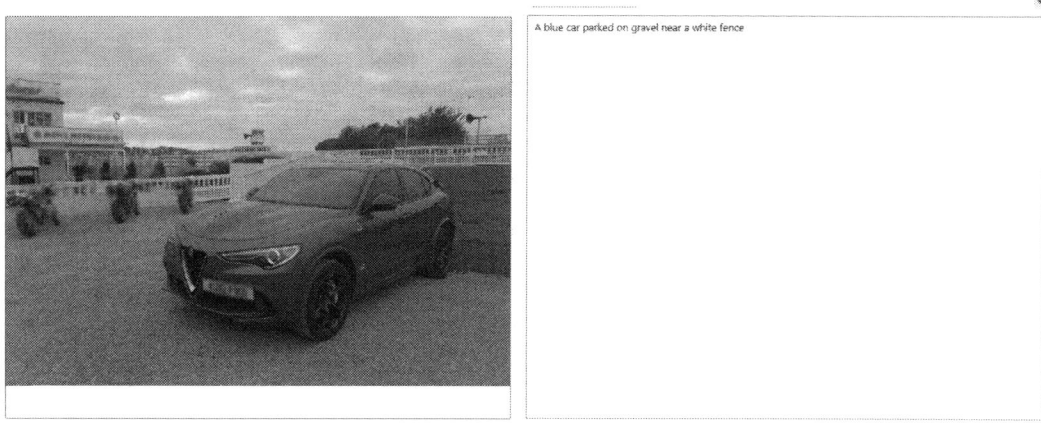

Figure 6.5 – Image classified as a car

The following is an extract of the corresponding API's JSON response for the image classification from *Figure 6.5*:

```
{
  "aim-request-id": "0df7e99e-29e4-48ea-a11e-c66bec449dd9",
  "content-length": "174",
  "content-type": "application/json; charset=utf-8",
  "modelVersion": "2023-10-01",
  "captionResult": {
    "text": "a blue car parked on gravel near a white fence",
    "confidence": 0.737828254699707
  },
  "metadata": {
    "width": 1420,
    "height": 1047
  }
}
```

From this JSON output, you can see the "caption" result returned for this image, along with a confidence rating. Note that there are no "location" coordinates; this will be covered in the *Identifying features of object detection solutions* section.

You could train an ML model to identify which *type* of *transportation* category is shown, such as **car**, **bus**, and **bicycle**. Another example could be to identify a *type* of *animal*, such as a **bird**, **cat**, **dog**, or **horse**, or identify a species of animal.

It should be noted that a **classification model** is used; with this model, `categories` can be predicted using a **supervised ML (SML)** model.

An **unsupervised ML (UML) clustering** model based on grouping features would not be appropriate for this use case; neither would a **regression** model, as this model would be used for any type of *number value* estimation.

Use case: This may be useful in the scenario where you need to know if an image contains an animal, a building, people, and so on; identifying species of plants or birds could also be a use case for image analysis.

This section looked at identifying features of image classification solutions using CV. In the next section, you will learn about identifying features of object detection solutions.

Identify features of object detection solutions

The CV capabilities of Azure Machine Learning can be used as a solution for object detection.

In the previous section, you learned that **image classification** provides us with categorization and can tell us of singular, binary information (that is, this is a person, a car, a dog or cat, and so on in the image), whereas **object detection** provides individual location information (in *pixels*) for objects in the image through a "bounding box" surrounding each identified object, as well as assigning tag information with a confidence rating.

While both **classification** and **detection** of images share a common objective of analyzing and interpreting image content, the difference is in the amount of detail returned; in addition to the categorization and caption labels that describe the image provided by the classification, the tag information has a percentage value on the confidence of what is the object detected.

> **Note**
> We will look at an example of object detection API operation information returned in more detail using the **Azure AI Vision service** using **Azure Vision Studio** in *Chapter 7, Identify Azure Tools and Services for Computer Vision Tasks*.

You can see in *Figure 6.6* a simple scenario for object detection:

Identify features of object detection solutions   121

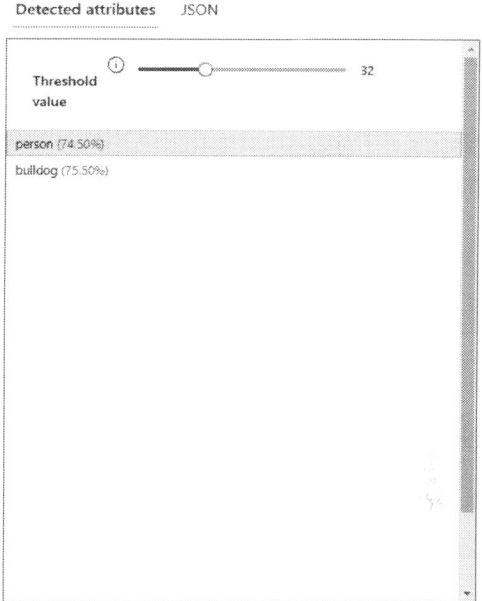

Figure 6.6 – Objects located within an image

From *Figure 6.6*, you can see that two objects have been detected and that each has a **bounding box** surrounding them. You will see that it has assigned detected attributes (tags) to each object and provided a percentage of confidence of what the object is categorized as. The **person** tagged object is correctly identified as a person, but the model is returning a percentage figure of only **74.50%**; this will be largely due to **occlusion**, meaning that the object's view is partially obscured and is not prominent. In this object's case, the glasses on the person object and the position in the background are partially covered by the second detected object tagged **bulldog** in the foreground.

Some of you may have already noticed a flaw in the **bulldog** detected object, which will highlight the caution needed when working with AI models and why the responsible AI principle of "reliability and safety" is so critical. The issue to be flagged here is that the API has returned that the model has predicted that the detected object is a bulldog, but is only **75.50%** certain that is the breed, when the breed is, in fact, a boxer. This would require the model to be trained further with more images to have a more accurate score and return the correct breed attribute.

The following is the corresponding API's JSON response for the object detection from *Figure 6.6*:

```
{"apim-request-id": "de342447-63a1-4a7b-a922-34a758d66f53",
  "content-length": "289",
  "content-type": "application/json; charset=utf-8",
  "modelVersion": "2023-10-01",
```

```json
    "metadata": {
      "width": 1347,
      "height": 1106
    },
    "objectsResult": {
      "values": [
        {
          "boundingBox": {
            "x": 567,
            "y": 306,
            "w": 555,
            "h": 795
          },
          "tags": [
            {
              "name": "person",
              "confidence": 0.745
            }
          ]
        },
        {
          "boundingBox": {
            "x": 0,
            "y": 365,
            "w": 840,
            "h": 729
          },
          "tags": [
            {
              "name": "bulldog",
              "confidence": 0.755
            }
          ]
        }
      ]
    }
}
```

In this JSON output, you can see additional information that is returned than when using **image classification**; you can see the "location coordinates" in pixels for each object detected, a tag for each object, and a confidence rating for that applied tag for the object. As mentioned, the model should be trained further to increase the confidence score so that the correct tag can be applied to the object; in this case, the tag should have been *boxer* and not *bulldog*.

It should be noted that object detection does not use a **regression** or **clustering** model but an **image analysis** model.

As well as a **pre-trained** CV model for object detection, a **custom** model can be trained using our own images; it could be trained to identify products or multiple instances of products, or certain aspects of products such as orientation, flaws, damage, and so on.

Use case: This may be useful in the scenario where you need to determine the location, placement, positioning, orientation, or spatial relationships of the categorized object(s) in the image.

This section looked at identifying the features of object detection solutions using CV. In the next section, you will learn about identifying features of OCR solutions.

Identify features of OCR solutions

The Computer Vision (CV) capabilities of Azure Machine Learning can be used as a solution for OCR.

The **OCR** solution can be used to extract "text" from an image. Letters and numbers are identified from shapes and then converted into *machine-encoded text* that can then be further utilized for processing by applications or users.

An example of OCR for an image can be seen in *Figure 6.7*:

Figure 6.7 – Extracting text from an image with OCR capability

The OCR model is trained to recognize elements of text, including punctuation, as well as numerals from individual shapes, and then produce an output as text. An example of a text output produced by an OCR model is shown in *Figure 6.8*:

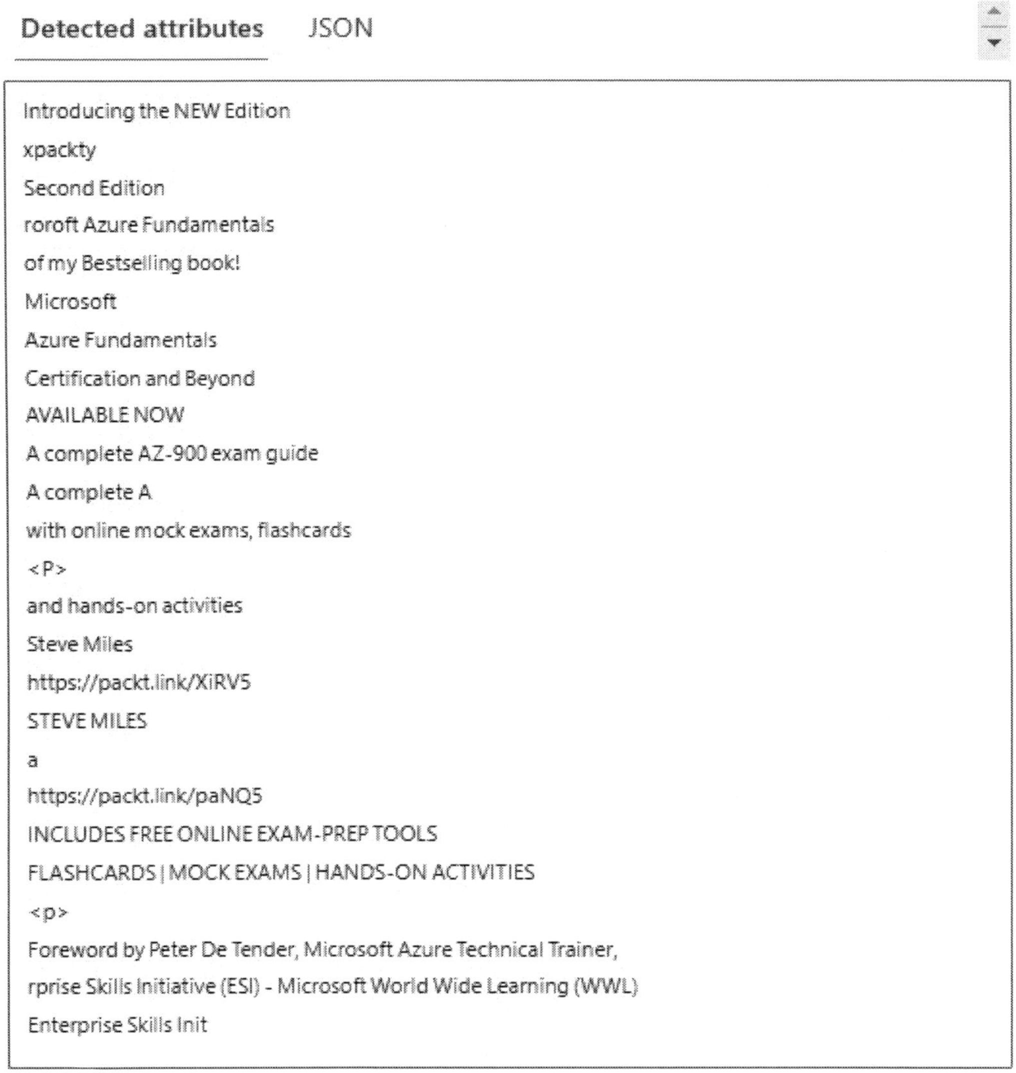

124 Identify Common Types of Computer Vision Solutions

Detected attributes JSON

```
Introducing the NEW Edition
xpackty
Second Edition
roroft Azure Fundamentals
of my Bestselling book!
Microsoft
Azure Fundamentals
Certification and Beyond
AVAILABLE NOW
A complete AZ-900 exam guide
A complete A
with online mock exams, flashcards
<P>
and hands-on activities
Steve Miles
https://packt.link/XiRV5
STEVE MILES
a
https://packt.link/paNQ5
INCLUDES FREE ONLINE EXAM-PREP TOOLS
FLASHCARDS | MOCK EXAMS | HANDS-ON ACTIVITIES
<p>
Foreword by Peter De Tender, Microsoft Azure Technical Trainer,
rprise Skills Initiative (ESI) - Microsoft World Wide Learning (WWL)
Enterprise Skills Init
```

Figure 6.8 – OCR model text extraction output

The following is an extract of the corresponding API's JSON response for the object detection from *Figure 6.8*:

```
{
  "words": [
    {
      "text": "roroft",
      "boundingPolygon": [
```

```json
        {
          "x": 5349,
          "y": 214
        },
        {
          "x": 5347,
          "y": 351
        },
        {
          "x": 5295,
          "y": 354
        },
        {
          "x": 5299,
          "y": 217
        }
      ],
      "confidence": 0.68
    },
    {
      "text": "Azure",
      "boundingPolygon": [
        {
          "x": 5347,
          "y": 361
        },
        {
          "x": 5346,
          "y": 490
        },
        {
          "x": 5294,
          "y": 494
        },
        {
          "x": 5295,
          "y": 364
        }
      ],
      "confidence": 0.981
    },
```

From this JSON output, as you saw in the object detection solution, there is still some inaccuracy in the text output that could be improved, such as "*roroft*" instead of "*Microsoft*", which showed a confidence rating of *0.68* in recognizing the shapes into a recognized word. This can be achieved with further training of a model, which highlights again the caution needed with AI models and why the responsible AI principle of "reliability and safety" is so critical.

We use the generic word "images," but the capability can be used to extract *printed* and *handwritten* text from photos, documents, note paper, TIFF files, and scanned PDF files.

Use case: This capability of "text extraction" may be useful in the scenario where you need to provide an inventory for a book collection, read a receipt for expense submission, extract invoice information, digitize historical documents for archival purposes, digitize handwritten report notes, extract names from road signs or movie posters, extract numbers from sporting event competitors, extract vehicle number plate numbers from CCTV, and so on.

This section looked at identifying the features of OCR using CV. The next section will explore facial detection and analysis.

Identify features of facial detection and facial analysis solutions

CV aspects using Azure Machine Learning algorithms can be utilized as a solution for creating image and video facial detection, analysis, and recognition capabilities in applications.

Face detection and analysis capabilities in ML can be used in the areas of identity verification and security. The capabilities can provide security access controls by determining the level of access by identifying and verifying the person's face. You could think of this like **role-based access control** (**RBAC**), but instead of controlling access based on a user's role, the level of access is determined by their face.

Use case: This may be useful in the scenario where you wish to tag recognized friends in social media photographs; for identifying and targeting demographic groups for use in advertising; identifying celebrities; locating missing or wanted persons using CCTV footage; for intelligent monitoring of face pose; attribute detection such as mask wearing.

Facial detection

The capability of **facial detection** in **Computer Vision** (**CV**) can take an image and identify human faces within it. Faces that are detected have a square box around them, and the location of faces can be provided with "bounding box" coordinates returned, which can help inform a relationship between the images.

It is important to know that this operation of *detection* is the first-stage capability for performing all other face service capabilities such as *analysis* and *recognition*; that is, we must first detect a face or faces to be able to derive any further information or understanding.

Figure 6.9 shows an example of facial detection by CV to extract the human faces located in the image:

Figure 6.9 – Detecting faces capability of CV

Figure 6.9 shows the returned face objects and also the value of no for the Face mask attribute.

The following is an extract (not a full response) of the corresponding API's JSON response for the object detection from *Figure 6.9*:

```
[
  {
    "recognitionModel": "recognition_01",
    "faceRectangle": {
      "width": 58,
      "height": 75,
```

```
            "left": 280,
            "top": 297
        },
        "faceLandmarks": {
          "pupilLeft": {
            "x": 291.3,
            "y": 332.8
          },
          "pupilRight": {
            "x": 315.2,
            "y": 327.2
          },
          "noseTip": {
            "x": 301.8,
            "y": 340.1
          },
          "mouthLeft": {
            "x": 297.1,
            "y": 355.8
          },
        },
        "faceAttributes": {
          "mask": {
            "type": "noMask",
            "noseAndMouthCovered": false
          }
        }
      }
    ]
```

From this JSON output, you can see the "bounding box" coordinates (in pixels) for the face object and the "face attributes" returned values; the "face landmark" value returned is part of facial analysis, which you will explore in the next section.

This section looked at identifying the features of facial detection solutions using CV. Next, you will learn about facial analysis.

Facial analysis

With ML models, the **facial analysis** capability can take an image and provide information on facial features, also referred to as **landmarks**, including categories of **mouth**, **lips**, **nose**, **eyes**, and **eyebrows**:

Identify features of facial detection and facial analysis solutions | 129

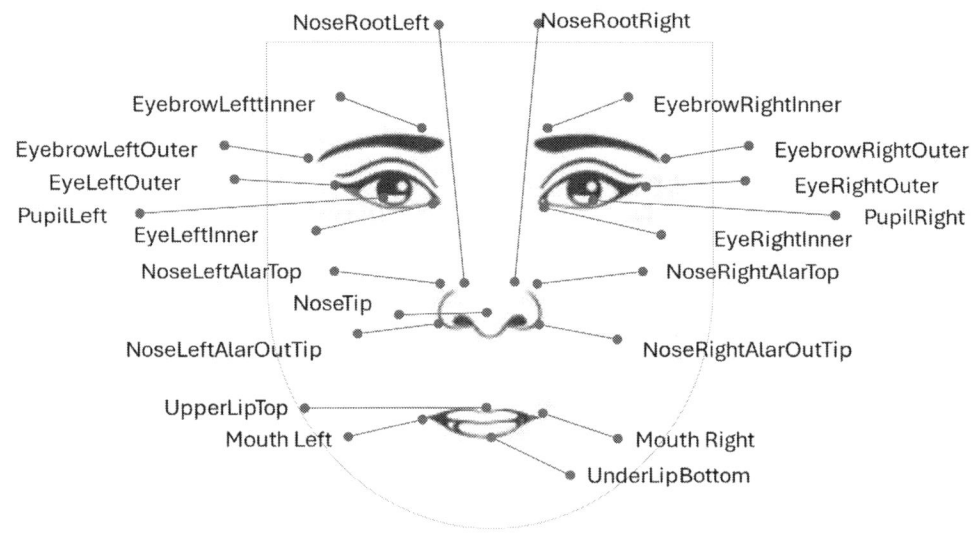

Figure 6.10 – Detecting facial landmarks capability using CV

Figure 6.10 shows the facial features that can be used for ML model training of facial analysis using CV.

This section looked at identifying the features of facial analysis solutions using CV. Next, you will learn about facial recognition.

Facial recognition

Facial recognition involves known individuals being identified from their facial features in an image. This works by training an ML model with that individual's images; then, for all new images on which the model has not been trained, they can be identified by the trained model in those images. This capability is illustrated in *Figure 6.11*:

Figure 6.11 – Identifying individuals using CV

Figure 6.11 shows an example of facial recognition to identify the **Microsoft Certified Trainer** (**MCT**) using a trained ML model using CV to identify known individuals located in the image; this can be customized to identify the student(s) from the trainer(s).

Summary

This chapter provides comprehensive coverage on the identification of common types of computer vision solutions.

In this chapter, you were introduced to CV solutions, including image classification, object detection, and OCR. We then concluded your learning for this chapter with information about CV solutions for facial detection and facial analysis solutions.

In the next chapter, you learn to describe the capabilities of the following Azure AI services: Azure AI Vision, Azure AI Face, and Azure AI Video Indexer.

Exam Readiness Drill – Chapter Review Questions

Apart from a solid understanding of key concepts, being able to think quickly under time pressure is a skill that will help you ace your certification exam. That is why working on these skills early on in your learning journey is key.

Chapter review questions are designed to improve your test-taking skills progressively with each chapter you learn and review your understanding of key concepts in the chapter at the same time. You'll find these at the end of each chapter.

> **Before you proceed**
>
> If you don't have a Packt Library subscription or you haven't purchased this book from the Packt store, you will need to unlock the online resources to access the exam readiness drills. Unlocking is free and needs to be done only once. To learn how to do that, head over to the chapter titled *Chapter 12, Accessing the Online Resources*.

To open the Chapter Review Questions for this chapter, perform the following steps:

1. Click the link – `https://packt.link/AI-900_CH06`.

    Alternatively, you can scan the following QR code (*Figure 6.12*):

Figure 6.12– QR code that opens Chapter Review Questions for logged-in users

2. Once you log in, you'll see a page similar to the one shown in *Figure 6.13*:

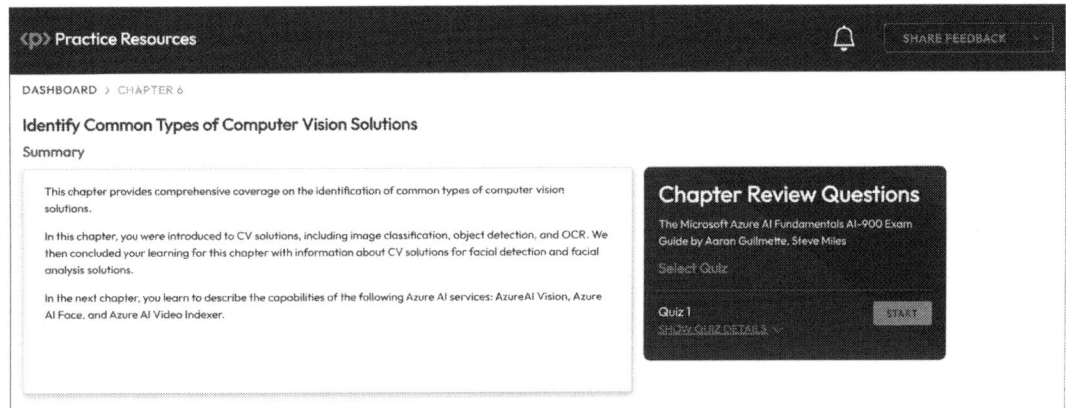

Figure 6.13 – Chapter Review Questions for Chapter 6

3. Once ready, start the following practice drills, re-attempting the quiz multiple times.

Exam Readiness Drill

For the first three attempts, don't worry about the time limit.

ATTEMPT 1

The first time, aim for at least **40%**. Look at the answers you got wrong and read the relevant sections in the chapter again to fix your learning gaps.

ATTEMPT 2

The second time, aim for at least **60%**. Look at the answers you got wrong and read the relevant sections in the chapter again to fix any remaining learning gaps.

ATTEMPT 3

The third time, aim for at least **75%**. Once you score 75% or more, you start working on your timing.

> **Tip**
> You may take more than **three** attempts to reach 75%. That's okay. Just review the relevant sections in the chapter till you get there.

Working On Timing

Your aim is to keep the score the same while trying to answer these questions as quickly as possible. Here's an example of how your next attempts should look like:

Attempt	Score	Time Taken
Attempt 5	77%	21 mins 30 seconds
Attempt 6	78%	18 mins 34 seconds
Attempt 7	76%	14 mins 44 seconds

Table 6.1 – Sample timing practice drills on the online platform

> **Note**
> The time limits shown in the above table are just examples. Set your own time limits with each attempt based on the time limit of the quiz on the website.

With each new attempt, your score should stay above **75%** while your "time taken" to complete should "decrease". Repeat as many attempts as you want till you feel confident dealing with the time pressure.

7
Identify Azure Tools and Services for Computer Vision Tasks

In *Chapter 6*, *Identify Common Types of Computer Vision Solutions*, you learned how to identify common types of computer vision solutions capabilities surrounding image classification, object detection, **optical character recognition** (**OCR**), facial detection, and facial analysis.

In this chapter, you will explore the use of the **Azure AI Vision Studio tool** and the **Azure AI Vision** service, which allows you to analyze images, read text, and provide spatial analysis. You will then explore the **Azure AI Face** service, which allows you to detect and recognize faces and attributes in images. Finally, you will discover the **Azure AI Video Indexer** service, which is a video and audio analytics service that allows insights to be extracted using machine learning models.

This content requires some understanding of machine learning principles; if you have skipped straight to this chapter and are new to machine learning or just want to refresh on some existing knowledge, then please refer to *Part 2 – Fundamental Principles of Machine Learning on Azure*, as a machine learning primer before you continue with this chapter.

The Azure AI services of **Vision**, **Face**, and **Video Indexer** provide *pre-built* and *customizable* machine learning models that can be used by developers to enhance their applications. This allows you to add AI services with fewer skills, cost, and complexity and provides faster time to value and faster time to market, providing a competitive edge.

The objectives and skills we'll cover in this chapter are as follows:

- Describe capabilities of the Azure AI Vision service
- Describe capabilities of the Azure AI Face service
- Describe capabilities of the Azure AI Video Indexer service

By the end of this chapter, you should be aware of the capabilities of the aforementioned Azure AI services.

Technical requirements

To get started with the **Azure AI services** mentioned in this chapter, you will need an **Azure subscription** with sufficient access to create and delete resources. You can create a free Azure account for evaluation by going to `https://azure.microsoft.com/free/`.

This free Azure account provides the following:

- $200 credit to explore Azure for 30 days
- 12 months of free popular services
- 55+ other services that are always free

Once you have an Azure subscription in place, you need either the **Owner** or **Contributor** role at the *resource group* or *resource* level.

To evaluate computer vision, you can create a "single service resource" or a "multi-service resource"; each can be explained as follows:

- **Azure AI Vision**: This is an example of a specific *single service resource*. This resource can be used with the "free tier" of the Azure AI services you may wish to evaluate; it uses an *endpoint* and a *key* that are unique for *each single* Azure AI service. So, if you use multiple Azure AI services, then you will have multiple endpoints and keys (one endpoint and key for each service).

- **Azure AI Services**: This is a general *multi-service resource*. This resource provides billing consolidation for *all used service resources* through the use of a *single key* and *endpoint*. So, if you use multiple Azure AI services, then you will have just one endpoint and just one key that can access all the services.

Understanding workspaces or compute resources isn't required; only an Azure AI resource needs to be created within your Azure subscription.

You can learn more about service resources at `https://learn.microsoft.com/en-us/azure/ai-services/multi-service-resource`.

Now that we've looked at the technical requirements for working with the Azure AI services that will be covered in this chapter, let's discover the first of the Azure AI services: Azure AI Vision.

Describe capabilities of the Azure AI Vision service

The **Azure AI Vision** service is a *cloud-based Microsoft-hosted AI* service that provides machine learning algorithms that allow you to analyze the visual features and characteristics of an image, moderate image content, and extract text from images.

The Azure AI Vision service provides the following:

- **Image Analysis**: This capability can be used to return information on image characteristics and visual features. It includes the following model capabilities:

    - Add captions and dense captions to images
    - Assign labels to images with tags
    - Detect objects in images, such as people
    - Detect multiple instances of products
    - Detect brands
    - Detect color schemes
    - Detect sensitive information in images, such as adult content (including "racy" or "gory" content)
    - Create custom image classification and object detection models that can be trained on your collection of images
    - Detect damaged/non-conforming products using custom models

    You can learn more at `https://learn.microsoft.com/en-us/azure/ai-services/computer-vision/overview-image-analysis`.

- **OCR**: This capability, sometimes also referred to as text recognition or text extraction, is based on machine learning and allows printed or handwritten text to be extracted from the likes of **documents**, such as forms, invoices, expense receipts, and **images**, which could include vehicle number plates, street signs, product brand labels, names on movie posters, and more.

    You can learn more at `https://learn.microsoft.com/en-us/azure/ai-services/computer-vision/overview-ocr`.

- **Face**: This capability provides machine learning for detecting human faces in an image; it can provide recognition and analysis to extract attributes such as age, glasses, facial hair, and pose.

    You can learn more at `https://learn.microsoft.com/en-us/azure/ai-services/computer-vision/overview-identity`.

The Foundation model that's used for the tasks of computer vision is the **Microsoft Florence model**. It is "pre-trained" on vast amounts of captioned internet images to build models that can be used for image analysis tasks, such as the following:

- **Image classification**: Identify an image category and add labels to the image
- **Object detection**: Identify an object's location in an image, photo, or video
- **Captioning**: Generate human-readable descriptions for everything that appears in images, such as a photo
- **Tagging**: Generate a list of tags that can be associated with an image for its detected attributes

Image classification

The capabilities for the models of the **Azure AI Vision** service can analyze an image, at which point one more **label** can be applied based on its understanding of the contents.

Labels are identified as belonging to an image; the image can be associated with one or more labels. You can think of this as adding **attributes** to the image. The service's capabilities mean it can also be used with documents as well as photographs.

Azure AI Vision Studio, shown in *Figure 7.1*, is a public web-based portal that can be used to perform image analysis tasks:

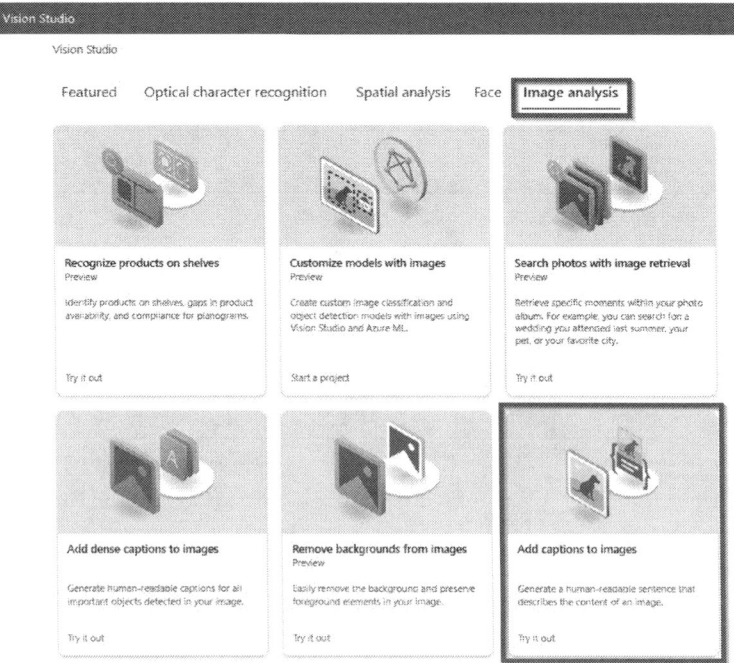

Figure 7.1 – The Azure AI Vision Studio portal

You can get started with **Azure AI Vision Studio** at `https://portal.vision.cognitive.azure.com/`.

Figure 7.2 shows an example of **image analysis** when using the **Azure AI Vision** service. It can generate a human-readable sentence as a description of the image:

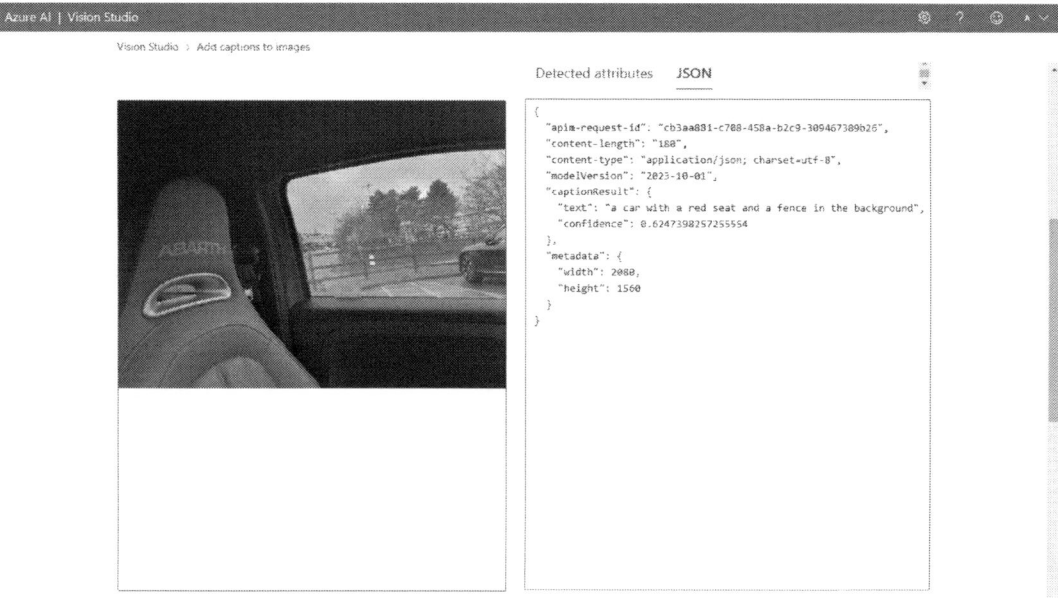

Figure 7.2 – Image captioning information provided via Azure AI Vision Studio

Figure 7.2 shows an example of image analysis using the **Azure AI Vision** service. It can **caption** an image and generate a human-readable **sentence** that acts as the **description** of the image; the caption reads "a car with a red seat and a fence in the background."

The **Azure AI Vision** service models' capabilities can analyze an image; a **label** can be applied based on its understanding of the contents.

Categorization is a "parent/child hierarchy structure;" there are *86 categories*, with all the names in English. *Figure 7.3* shows an example of this category's taxonomy and structure:

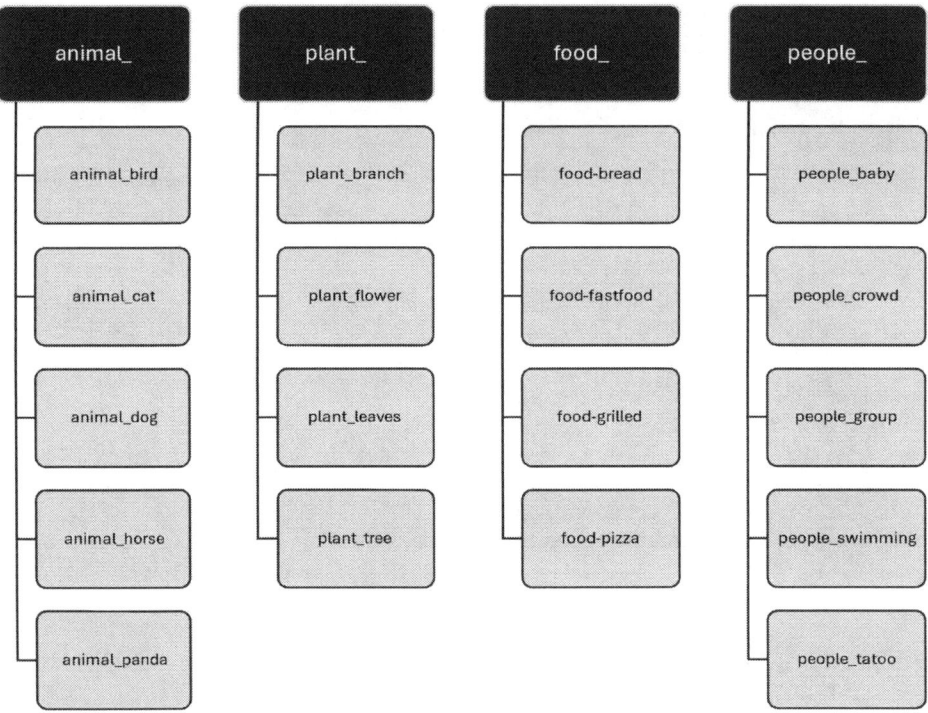

Figure 7.3 – Category topology example

The full "text format" topology shown in *Figure 7.3* can be found at https://learn.microsoft.com/en-us/azure/ai-services/computer-vision/category-taxonomy.

You can learn more about how images are categorized at https://learn.microsoft.com/en-us/azure/ai-services/computer-vision/concept-categorizing-images.

In this subsection, you discovered image classification when using the Azure AI Vision service. In the next subsection, you'll learn about object detection.

Object detection

Where **image classification** provides us with categorization and can tell us of singular information – that is, there is a "person," "car," "cat," and so on in the image – **object detection** provides individual **location information** for objects in the image, in addition to the "categorization" and "caption labels" provided by the classification.

Multiple objects can also be identified in an image. For each object that's found in the image, the detected attributes will be returned by the API. The individual location of the object in the image is found by providing the coordinates of a **bounding box** (*in pixels*) returned by the **Image Analysis API**. This information can be used to provide a relationship between objects in the image.

Azure AI Vision Studio, shown in *Figure 7.4*, is a public web-based portal that can be used to perform object detection tasks:

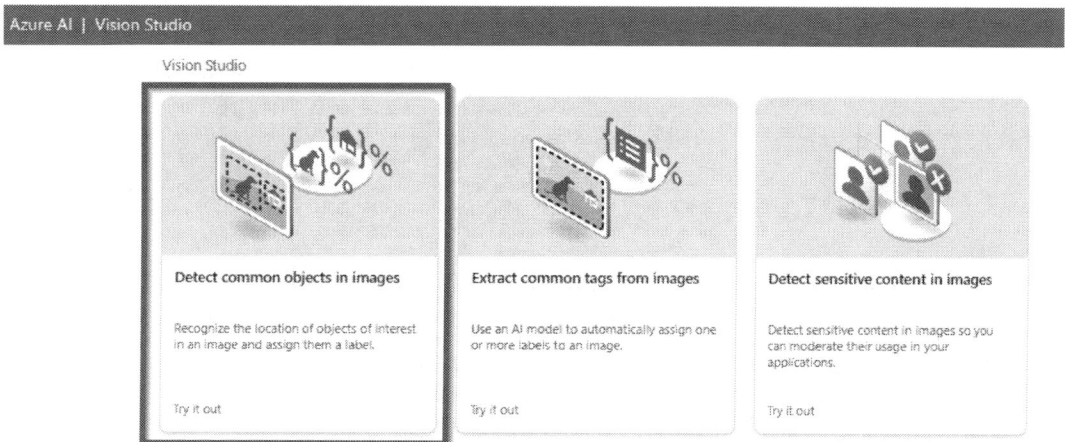

Figure 7.4 – The Azure AI Vision Studio portal

You can get started with **Azure AI Vision Studio** at `https://portal.vision.cognitive.azure.com/`.

Figure 7.5 shows an example of using object detection in an image via **Azure AI Vision Studio**:

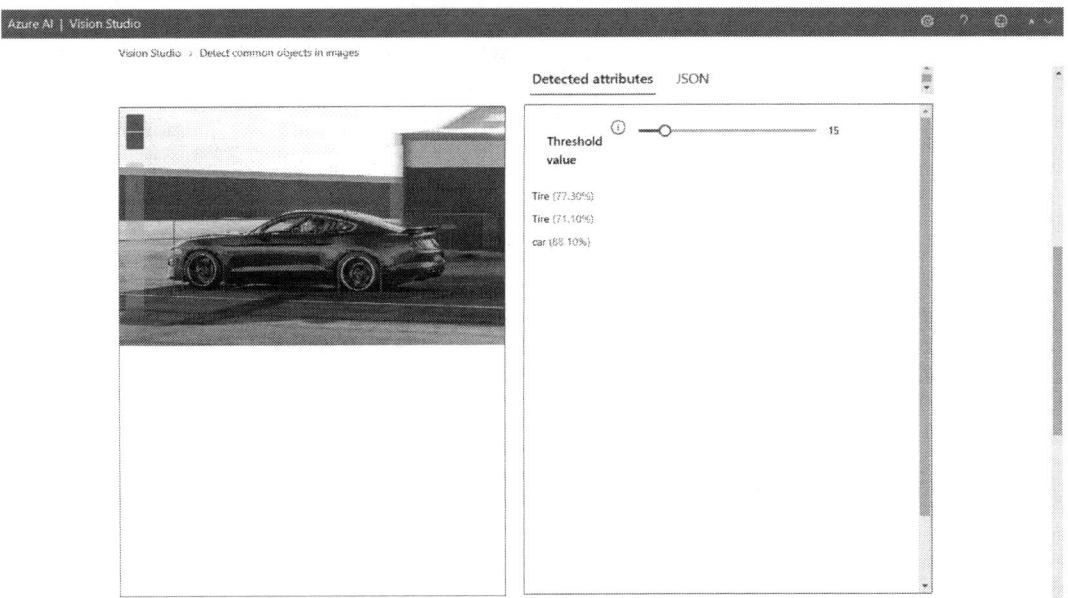

Figure 7.5 – Object detection information provided via Azure AI Vision Studio

Figure 7.5 shows an example of **image analysis** when using the **Azure AI Vision** service to generate detections regarding **car** and **Tire**.

The object's location is provided within a **bounding box** as a **pixel value** within the image; **Tag** information will also be retrieved from the image. The **JavaScript Object Notation (JSON)** information that's returned by the API is as follows for the image shown in *Figure 7.5*:

```
{
    "modelVersion": "2023-10-01",
    "metadata": {
        "width": 1921,
        "height": 1172
    },
    "objectsResult": {
        "values": [
            {
                "boundingBox": {
                    "x": 323,
                    "y": 699,
                    "w": 206,
                    "h": 205
                },
```

```
          "tags": [
            {
              "name": "Tire",
              "confidence": 0.773
            }
          ]
        },
        {
          "boundingBox": {
            "x": 1095,
            "y": 715,
            "w": 207,
            "h": 209
          },
          "tags": [
            {
              "name": "Tire",
              "confidence": 0.711
            }
          ]
        },
        {
          "boundingBox": {
            "x": 282,
            "y": 501,
            "w": 1363,
            "h": 414
          },
          "tags": [
            {
              "name": "car",
              "confidence": 0.881
            }
          ]
        }
      ]
    }
}
```

It should be noted that this service does not use a **regression** or **clustering** model but an **Image Analysis** model.

142   Identify Azure Tools and Services for Computer Vision Tasks

You can learn more at the following URLs:

- `https://learn.microsoft.com/en-us/azure/ai-services/computer-vision/concept-object-detection-40`
- `https://learn.microsoft.com/en-us/azure/ai-services/computer-vision/concept-describe-images-40`

This section identified the capabilities of object detection solutions using the Azure AI Vision service. In the next section, you will learn how to identify the capabilities of OCR solutions using Azure AI Vision.

OCR solutions

The **Azure AI Vision service** can be used as a solution for **OCR**.

Through the capabilities of OCR, this service enables you to "extract" text information from photographs, scanned documents, or any other visual content. The **Read API** can recognize printed and handwritten text across languages.

Azure AI Vision Studio, shown in *Figure 7.6*, is a public web-based portal that can be used to perform OCR tasks:

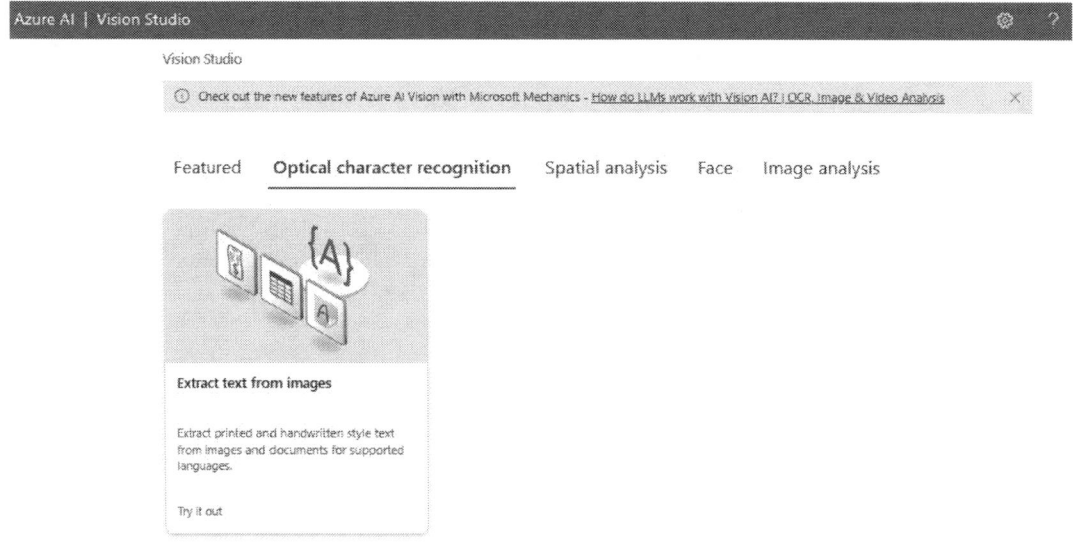

Figure 7.6 – The Azure AI Vision Studio portal

You can get started with **Azure AI Vision Studio** at `https://portal.vision.cognitive.azure.com/`.

Figure 7.7 shows an example of using **OCR** via **Azure AI Vision Studio** to extract the "printed text" located in the image:

Figure 7.7 – Extracting text from an image by using the OCR capability via Azure AI Vision Studio

You can learn more at `https://learn.microsoft.com/en-us/azure/ai-services/computer-vision/overview-ocr`.

This section looked at identifying the capabilities of OCR solutions using the Azure AI Vision service. In the next section, you will learn how to identify the capabilities of face detection via the Azure AI Face service.

Describe the capabilities of the Azure AI Face service

The **Azure AI Face** service is a part of **Microsoft Azure's AI** services.

The **Face** service provides capabilities for detecting and recognizing human faces in images, as well as extracting various facial attributes. Some key features and functionalities of the Microsoft Azure AI Face service are as follows:

- **Face Detection**: Identify and locate human faces within an image
- **Face Recognition**: Associate detected faces with previously known faces in a dataset
- **Face Verification**: Confirm whether two faces in an image are of the same person or not

- **Facial Landmarks Detection**: Identify key facial features such as eyes, nose, and mouth
- **Face Similarity Matching**: Determine the similarity between faces for potential use in applications such as face-based authentication

Developers can integrate the **Azure AI Face** service into their applications using a **REST API**.

In this section, you were introduced to the Azure AI Face service. In the next section, you will understand what you'll need to start using it.

Getting started

To get started with Face, you will need to create resources within an Azure subscription, as covered in the *Technical requirements* section. One of the following is required:

- **Face Azure resource**: This resource will be used to create a *dedicated* endpoint and key for this *specific* Azure AI service. You will be billed for the consumption of this AI service independently of any other Azure AI service. This is best suited if you're not using any other Azure AI services.
- **Azure AI services Azure resource**: This resource will be used to create a *shared* endpoint and key that will be used for all Azure AI services you wish to use. You will have an aggregated bill for the consumption of all AI services you use.

Azure AI Vision Studio, shown in *Figure 7.8*, is a public web-based portal that can be used to perform these tasks:

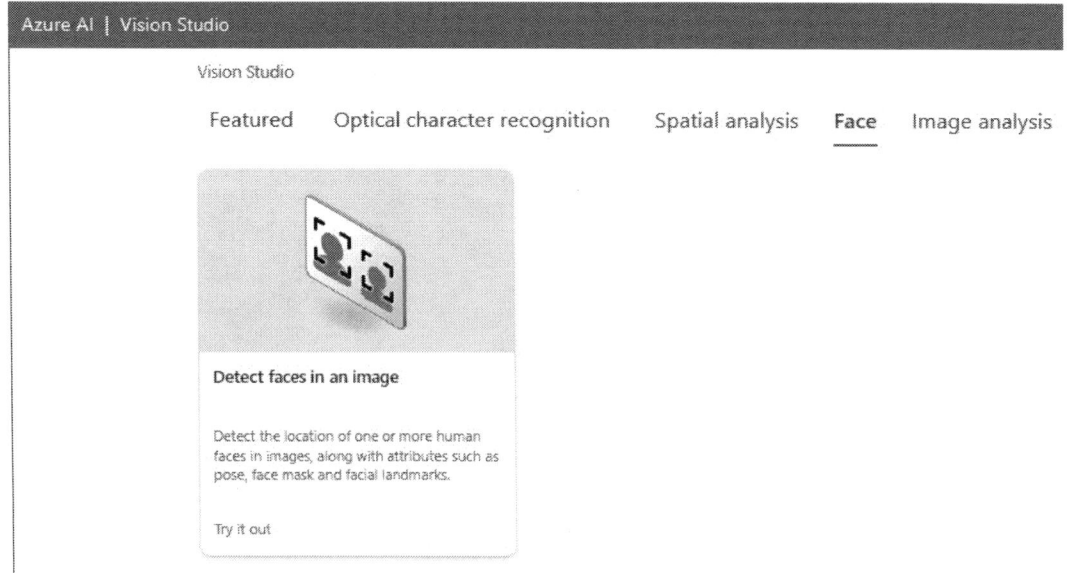

Figure 7.8 – The Azure AI Vision Studio portal

You can get started with **Azure AI Vision Studio** at `https://portal.vision.cognitive.azure.com/`.

In this section, you learned what's required to get started with the Azure AI Face service. We will look at the Azure AI Face service's capabilities in the following subsections.

Facial detection

This capability can take an image and identify human faces within it.

The **Azure AI Face** service provides an API for facial detection and recognition within images. It can detect attributes and return the pixel coordinates to locate the face(s) in the image. *Figure 7.9* illustrates this capability:

Figure 7.9 – Detecting faces using Azure AI Vision Studio

Figure 7.9 shows an example of **face detection** using the **Azure AI Face** service to extract the human faces located in the image.

Here's an example of the **JSON** information that's returned by the API. Note that the face location is provided within bounding box coordinates and that the identifying face landmarks are returned for each face, as well as an attribute, such as `mask`, under `faceAttributes`:

```
[
  {
    "recognitionModel": "recognition_01",
    "faceRectangle": {
      "width": 144,
      "height": 209,
      "left": 305,
      "top": 473
    },
    "faceLandmarks": {
      "pupilLeft": {
        "x": 327.9,
        "y": 548.7
      },
      "pupilRight": {
        "x": 379.3,
        "y": 559.1
      },
      "noseTip": {
        "x": 325.9,
        "y": 588
      },
    ----<<<< Full code removed for brevity >>>>----
    "faceAttributes": {
      "mask": {
        "type": "noMask",
        "noseAndMouthCovered": false
      }
    }
  }
]
```

Please note that the full JSON response that was returned was not included; this snippet has only been included for illustrative purposes.

Machine learning algorithms that are *pre-built* with the **Azure AI Face** service can identify the following face-related attributes:

- **Accessories**: This refers to whether the face is wearing accessories, such as headwear, glasses, or a mask; a confidence score will also be returned
- **Blur**: This refers to whether there is a lack of focus on the image
- **Exposure**: This refers to whether faces in the image are overexposed or underexposed
- **Occlusion**: This refers to whether the face may be blocked by an object
- **Noise**: This refers to visual noise, where an image has reduced clarity through tiny dots, and grainy appearance, such as for photos with darker settings where a high ISO has been used
- **Pose**: This refers to the face's orientation

> Important note
> Refer to the *Responsible AI* section to learn more about how to retire attribute detection such as emotion, age, and facial hair.

The following should be considered for better detection results for the image:

- **Format**: BMP, GIF (*first frame*), JPEG, PNG
- **File size**: 6 MB maximum
- **Face size**: 36 x 36 minimum and 4,096 x 4,096 maximum size range to be able to be detected
- **Rotation**: Images must be rotated correctly; for some images, such as those in JPEG format, this may be done automatically through their **Exchangeable Image File Format** (**EXIF**) metadata
- **Additionally**: The accuracy will be reduced when the images have extreme face angles, lighting, and object blocking (occlusion)

In addition to the *video input*, the following settings should be considered for clearer video frame results:

- **Shutter angle**: A lower shutter angle should be used
- **Shutter speed**: Reduce the amount of motion between frames
- **Smoothing**: This should be turned off

For each face that's detected in an image by the Face service, you can request a **Face ID** via the **Face Detect API**. This is a *unique identifier* string.

The following API operations can be performed using the Face service:

- **Identify**: This is a one-to-many operation to find the match closest to a queried person from a known person database/security repository (**Person group**). This takes **Face IDs** from a **Detected Face** object and returns a list of **Person objects** with a **confidence prediction** value that the detected face may belong to – that is, is this the person being claimed?

    Each **Person group** (security repository/database of person objects) can have a maximum number of Person objects of 1 million; a maximum of 248 faces can be registered for each Person object in the Person group.

- **Verify**: This a one-to-one operation that validates if the Face ID for the detected face in the image matches the Person object from the security repository/database – that is, are these two faces the same person?

- **Find Similar**: This is a face search operation that can take a Face ID and find other candidates' face images in a face list that are matched as similar; it can answer the questions of whether all the faces belong together, or whether this person looks like other people. The working modes are as follows:

    - **matchPerson**: This uses the **Verify API** to return filtered similar faces. This means the results that are returned can only be images of the target face.

    - **matchFace**: This returns a list of candidates' faces similar to the Face ID, but they may not be the face of that person; the filter of **same-person** is ignored. This means the results will not necessarily contain the target face in the returned images.

- **Group**: This is an operation that's based on similarity; unknown faces of similar candidates are divided into smaller groups. This means the likelihood is that all returned faces are of the same person, but that person can have different groups where a factor such as a facial expression can be used to differentiate.

The **Azure AI Face service** can analyze two faces and determine whether they belong to the same person; if the face that's identified is verified against an identity data store, then some action could be taken based on this verification.

These actions form the basis of security protocols through **Authentication** (**AuthN**) and **Authorization** (**AuthZ**) – that is, verifying "who you say you are" and "what you have access to,"

You can learn more at `https://learn.microsoft.com/en-us/azure/ai-services/computer-vision/overview-identity`.

You can try out face detection at `https://portal.vision.cognitive.azure.com/gallery/face`.

Responsible AI

While the previous capabilities are available to all to use, to support Microsoft's **Responsible AI Standard**, there are additional **Face Service** capabilities for face matching and identifying named individuals available to "Managed Microsoft" customers through a limited access policy.

You can learn more at `https://aka.ms/facerecognition`.

You should be aware that the capabilities of facial recognition, such as emotion, smile, gender, age, makeup, facial hair, and hair, and others, which can infer emotional states and identity attributes, have been retired by Microsoft so that they're not misused as this may lead to a denial of service attack, discrimination, and stereotyping.

You can learn more at `https://azure.microsoft.com/en-us/blog/responsible-ai-investments-and-safeguards-for-facial-recognition/`.

The following guiding principles of responsible AI are adhered to:

- Accountability
- Inclusiveness
- Reliability and safety
- Fairness
- Transparency
- Privacy and security

In this section, you learned about Microsoft's positioning on responsible AI. Next, we will look at the Azure AI Video Indexer service.

Describe capabilities of the Azure AI Video Indexer service

The computer vision capabilities of Azure ML can be used as a solution for analyzing and extracting insights and metadata from video and audio media files, as well as detecting and identifying faces in video.

The use cases for the **Azure AI Video Indexer** service are as follows:

- Accessibility
- Content creation
- Content moderation

- Deep search
- Monetization
- Recommendation

The **Azure AI Video Indexer** service uses machine learning algorithms and can be used to perform these tasks. It is built on the **Azure AI services** of **Azure AI Vision**, **Face**, **Speech**, and **Translator**. There are 30+ models available that retrieve video and audio content insights.

The **Azure AI Video Indexer service** can retrieve insights from video files using the following models:

- Account-based face identification
- Black frame detection
- Celebrity identification
- Editorial shot type detection
- Face detection
- Keyframe extraction
- Labels identification
- Matched person
- OCR
- Observed people tracking
- Rolling credits
- Scene segmentation
- Shot detection
- Slate detection
- Textual logo detection
- Thumbnail extraction for faces
- Visual content moderation

The **Azure AI Video Indexer** service can retrieve insights from audio files using the following models:

- Audio effects detection
- Automatic language detection
- Audio transcription
- Closed captioning

- Multi-language speech identification and transcription
- Noise reduction
- Speaker enumeration
- Speaker statistics
- Text-based emotion detection
- Textual content moderation
- Translation
- Two-channel processing

The following multi-channel (*audio and video*) models are available:

- Artifacts
- Keywords extraction
- Named entities extraction
- Sentiment analysis
- Topic inference

The Azure AI Video Indexer service can be tried out at `https://www.videoindexer.ai/`.

You can learn more at `https://learn.microsoft.com/en-us/azure/azure-video-indexer/`.

Summary

This chapter provided complete coverage of the *Describe features of computer vision workloads on Azure* AI-900 Azure Fundamentals skills area.

In this chapter, you were introduced to the Azure AI Vision Studio tool and discovered the capabilities of the Azure AI Vision service regarding image classification, object detection, and OCR. You then learned about the Azure Face service, which can be used for facial detection, facial analysis, and recognition. Finally, we covered the Azure AI Video Indexer service, which can extract insights from video and audio files, as well as Microsoft's positioning on responsible AI.

In the next chapter, you will learn how to describe the various features of **natural language processing (NLP)** workloads on Azure. NLP supports many of the popular commercial AI services available today.

Exam Readiness Drill – Chapter Review Questions

Apart from a solid understanding of key concepts, being able to think quickly under time pressure is a skill that will help you ace your certification exam. That is why working on these skills early on in your learning journey is key.

Chapter review questions are designed to improve your test-taking skills progressively with each chapter you learn and review your understanding of key concepts in the chapter at the same time. You'll find these at the end of each chapter.

> **Before you proceed**
>
> If you don't have a Packt Library subscription or you haven't purchased this book from the Packt store, you will need to unlock the online resources to access the exam readiness drills. Unlocking is free and needs to be done only once. To learn how to do that, head over to the chapter titled *Chapter 12, Accessing the Online Resources*.

To open the Chapter Review Questions for this chapter, perform the following steps:

1. Click the link – `https://packt.link/AI-900_CH07`.

    Alternatively, you can scan the following QR code (*Figure 7.10*):

    Figure 7.10 – QR code that opens Chapter Review Questions for logged-in users

2. Once you log in, you'll see a page similar to the one shown in *Figure 7.11*:

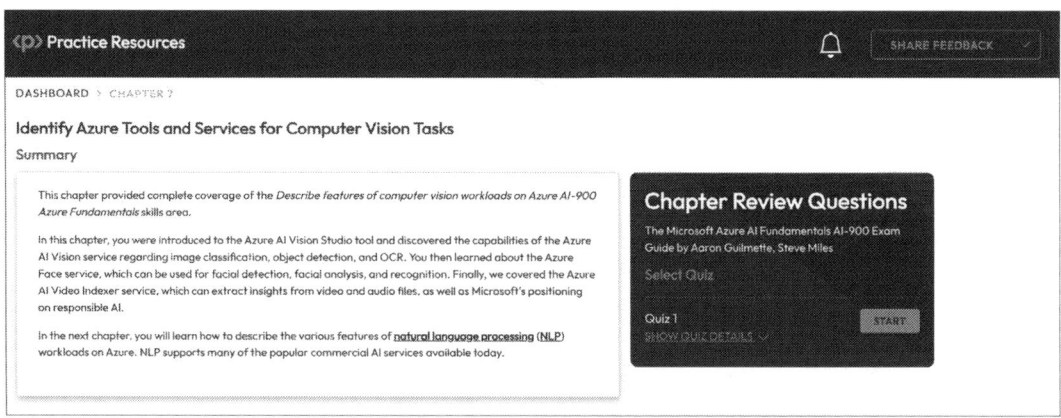

Figure 7.11 – Chapter Review Questions for Chapter 7

3. Once ready, start the following practice drills, re-attempting the quiz multiple times.

Exam Readiness Drill

For the first three attempts, don't worry about the time limit.

ATTEMPT 1

The first time, aim for at least **40%**. Look at the answers you got wrong and read the relevant sections in the chapter again to fix your learning gaps.

ATTEMPT 2

The second time, aim for at least **60%**. Look at the answers you got wrong and read the relevant sections in the chapter again to fix any remaining learning gaps.

ATTEMPT 3

The third time, aim for at least **75%**. Once you score 75% or more, you start working on your timing.

> Tip
> You may take more than **three** attempts to reach 75%. That's okay. Just review the relevant sections in the chapter till you get there.

Working On Timing

Your aim is to keep the score the same while trying to answer these questions as quickly as possible. Here's an example of how your next attempts should look like:

Attempt	Score	Time Taken
Attempt 5	77%	21 mins 30 seconds
Attempt 6	78%	18 mins 34 seconds
Attempt 7	76%	14 mins 44 seconds

Table 7.1 – Sample timing practice drills on the online platform

> **Note**
> The time limits shown in the above table are just examples. Set your own time limits with each attempt based on the time limit of the quiz on the website.

With each new attempt, your score should stay above **75%** while your "time taken" to complete should "decrease". Repeat as many attempts as you want till you feel confident dealing with the time pressure.

Part 4: Describe Features of Natural Language Processing (NLP) Workloads on Azure

Natural language processing (NLP) is the technology that allows computers to identify and understand the relevant parts of human language, including text recognition, text analysis, text-to-speech, and speech synthesis. In this part, you'll learn about the NLP capabilities in Azure.

This part includes the following chapters:

- *Chapter 8, Identify Features of Common NLP Workload Scenarios*
- *Chapter 9, Identify Azure Tools and Services for NLP Workloads*

8

Identify Features of Common NLP Workload Scenarios

In *Chapter 7, Identify Azure Tools and Services for Computer Vision Tasks*, you discovered the usage of the Azure AI services of Vision and Face using the Azure AI Vision Studio tool, you then learned about the Azure AI Video Indexer service.

In this chapter, you will learn to identify features of **Natural Language Processing** (**NLP**) capabilities such as *key phrase extraction, entity recognition, sentiment analysis, language modeling, speech recognition,* and *translation*, which are all common NLP workload scenarios that can be applied to Azure.

The objectives and skills we'll cover in this chapter include the following:

- Introduction to NLP
- Identify features and uses for key phrase extraction
- Identify features and uses for entity recognition
- Identify features and uses for sentiment analysis
- Identify features and uses for language modeling
- Identify features and uses for speech recognition and synthesis
- Identify features and uses for translation

By the end of this chapter, you should be able to identify the features and uses of Natural Language Processing (NLP) AI services.

Introduction to NLP

NLP is an area of **artificial intelligence** (**AI**) that deals with spoken and written language meaning. This utilizes a machine's ability to analyze, understand, infer, and manipulate interactions that are human-like with their language response. With NLP, *algorithms* and *computing models* are built and deployed that enable computers to understand, interpret, and create human language according to a certain meaning.

The discipline of AI is nothing new and is based on computer sciences from many previous decades ago. The history and lineage of **machine learning** (**ML**) are rooted within the mathematics, statistics, and logic disciplines.

Back in time, and only until recently, we used the term *cognitive* in our language in expressing AI topics; this was to reflect the close relationship between human beings' cognitive abilities and the machines' goals of emulating these. AI could be seen by some to be a reference to a "marketing" or "business" term to describe this public face of the discipline of ML.

We should understand that AI is an encompassing term for ML, which itself has **deep learning** (**DL**) as a subset discipline. AI describes the "emulation of human intelligence" with machines.

The diagram in *Figure 8.1* depicts the relationship and intersection between **NLP**, **AI**, **computer science**, and **human language**:

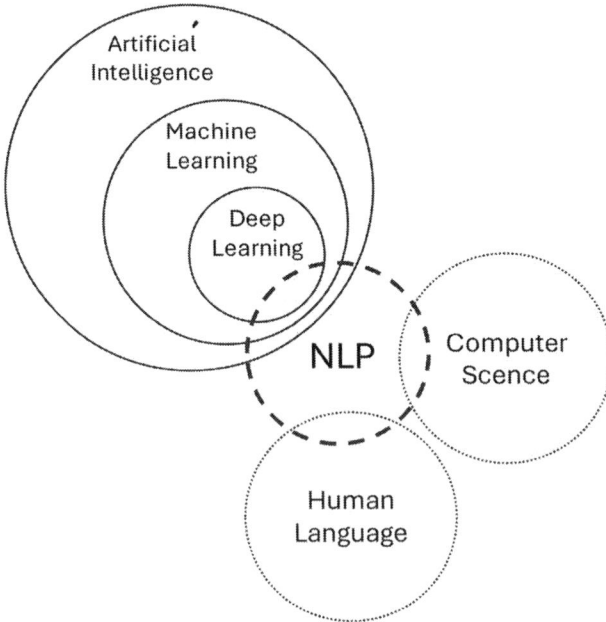

Figure 8.1 – NLP relationship with other disciplines

Now that you understand the relationship of NLP and its interconnection with other related disciplines, you should be aware of some of the areas of AI where NLP can provide support. Next, you will understand the concepts of NLP.

NLP concepts

The earliest example of *text analytics* techniques is where a body of text (a *corpus*) uses statistical analysis to have some form of semantic meaning inferred. This technique is a form of *summarization* and *classification* for all words that appear in a document; it can extract the commonality and frequency of words that appear to derive meaning from the topic and what the content of the document is about. This "extraction" and "processing" is referred to as **tokenization**, which is an analysis technique you will explore next.

The techniques and NLP solution for spoken and written language meaning start with the ingestion of raw text for *processing*, *tokenizing*, and *model training*. The components in a generalized NLP solution that deliver the outcome of common NLP tasks such as *text analysis*, *opinion mining*, *machine translation*, *summarization*, and *conversational AI* can be represented as per the diagram in *Figure 8.2*:

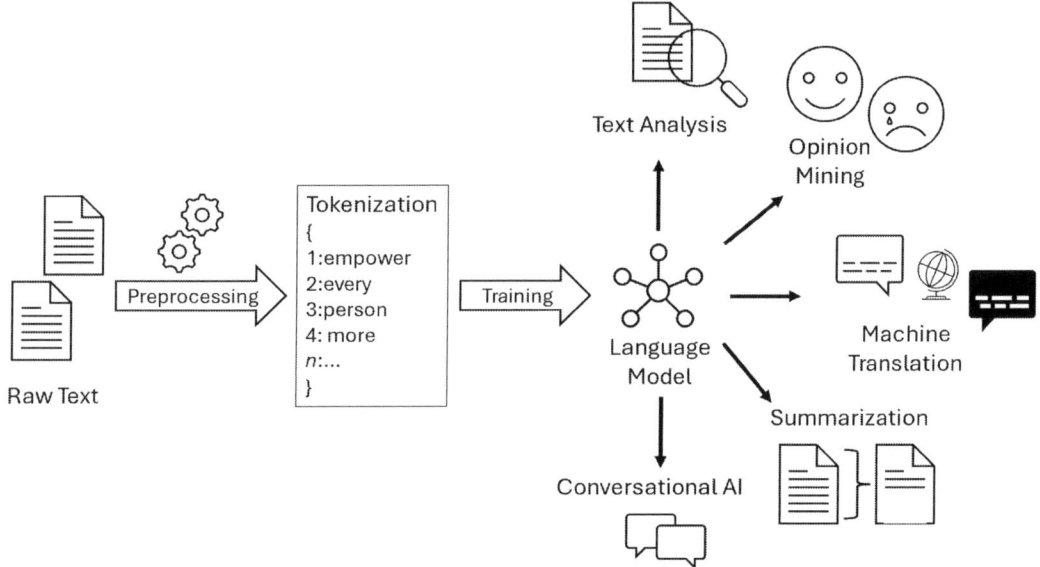

Figure 8.2 – NLP relationship with other disciplines

Tokenization, as seen in *Figure 8.2*, is a foundational component of the concept of NLP and is core to your understanding going forward as you progress your AI skills.

Tokens are used to *break down* the body of raw training text (the *corpus*); each distinct or partial word, or combination of words, is a **token**.

The following phrase, which is the Microsoft mission statement, will be used as an example of **tokenization**:

"Our mission is to empower every person and every organization on the planet to achieve more."

For this mission statement example phrase, the following breakdown can be derived:

1. `our`
2. `mission`
3. `is`
4. `to`
5. `empower`
6. `every`
7. `person`
8. `and`
9. `every`
10. `organization`
11. `on`
12. `the`
13. `planet`
14. `achieve`
15. `more`

Note that each word is represented as a token with an identifier that is numeric. You will see from the token list that the `to` token is used only **once** but in the corpus (*body of text*), the word "to" appears **twice**; this is because it is a common word, and the numeric identity is used and substitutes the actual word value, much like a **variable** in coding that can store a *string value*.

So, how does this help us? This means that the phrase (*the body of text, or corpus*) can be represented by the following tokens: 1, 2, 3, 4, 5, 6, 7, 8, 9, 10, 11, 12, 13, 14, 15. You will see that there are **16 words** in the phrase, but **15 tokens**; that is because the *token ID #4* is used to represent the word "to," which appears as a count twice in the phrase.

To illustrate this aspect a little further, if the text were a simple string where a distinct word is just repeated, such as in Microsoft's Steve Ballmer's infamous conference chant back in 2006 of "*Developers, Developers, Developers, Developers*" then the tokens would appear as follows:

1. `Developers`

In this example, in contrast to the previous Microsoft mission statement phrase example, only **one token** needs to be used to represent the entire corpus (body of text).

When applied to the case where a machine needs to output a phrase from a token sequence, if is it asked to display the four-worded phrase, it knows just to use the *token ID #1* four times repeatedly; that is, everywhere we need to display or represent the word "Developer," we can ask it to use the token.

Now that you have learned a simple example, you will need to explore some more advanced and complex examples using the concepts of **preprocessing text normalization** (such as changing text to lowercase; punctuation removal), **stop word removal** (such as *a, and, the, it*), **n-grams** (such as *they had, it was*), and **stemming** (such as *develop, developer, development, developing*). These concepts are beyond the scope of the content for this chapter; however, you can learn more at this URL:

```
https://learn.microsoft.com/en-us/azure/machine-learning/component-
reference/preprocess-text
```

Now that you have discovered the concepts of NLP, in the next section, you will explore core NLP use-case scenarios.

NLP scenarios

The three key AI areas and tasks that can be provided by NLP are as follows:

- **Language**
  - Language detection
  - Key phrase extraction (*main topics of discussion*)
  - **Named entity detection**: Identify and extract mentioned names from unstructured text documents (such as contracts, support cases), companies, and frequency; person type, skill, location, date time, and quantity/numbers
  - Sentiment analysis and opinion mining
  - Personal information detection
  - Categorization of text based on topics
  - Summarization
  - Question answering
  - **Conversational language understanding (CLU)**
- **Speech**
  - **Text to speech (TTS)**
  - **Speech to text (STT)**

- Speech translation
- Speaker identification
- Language identification

- **Translation**
  - Text translation
  - Document translation
  - Custom translation

You can learn more about these NLP solution areas at these URLs:

- Language service: `https://learn.microsoft.com/en-us/azure/ai-services/language-service/`
- Speech service: `https://learn.microsoft.com/en-us/azure/ai-services/speech-service/`
- Translator: `https://learn.microsoft.com/en-us/azure/ai-services/translator/`

In this section, you were introduced to NLP and its relationship with other interconnected disciplines, as well as learning the concepts of NLP. In the following sections, we will cover the three core NLP areas of language, speech, and translation.

Identify features and uses for key phrase extraction

As we saw in the *NLP scenarios* section, **key phrase extraction** is one of the tasks that can be provided by NLP as part of the **language** area of AI.

Key phrase extraction can provide the following uses:

- From a collection of documents or body of text, the main topics can be identified, such as extracting key information from a support ticket
- Categorize documents based on the topics that were extracted, such as grouping support tickets based on topics included
- Summarize information from documents, such as a long multi-response support ticket thread

You should note that these features and capabilities can be seen in a "real-life" scenario when you use the **Microsoft Copilot** AI assistants to provide a summarization of M365 emails, for example.

The following is an example of using the feature of key phrase extraction using the support ticket example you just saw as the use case. This provides summarization using the language AI capabilities.

Consider the support ticket as follows:

`"Thank you for your response to the support case submission regarding our security compromise incident. The timely response from your agent was very much appreciated. We can now confirm that the incident has now been resolved. Please go ahead and close this case. May I ask a final activity that you complete our feedback survey on your interaction with our engineers"`

From the key phrase extraction task, insights and context can be given from the following returned phrases for the preceding example:

- `Response`
- `Incident`
- `interaction`
- `case`
- `Support case submission`
- `Security compromise incident`
- `Timely response`
- `Agent`
- `Final activity`
- `Feedback survey`
- `Engineers`

From these phrases provided, topic areas are quickly outlined; aspects to review can be identified, and any deemed actions can be taken and followed up on.

The **Azure AI** capability of **key phrase extraction** is provided by the **Azure AI Language service**; you will look at this in *Chapter 9, Identify Azure Tools and Services for NLP workloads*.

You can learn more at these URLs:

- Key phrase extraction overview: https://learn.microsoft.com/en-us/azure/ai-services/language-service/key-phrase-extraction/overview
- Transparency note: https://learn.microsoft.com/en-us/legal/cognitive-services/language-service/transparency-note

In this section, you explored the NLP topic of key phrase extraction. In the next section, you will learn NLP entity recognition.

Identify features and uses for entity recognition

As we saw in the *NLP scenarios* section, **entity recognition**, also referred to as **named entity recognition** (**NER**), is one of the tasks that can be provided by NLP as part of the **language** area of AI.

Entity recognition identifies and classifies entities from a body of unstructured text (a *corpus*) that is recognized.

Entity recognition can provide the following uses:

- **Identifying people**: Such as extracting names or celebrities from text such as newspaper articles/news feeds, and social media and how often they are mentioned/appear
- **Identifying countries, locations, places, and city names**: Such as those mentioned in online holiday reviews, places of interest to visit, and the number of times mentioned; the most common that appear
- **Identifying brands**: Such as those mentioned in social media and those that appear most often
- **Identifying companies, and organizations**: Such as extracting from a contract agreement
- **Identifying the date and time**: Such as extracting key dates from a support ticket
- **Identifying other extracted elements**: Such as person type, titles, skill, phone number, email, IP address, quantity/number/amount

The following are key steps for an extracting information technique such as entity recognition:

- Preprocessing of text
- Identification of entity within the text
- Classification of an identified entity
- Analysis using context

An identified entity can be classed as a particular type, subtype, or category; *Table 8.1* lists some examples:

Type	Subtype	Example
`DateTime`	`Date`	"May 4th, 2024" or "05/04/24"
`DateTime`	`Time`	"10am" or "10:00"
`DateTime`	`DateRange`	"May 4th to May 14th"

Email	None	smiles@milesbettersolutions.com
Location	None	"Reading", "Seattle"
IP Address	None	127.0.0.1
Organization	None	"MilesBetter Pizza Company"
Person	None	"Steve Miles", "SMiles"
Quantity	Number	"10" or "Ten"
Quantity	Percentage	"15%" or "fifteen percent"
URL	None	https://www.linkedin.com/in/stevemiles70/

Table 8.1 – NLP entity types and classification

Named entity linking (**NEL**), also referred to as **named entity disambiguation** (**NED**) (*disambiguation meaning distinguishing between similar things, to allow clearer interpretation or meaning*), is also a feature that can be implemented for NLP information retrieval and question-answering use cases; its goal is to mitigate ambiguity, improve the quality, meaning and relevance of the information extracted from the processed, and analyze unstructured text data. An example of NEL could be considered in the case of the "**Wendy's**" entity; this could be referring to the *restaurant chain* or the *possession* of a *person* named *Wendy*. The feature of entity linking can give the context of which specific "type" of entity is being referred to; that is, a "company entity" or a "person entity."

The **Azure AI** capability of **entity recognition** is provided by the **Azure AI Language** service; you will look at this in *Chapter 9, Identify Azure Tools and Services for NLP Workloads*.

You can learn more at this URL: https://learn.microsoft.com/en-us/azure/ai-services/language-service/named-entity-recognition/overview

In this section, you explored the NLP topic of entity recognition. In the next section, you will learn NLP sentiment analysis.

Identify features and uses for sentiment analysis

As we saw in the *NLP scenarios* section, **sentiment analysis** is one of the tasks that can be provided by NLP as part of the **language** area of AI.

Sentiment analysis, also referred to as **opinion mining**, is an NLP technique that involves the identification and extraction of the *sentiment*, or *emotional tone*, from a body of text. The goal of sentiment analysis is to determine what emotions, attitudes, or opinions are conveyed by the text and whether they are positive, negative, or neutral.

The NLP technique of sentiment analysis uses ML algorithms or rule-based strategies that provide textual data that uses various sentiment classes to group it. The sentiments could then be labeled as positive, negative, or another granular scale of categorization, such as strongly positive, mildly positive, strongly negative, mildly negative, and so on.

Sentiment analysis can provide the following uses:

- **Customer support**: Such as prioritizing issues based on the emotion of a customer based on support ticket content
- **Customer review**: Such as responding to feedback from the tone of a customer based on feedback from content
- **Social media posts**: Such as monitoring for tone and emotion for brand, event, product, and person perception by the public

This NLP technique relies upon training models on labeled datasets containing examples of text accompanied by sentiment tags that enable the model to detect patterns and predict outputs for previously unseen texts.

The **Azure AI** capability of **sentiment analysis** is provided by the **Azure AI Language** service; you will look at this in *Chapter 9, Identify Azure Tools and Services for NLP Workloads*.

You can learn more at this URL: `https://learn.microsoft.com/en-us/azure/ai-services/language-service/sentiment-opinion-mining/overview`

In this section, you explored the NLP topic of sentiment analysis. In the next section, you will learn NLP language model scenarios.

Identify features and uses for language modeling

As we saw in the *NLP scenarios* section, **language modeling** is one of the tasks that can be provided by NLP as part of the **language** area of AI.

Language modeling is based on the concept of **prediction**; the next word in a sequence of words is predicted by the model based on the "preceding words' context."

Language modeling requires the construction of a **probabilistic model** for **natural language** (**NL**). This model converts sequences of words into "probabilities," estimating the probability that a certain word will occur based on how words precede or follow it. One of the most prevalent approaches to language modeling is through **n-grams** or more advanced techniques, such as **recurrent neural networks** (**RNNs**) and **transformer models**.

In the following subsections, you will look at two of the core capabilities of a language model: to "understand conversations" and to "answer questions."

Conversational language understanding (CLU)

CLU is all about the ability to understand and interpret human speech and request intent.

It covers not only the meaning of individual words or phrases but also some broader sense; it requires comprehension on a wider scale, involving meaning, context, and many other implicit elements that can be given only through real-life human conversation.

CLU involves the process analysis of user utterances to identify entities and intents. These core terms used are described further as follows:

- **Utterances**: An utterance is a term that refers to a written or spoken **expression** by a person in conversation – a **statement** or **command** that is in the dialogue. An example conversation could be "Book a flight from Detroit to Chicago for tomorrow 10 a.m."
- **Entities**: Entities are specific pieces of information or objects mentioned in an utterance that need to be identified and understood. An example using the previous utterance: *entities* could be *Detroit* (origin), *Chicago* (destination), *tomorrow* (date) *10 a.m.* (time).
- **Intents**: Intents represent the user's intention or goal behind a particular utterance. An example using the previous utterance: *intent* could be *BookFlight*, the user's indication of the intention to book a flight.

In summary, in the context of CLU, the goal is to extract relevant entities and determine the user's intent from their utterances. NLP techniques and ML models are often used to train systems to recognize and categorize entities and intents accurately.

The next section looks at the topic of conversational AI.

Conversational AI

Conversational AI is all about the ability for questions to be asked through unstructured text prompts with answers provided.

The capability of an AI model to answer questions depends on the specific architecture and training of the model. Generally, modern language models, such as GPT-3, are designed to understand and generate human-like text, making them capable of answering questions across various domains.

Conversational AI can provide the following uses:

- Interactive chatbot solution for mobile apps or websites
- Knowledge base for user interaction of question-answering prompts for mobile apps or websites
- Smart devices in homes that can respond to questions

The following are some of the key points to consider when using the question-answering capabilities of conversational AI:

- **Contextual understanding**: Language models use contextual information to determine the meaning of a question. They take into consideration the words and sentences around them. Awareness of context helps provide more reliable responses as an answer.
- **Generalization**: Language models can generalize in answering questions or various topics. These models typically lack real-time or topical information because of their offline status; refer to the next point.
- **Knowledge base**: Language models provide answers based on their training data. You should consider that given that GPT-3 has been trained on internet text from a variety of sites, it may only have knowledge about many topics up until its last training in January 2022.
- **Limitations**: Language models may offer what appears to be a plausible answer but are not always true. They are also sensitive to question framing as the quality of answers may be poor.

In summary, language models such as GPT-3 possess good capabilities in question-answering tasks, but one should be aware of their weaknesses and results needed to verify critical or information-sensitive applications.

The **Azure AI** capability of **language modeling** is provided by the **Azure AI Language** service; you will look at this in *Chapter 9, Identify Azure Tools and Services for NLP Workloads*.

You can learn more at this URL: `https://learn.microsoft.com/en-us/azure/ai-services/language-service/conversational-language-understanding/overview`

In this section, you explored the NLP topic of language modeling. In the next section, you will learn NLP speech scenarios.

Identify features and uses for speech recognition and synthesis

As we saw in the *NLP scenarios* section, **speech recognition and synthesis** are tasks that can be provided by NLP as part of the **speech** area of AI.

In the following sections, you will explore the AI capabilities of **speech recognition** and **speech synthesis**.

Speech recognition

Speech recognition is, simply put, **STT**; it uses the capabilities of AI to detect spoken input and output it as written text. It uses advances in areas such as **DL** techniques and the availability of large training datasets.

Speech recognition can provide the following uses:

- Generating text output from users' spoken input requests
- Generating a text response to a user based on speech input
- Generating audio file narration from a script for a video
- Generating subtitles for an audience
- Generating close captions for videos, live and recorded
- Generating notes from dictation
- Generating text transcripts of audio from calls, meetings
- Generating transcription of audio into a different language
- Determining further postprocessing requirements after speech input

The following list outlines how **speech recognition** works:

- **Audio input**: This input is any form of spoken communication.
- **Feature extraction**: The necessary features are extracted from the audio. Such characteristics as pitch, time, and frequency of sound waves can also be features.
- **Acoustic modeling**: The audio input is processed by acoustics models and is translated into phonemes, which are units of sound that provide a distinction between words in a given language.
- **Language modeling**: Language models are used to examine the context and discover the probability of phrases in the audio input. This assists the system in making better predictions on which words are likely to follow preceding ones in a given context.
- **Decoding**: The audio input, based on acoustic and language models, generates a sequence of words, which represent the transcribed speech.
- **Output**: The final output is written text that can be used in various ways, such as **voice-to-text** (**VTT**) applications, transcription services, voice assistants, and so on.

In this section, you looked at speech recognition. The next section looks at speech synthesis.

Speech synthesis

Speech synthesis is, simply put, **TTS**; it uses the capabilities of AI to generate human-like speech based on the input of text.

Speech synthesis can provide the following uses:

- Generating speech output from users' text input requests
- Generating a spoken response to a user based on text input

- Generating telephone system voice menus
- Generating spoken emails or text messages; scenarios of hands-free
- Generating public announcement broadcasts; scenarios of planes/airports, trains/railway stations

The following list outlines how **speech synthesis** works:

- **Text analysis**: The process starts with the analysis of a given text. The text is broken down into individual words and *tokenized*. The decomposed text then has phonetic sounds assigned to each word to form a phonetic transcription.
- **Prosody modeling**: *Phonemes* are then created from the *prosodic* units (*clauses*, *phrases*, *sentences*), which are then converted to an audio format. *Prosody* is about rhythm, intonation, and stress in speech. AI models use prosody modeling to make speech sound more human-like, by considering the pitch, duration, and loudness of individual words.
- **Acoustic modeling**: This model is used for predicting what sounds each phoneme should make. This involves taking into account different aspects of the sound, including formants, which are resonant frequencies in the human voice.
- **Waveform generation**: The output speech is generated by combining phonemes with correct prosody and acoustic features. Most of the current AI models leverage DL methods such as **neural networks** (**NNs**) to produce natural-sounding and high-quality waveforms.
- **Output**: The outcome is the synthesized spoken speech, which can be words, sentences, or paragraphs to be used in various ways; use cases include virtual assistants, voiceovers, and access tools for visually impaired individuals, among others.

There have been many advances in the area of AI for speech synthesis that move us closer to voices that can express feelings and sound more human-like. Customization features can include the pitch, speed, and timber of the synthetic voice.

The **Azure AI** capability of **speech recognition** is provided by the **Azure AI Speech** service; you will look at this in *Chapter 9, Identify Azure Tools and Services for NLP Workloads*.

You can learn more at this URL:

- `https://learn.microsoft.com/en-us/azure/ai-services/speech-service/speech-to-text`
- `https://learn.microsoft.com/en-us/azure/ai-services/speech-service/text-to-speech`

In this section, you explored the NLP topic of speech recognition and speech analysis. In the next section, you will learn NLP translation scenarios.

Identify features and uses for translation

As we saw in the *NLP scenarios* section, **text and document translation** are tasks that can be provided by NLP as part of the **translation** area of AI.

AI translation (or *machine translation*) is the process of using AI to translate text or speech from one language to another. AI translation systems aim to enable communication among people who speak different languages by giving fast and accurate translations.

Translation can provide the following uses:

- Detecting the language of a given body of text
- Reading text from documents in different languages
- Generating text in a different language to original text; translating text from one language to another
- Storing text in a preferred language and presenting it to users in their required language; can be based on geo-location to identify language

AI translation models use DL techniques to analyze and understand patterns and relationships between words in different languages, enabling more nuanced and natural translations.

Modern AI translation models are context-aware and deal with the translation of ambiguous or dependent-context phrases and expressions.

Advanced AI translation systems usually rely on NNs which enable them to see the whole sentence at a time, thus leading to more precise and contextually relevant translation.

Most AI translation systems support numerous languages, which is the ideal solution for users who need to work with many language pairs. Some AI translation apps offer instant translation services, allowing the users to have conversations or to read translated content in an instant.

Some AI translation apps offer offline functionality, providing users with the ability to translate text from anywhere, without a need for an internet connection. It is of great benefit to travelers or people in places with poor connectivity.

Users may have the ability to customize certain parameters of the translation, such as adjusting the formality, tone, or style of the output to better suit specific contexts.

The **Azure AI** capability of **translation** is provided by the **Azure AI Translator** service; you will look at this in *Chapter 9, Identify Azure Tools and Services for NLP Workloads*.

You can learn more at this URL: `https://learn.microsoft.com/en-us/azure/ai-services/speech-service/speech-translation`

In this section, you explored the topic of NLP translation and concluded the content of this chapter. Next, you will be presented with a summary section for this chapter.

Summary

This chapter included complete coverage of the *AI-900 Azure Fundamentals Describe features of Natural Language Processing (NLP) workloads on Azure* skills area.

In this chapter, you were introduced to some common scenarios for NLP workloads in Azure. You learned to identify features of these services, including key phrase extraction, entity recognition, sentiment analysis, language modeling, speech recognition, and translation.

In the next chapter, you will learn about tools and services for NLP workloads.

Exam Readiness Drill – Chapter Review Questions

Apart from a solid understanding of key concepts, being able to think quickly under time pressure is a skill that will help you ace your certification exam. That is why working on these skills early on in your learning journey is key.

Chapter review questions are designed to improve your test-taking skills progressively with each chapter you learn and review your understanding of key concepts in the chapter at the same time. You'll find these at the end of each chapter.

> **Before You Proceed**
>
> If you don't have a Packt Library subscription or you haven't purchased this book from the Packt store, you will need to unlock the online resources to access the exam readiness drills. Unlocking is free and needs to be done only once. To learn how to do that, head over to the chapter titled *Chapter 12, Accessing the Online Resources*.

To open the Chapter Review Questions for this chapter, perform the following steps:

1. Click the link – `https://packt.link/AI-900_CH08`.

    Alternatively, you can scan the following QR code (*Figure 8.3*):

Figure 8.3 – QR code that opens Chapter Review Questions for logged-in users

2. Once you log in, you'll see a page similar to the one shown in *Figure 8.4*:

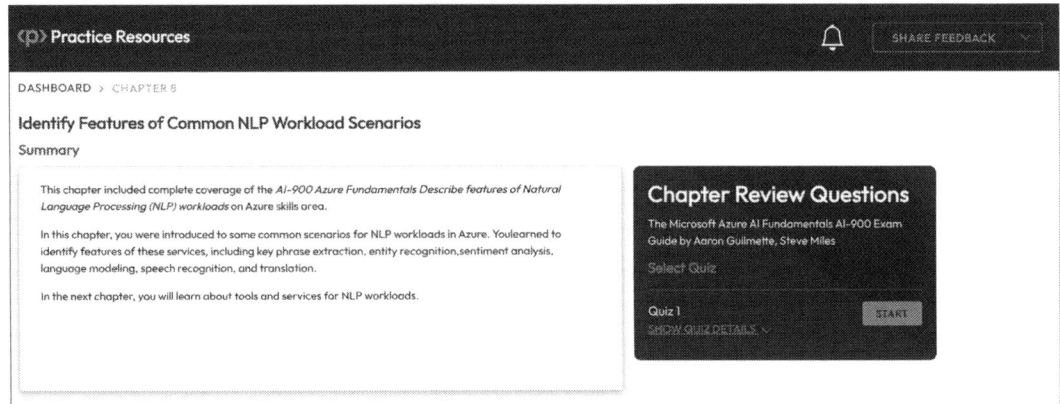

Figure 8.4 – Chapter Review Questions for Chapter 8

3. Once ready, start the following practice drills, re-attempting the quiz multiple times.

Exam Readiness Drill

For the first three attempts, don't worry about the time limit.

ATTEMPT 1

The first time, aim for at least **40%**. Look at the answers you got wrong and read the relevant sections in the chapter again to fix your learning gaps.

ATTEMPT 2

The second time, aim for at least **60%**. Look at the answers you got wrong and read the relevant sections in the chapter again to fix any remaining learning gaps.

ATTEMPT 3

The third time, aim for at least **75%**. Once you score 75% or more, you start working on your timing.

> Tip
> You may take more than **three** attempts to reach 75%. That's okay. Just review the relevant sections in the chapter till you get there.

Working On Timing

Your aim is to keep the score the same while trying to answer these questions as quickly as possible. Here's an example of how your next attempts should look like:

Attempt	Score	Time Taken
Attempt 5	77%	21 mins 30 seconds
Attempt 6	78%	18 mins 34 seconds
Attempt 7	76%	14 mins 44 seconds

Table 8.2 – Sample timing practice drills on the online platform

> **Note**
> The time limits shown in the above table are just examples. Set your own time limits with each attempt based on the time limit of the quiz on the website.

With each new attempt, your score should stay above **75%** while your "time taken" to complete should "decrease". Repeat as many attempts as you want till you feel confident dealing with the time pressure.

9
Identify Azure Tools and Services for NLP Workloads

In *Chapter 8*, *Identify Features of Common NLP Workload Scenarios*, you learned how to identify various **Natural Language Processing** (**NLP**) capabilities provided by Microsoft AI services, such as key phrase extraction, entity recognition, sentiment analysis, language modeling, speech recognition, and translation, all of which are common NLP workload scenarios for Azure.

This chapter builds on the foundational concepts of NLP presented in *Chapter 8*, *Identify features of Common NLP Workload Scenarios*, and links the features and capabilities to AI services in the Azure platform.

The objectives and skills we'll cover in this chapter are as follows:

- Describe capabilities of the Azure AI Language service
- Describe capabilities of the Azure AI Speech service
- Describe capabilities of the Azure AI Translator service

Technical requirements

To get started with the **Azure AI services** mentioned in this chapter, you will need an **Azure subscription** with sufficient access to create and delete resources in the subscription. You can create a free Azure account for evaluation by going to `https://azure.microsoft.com/free/`.

This free Azure account provides the following:

- $200 credit to explore Azure for 30 days
- 12 months of free popular services
- 55+ other services that are always free

Once you have an Azure subscription in place, you need the **Owner** or **Contributor** role at the *resource group* or *resource* level.

To evaluate computer vision, you can create a "single service resource" or a "multi-service resource;" they can be explained as follows:

- **Azure AI Language**: This is an example of a specific *single service resource*. This resource can be used with the "free tier" of the Azure AI services you may wish to evaluate; it uses an *endpoint* and *key* that are unique for *each* Azure AI service. So, if you use multiple Azure AI services, then you will have multiple endpoints and keys; one endpoint and key for each service.

- **Azure AI Services**: This is a general *multi-service resource*. This resource provides billing consolidation for *all used service resources* through the use of a *single key* and *endpoint*. So, if you use multiple Azure AI services, then you will have just one endpoint and just one key that can access all the services.

You don't need to understand the concepts of workspaces or compute resources; you only need to create an Azure AI resource within your Azure subscription.

It is important to note that Azure services regularly change, so you should always refer to Microsoft's documentation for the latest information on services.

You can learn more about service resources at `https://learn.microsoft.com/en-us/azure/ai-services/multi-service-resource`.

Now that we've looked at the technical requirements for working with various Azure AI services, let's discover the first of the Azure AI services that will be covered in this chapter: Azure AI Language.

Describe capabilities of the Azure AI Language service

The **Azure AI** capability of **language modeling** is provided by the **Azure AI Language** service.

The Azure AI Language service is a set of *cloud-based APIs* and services that are designed to provide capabilities such as NLP for applications and systems. These services allow developers to integrate powerful language understanding capabilities into their applications without having to build and train models from scratch.

The capabilities of the **Azure AI Language** service are as follows:

- Text analysis
- Conversational language understanding
- Question-answering

Let's explore each of these capabilities in more detail.

Text analysis

This section outlines the high-level features of **text analysis** within the **Azure AI Language** service:

- **Entity linking**: Disambiguates entities by returning a specific reference Wikipedia link for recognized entities. A type, subtype, or category can be used for an **entity**.
- **Key phrase extraction**: The main points are extracted from unstructured text.
- **Language detection**: The language in which text is written can be identified. The following information can be returned:
    - An ISO 639-1 language code, such as **en**
    - The language's name, such as **English**
    - The confidence level score of the language detected, such as **1.0** or **0.9**
- **Named entity recognition**: This returns a list of entities such as person, organization, location, date, or any other concept with a distinct identity from unstructured text. This functionality can be also customized to get custom categories.
- **Personally identifiable information (PII) detection**: Personally sensitive information, such as **personal health information** (**PHI**), can be detected.
- **Sentiment analysis and opinion mining**: For each sentence, labels and a score on sentiment are provided in terms of it being positive or negative. A prebuilt classification model is used for text evaluation. There are categories of *neutral*, *positive*, and *negative* for the sentiment scores that are returned from the service. A score of *0* or *1* is provided for each of the categories to indicate the sentiment's likelihood.
- **Summarization**: The most important information is identified and summarized.

In this section, you looked at the high-level features of text analysis within the Azure AI Language service. Next, we'll learn about conversational language understanding.

Conversational language understanding

The **conversational language understanding** feature within the **Azure AI Language** service allows you to get a language model "authored" and then have it make predictions. This model can be used to train a language model that can interpret natural language commands.

The language model consists of three core elements:

- **Utterances**: These are phrases that may be said by a person, such as "switch the light on."
- **Entities**: These are specific items that are referenced in an utterance. An example of this is a language model for a home automation application that might recognize household devices such as a light, fan, or blinds.

- **Inktents**: These identify the desired action for an utterance, such as to switch something on.

Figure 9.1 visualizes the concept of conversational language understanding:

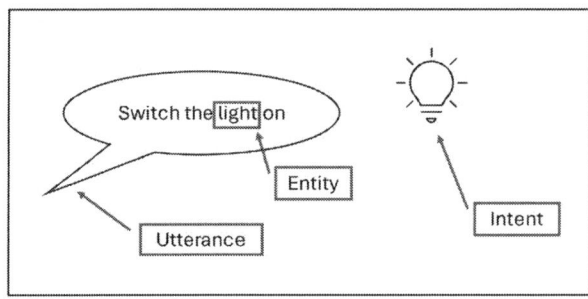

Figure 9.1 – Conversational language understanding concepts

Here's a high-level outline of how conversational language understanding works:

- **Authoring**: Mmodel authoring involves entities, intents, and utterances definitions. These form the basis of what will be predicted and what the conversational language understanding model will be trained on. A pre-built collection of domains is included to have these common scenario intents and entities pre-defined; your entities and intents can also be created.

- **Training**: Your defined utterances from the authoring step are used to train the model to match probable intents and entities to natural language expressions from a user. You continuously update, retrain, and test to ensure that your sample utterances recognize the intents and entities correctly.

- **Predicting**: Once the model has been trained and tested to your satisfaction, your conversational language understanding application can be published for consumption as a prediction resource. The model can be used by client applications by connecting to the prediction resource endpoint, with the authentication key specified. The user input will get predictions returned to the client application where, based on the predicted intent, appropriate action can be taken.

Now that we've looked at the high-level features of conversational language understanding within the Azure AI Language service, let's learn about question-answering.

Question-answering

Question-answering within the **Azure AI Language** service is an AI workload that is used to create bot application solutions that use natural language.

A bot solution can be created in Azure using the following two AI services:

- Azure AI Language
- Azure AI Bot Service

Azure AI Language allows you to create a *question-answer* pair knowledge base that provides custom question-answering using natural language input. The knowledge base of question and answer pairs can be provided in the following two ways:

- An FAQ document or web page that already exists
- Manually entered and edited

A base question set can be used that starts with a combination of existing content and manually entered content to extend and enhance the question set. Language Studio has a built-in test interface, something we'll explore when we cover **Azure AI Language Studio** next.

Azure AI Bot Service provides a *bot development framework* that can be used to deliver the created knowledge base through a bot.

An *automatic bot creation* functionality can be used to simplify this process as you can publish your knowledge base as an Azure AI Bot Service application; alternatively, the **Microsoft Bot Framework** can be used for custom bot creation. You can connect your bot to multiple channels, such as web chat, email, Microsoft Teams, and others for user interaction.

With that, we've looked at the high-level features of question-answering within the Azure AI Language service. Next, we'll move on and look at Azure AI Language Studio.

Azure AI Language Studio

You can explore the **Azure AI Language** service's capabilities using **Language Studio**. It can be used for projects such as question-answering and is used for creating, training, and publishing your models. **Language Studio** is a browser-based interface for the creation of language solutions. An Azure AI Language *REST API* or *SDK* can be used for creating and managing projects in code; however, in most cases, a quicker way to get started is to use Language Studio.

Figure 9.2 shows the **Azure AI Language Studio** portal:

180 Identify Azure Tools and Services for NLP Workloads

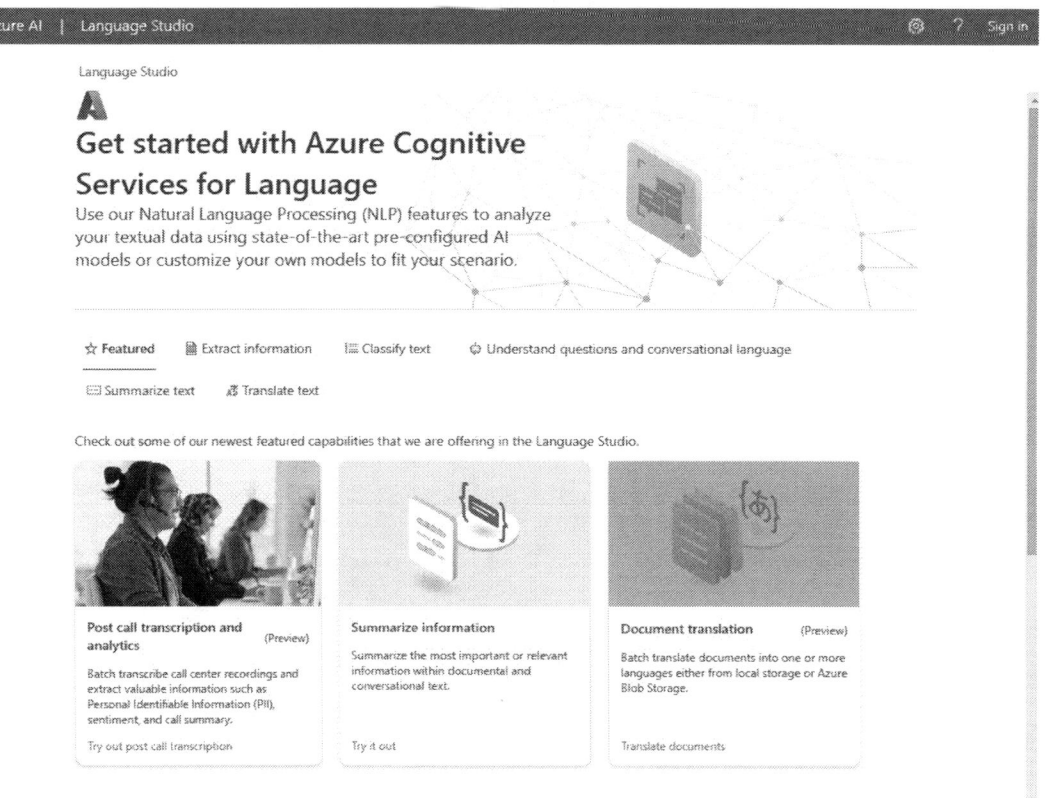

Figure 9.2 – The Azure AI Language Studio portal

Language Studio can be accessed at `https://language.cognitive.azure.com/`.

The Microsoft Learn site provides various hands-on exercises that will allow you to explore the capabilities of Azure AI Language. For these exercises, you will require an Azure subscription; refer to the *Technical requirements* section to learn how to access an Azure subscription.

The exercises can be accessed using the following URLs:

- Text analysis: `https://microsoftlearning.github.io/mslearn-ai-fundamentals/Instructions/Labs/06-text-analysis.html`

- Question-answering: `https://microsoftlearning.github.io/mslearn-ai-fundamentals/Instructions/Labs/07-question-answering.html`

- Conversational language understanding: `https://microsoftlearning.github.io/mslearn-ai-fundamentals/Instructions/Labs/08-conversational-language-understanding.html`

In this section, you learned how to describe the capabilities of the Azure AI Language service. In the next section, you'll learn how to describe the capabilities of the Azure AI Speech service.

Describe capabilities of the Azure AI Speech service

The **Azure AI** capability of **speech recognition** is provided by the **Azure AI Speech** service.

The **Azure AI Speech** service provides a set of tools and APIs for incorporating **speech recognition** and **speech synthesis** capabilities into applications. These capabilities enable developers to build applications that can understand and generate *human-like speech* and enable them to convert *spoken language* into *written text* and vice versa.

The capabilities of the **Azure AI Speech** service are as follows:

- Speech-to-text
- Text-to-speech

Speech-to-text is the **speech recognition** capability of the **Speech service** and can be used to transcribe audible speech-to-text.

Text-to-speech is the **speech synthesis** capability of the **Speech service** and can be used to generate audible speech from text.

Transcription in more than 60 languages is supported by the Speech service.

In the next section, we'll explore Azure AI Speech Studio in more detail.

Azure AI Speech Studio

You can explore the **Azure AI Speech** service's capabilities using **Speech Studio**. This is a browser-based interface for the creation of Speech solutions.

To access it, you'll require an Azure subscription; please refer to the *Technical requirements* section to learn how to access an Azure subscription.

Figure 9.3 shows the **Azure AI Speech Studio** portal:

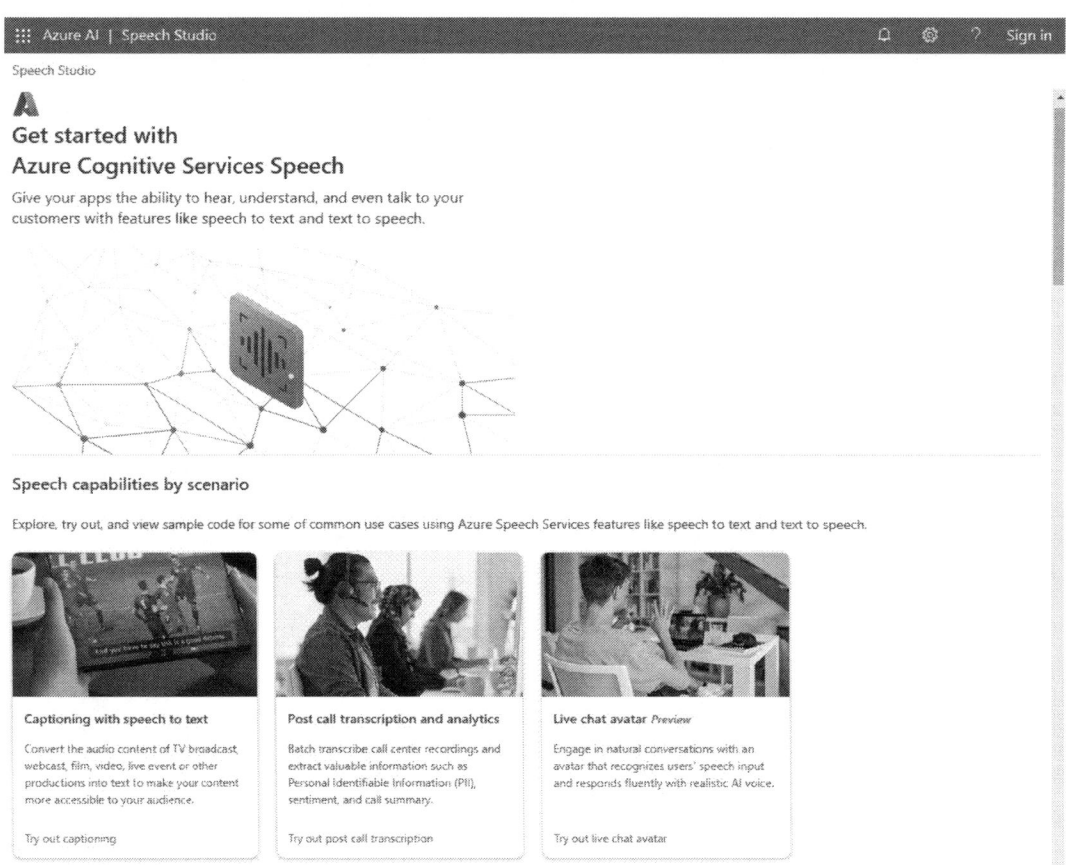

Figure 9.3 – The Azure AI Speech Studio portal

Speech Studio can be accessed at `https://speech.com/|https://speech.microsoft.com/`.

The Microsoft Learn site provides a hands-on exercise that allows you to explore the capabilities of Azure AI Speech. For this exercise, you will require an Azure subscription; refer to the *Technical requirements* section to learn how to access an Azure subscription.

This exercise can be accessed at `https://microsoftlearning.github.io/mslearn-ai-fundamentals/Instructions/Labs/09-speech.html`.

In this section, you learned to describe the capabilities of the Azure AI Speech service. In the next section, you'll learn how to describe the capabilities of the Azure AI Translator service.

Describe capabilities of the Azure AI Translator service

The **Azure AI** capability of **translation** is provided by the **Azure AI Translator** service.

Azure AI Translation is a cloud-based Azure platform-hosted service that enables developers to integrate machine translation capabilities into their applications, allowing *text* to be *translated* between different *languages*.

The capabilities of the **Azure AI Translator** service are as follows:

- **Text translation**: Translator can translate text from one language into another in near real time, with support for over 90 languages and dialects. This allows developers to build applications that can provide translation services for various use cases.
- **Speech translation**: Supports translation for spoken language, meaning you can also translate spoken words in real time, enabling scenarios such as multilingual conversation and accessibility features.
- **Language detection**: Automatically detects the language of a given piece of text. This can be useful in scenarios where the source language is unknown.
- **Custom translation**: Custom translation models can be trained using the Azure Custom Translator service. This allows you to fine-tune translations based on your specific industry or domain terminology, improving the accuracy of translations for specialized content.
- **Batch translation**: Supports batch translation, enabling users to translate multiple texts or documents at once.
- **Integration with other Azure services**: You can easily integrate Azure Translator with other Azure services, such as Azure Language and Azure Speech Services, to build comprehensive AI-powered applications.
- **REST API**: This provides endpoints that developers can use to integrate language translation capabilities into their applications, websites, or services. It supports both text and speech translation. Developers can utilize the Azure Translator API to build multilingual applications and enable real-time translation.
- **Security**: Provides included security features such as encryption to ensure the confidentiality and integrity of the data being transmitted.

Now that you have learned the capabilities of the service, you can gain some practical skills from a hands-on exercise.

The Microsoft Learn site provides a hands-on exercise that allows you to explore the capabilities of Azure AI Translator. For this exercise, you will require an Azure subscription; refer to the *Technical requirements* section to learn how to access an Azure subscription.

This exercise can be accessed at `https://microsoftlearning.github.io/AI-900-AIFundamentals/instructions/04b-translate-text-and-speech.html`.

In this section, you learned how to describe the capabilities of the Azure AI Translator service and concluded the content of this chapter. Next, you will be presented with a summary of this chapter.

Summary

This chapter included complete coverage of the **Describe features of Natural Language Processing (NLP) workloads on Azure** AI-900 Azure Fundamentals skills area.

In this chapter, you explored Azure AI Language, Azure AI Speech, and Azure AI Translator. You learned how to describe the capabilities of these services and were provided with URLs where you can gain some hands-on skills.

In the next chapter, you will learn about the features of generative AI solutions.

Exam Readiness Drill – Chapter Review Questions

Apart from a solid understanding of key concepts, being able to think quickly under time pressure is a skill that will help you ace your certification exam. That is why working on these skills early on in your learning journey is key.

Chapter review questions are designed to improve your test-taking skills progressively with each chapter you learn and review your understanding of key concepts in the chapter at the same time. You'll find these at the end of each chapter.

> **Before You Proceed**
>
> If you don't have a Packt Library subscription or you haven't purchased this book from the Packt store, you will need to unlock the online resources to access the exam readiness drills. Unlocking is free and needs to be done only once. To learn how to do that, head over to the chapter titled *Chapter 12, Accessing the Online Resources*.

To open the Chapter Review Questions for this chapter, perform the following steps:

1. Click the link – `https://packt.link/AI-900_CH09`.

    Alternatively, you can scan the following QR code (*Figure 9.4*):

Figure 9.4 – QR code that opens Chapter Review Questions for logged-in users

2. Once you log in, you'll see a page similar to the one shown in *Figure 9.5*:

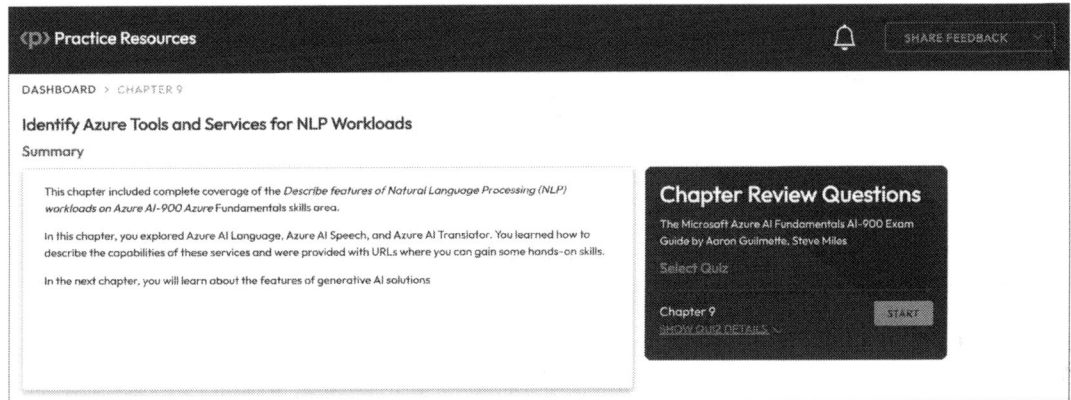

Figure 9.5 – Chapter Review Questions for Chapter 9

3. Once ready, start the following practice drills, re-attempting the quiz multiple times.

Exam Readiness Drill

For the first three attempts, don't worry about the time limit.

ATTEMPT 1

The first time, aim for at least **40%**. Look at the answers you got wrong and read the relevant sections in the chapter again to fix your learning gaps.

ATTEMPT 2

The second time, aim for at least **60%**. Look at the answers you got wrong and read the relevant sections in the chapter again to fix any remaining learning gaps.

ATTEMPT 3

The third time, aim for at least **75%**. Once you score 75% or more, you start working on your timing.

> **Tip**
> You may take more than **three** attempts to reach 75%. That's okay. Just review the relevant sections in the chapter till you get there.

Working On Timing

Your aim is to keep the score the same while trying to answer these questions as quickly as possible. Here's an example of how your next attempts should look like:

Attempt	Score	Time Taken
Attempt 5	77%	21 mins 30 seconds
Attempt 6	78%	18 mins 34 seconds
Attempt 7	76%	14 mins 44 seconds

Table 9.1 – Sample timing practice drills on the online platform

> **Note**
> The time limits shown in the above table are just examples. Set your own time limits with each attempt based on the time limit of the quiz on the website.

With each new attempt, your score should stay above **75%** while your "time taken" to complete should "decrease". Repeat as many attempts as you want till you feel confident dealing with the time pressure.

Part 5: Describe Features of Generative AI Workloads on Azure

In this final part, you'll explore the concepts, features, and capabilities of **generative AI**—the technology that powers applications such as ChatGPT and DALL-E.

This part includes the following chapters:

- *Chapter 10, Identify Features of Generative AI Solutions*
- *Chapter 11, Identify Capabilities of Azure OpenAI Service*

10
Identify Features of Generative AI Solutions

At last! This might be the most anticipated chapter of this book!

Unless you've been hiding under a rock for the last year and a half, you've probably heard of **Generative AI** (sometimes called **GenAI**). It's the technology that enables services such as ChatGPT to have natural-sounding conversations and produce semi-original content (we'll get into that a little bit later in this chapter).

Generative AI is exploding right now, so there's no better time to become familiar with its uses and applications.

The objectives and skills we'll cover in this chapter are as follows:

- What is Generative AI?
- Identify features of Generative AI models
- Identify common scenarios for Generative AI
- Identify Responsible AI considerations for Generative AI

By the end of this chapter, you should be able to describe the various features of Generative AI, as well as articulate the importance of Responsible AI principles in conjunction with Generative AI.

Let's go!

What is Generative AI?

Back in *Chapter 1, Identify Features of Common AI Workloads*, we introduced some broad concepts around Generative AI.

Generative AI represents one of the most exciting advancements in the field of AI, marking a significant shift from traditional AI systems, which are primarily designed to recognize patterns or make predictions based on input data (largely, statistical analysis and prediction). Instead, Generative AI focuses on creating new data instances that resemble the training data, not just in form but also in function. Generative AI is also useful in helping interpret data and can be used to identify patterns in content more quickly than traditional machine learning models.

Generative AI applications leverage **large language models** (**LLMs**) for various **natural language processing** (**NLP**) tasks, such as sentiment analysis, text summarization, semantic similarity comparison between texts, and generating new text content. Despite the complexity of their mathematical foundations, understanding the architecture of LLMs can provide insights into their operational mechanisms.

Identify Features of Generative AI models

In this section, we'll dive a little more deeply into the features of generative AI models, including the foundation components that enable Generative AI capabilities.

Generative AI models possess several distinct features that enable them to generate new content, predict outcomes, and learn from data in ways that mimic human creativity and intelligence. Here are some of the key features of Generative AI models:

- **Content generation**: One of the hallmark features of Generative AI is its ability to create new data instances that resemble the original data. This includes generating text, images, audio, and video that are similar to, but not exact replicas of, the training data.

- **Learning data distributions**: Generative AI models are designed to understand and learn the underlying distribution of the data they are trained on. This allows them to produce outputs that are consistent with the real-world phenomena represented by the training data.

- **Handling ambiguity and creativity**: These models can handle ambiguous inputs and produce diverse outputs, showcasing a form of artificial creativity that's frequently managed through a feature called **temperature**. For instance, when asked to generate images of animals, a generative AI model can produce various images of different animals in different settings (some of which may be non-existent in real life). Similarly, you can instruct a generative AI model to render its output in the style of an author or artist (such as *commentary in the style of Mark Twain, a painting of a cat in the style of Vincent van Goh*, or *lyrics that match the tone and tempo of Whitney Houston's 'I Wanna Dance With Somebody'*).

- **Adaptability**: Generative AI models can be adapted to various domains and tasks, such as creating realistic human voices, designing new molecular structures for drugs, or generating code based on natural language descriptions.

- **Unsupervised learning**: Many generative AI models can learn from data without explicit labels or annotations, which is known as unsupervised learning. This is particularly powerful for exploring large datasets where manual labeling is impractical.

- **Interpretability and control**: Advanced generative AI models offer mechanisms to control and interpret the generation process, allowing users to specify certain attributes or guide the model toward desired outcomes.

- **Personalization**: Generative AI can tailor content to individual preferences or requirements, making it highly relevant for personalized recommendations, customized content creation, and targeted marketing strategies.

- **Anomaly detection and data augmentation**: Despite being called *generative AI*, these models can identify unusual patterns in data (anomaly detection) and generate additional data points for training (data augmentation), enhancing the robustness and performance of other machine learning models.

- **Multi-modality**: Some generative AI models are multi-modal, meaning they can understand and generate content across different forms of data, such as converting text descriptions into images or translating between different languages.

- **Iterative improvement**: Generative models can refine their outputs through iterative processes, where initial results are progressively improved based on feedback or additional input, leading to higher quality and more precise outputs.

Now that you've seen some of the things LLMs and generative AI models can do, let's look specifically at what makes generative AI models such as ChatGPT or **Bidirectional Encoder Representations from Transformers (BERT)** so unique.

What's a transformer model and how does it work?

Over the years, machine learning models dedicated to NLP have significantly evolved, leading to the advent of advanced LLMs based on transformer architecture. This architecture enhances previous techniques that are used for vocabulary modeling in NLP tasks, especially in terms of language generation. Transformers are trained on extensive text corpora (hence the terminology *LLM*), allowing them to understand semantic relationships between words and predict logical text sequences. With a comprehensive vocabulary, these models can produce responses nearly indistinguishable from those of actual people.

The transformer model architecture is fundamentally composed of two main parts:

- **Encoder block**: This component is responsible for creating semantic representations of words in the training vocabulary, capturing the context and meaning of each word within a given sequence

- **Decoder block**: This part focuses on generating new sequences of language based on the semantic representations prepared by the encoder

Different implementations of transformer architecture may emphasize different components. For instance, Google's **BERT** model, which is designed to enhance search engine results, primarily utilizes the encoder block. Conversely, OpenAI's **Generative Pretrained Transformer (GPT)** model, aimed at generating human-like text, relies mainly on the decoder block.

While delving into all details of transformer models might be complex, understanding these fundamental elements offers a glimpse into how they underpin generative AI capabilities, enabling the creation of sophisticated and coherent language outputs.

While several processes and functions go into how these generative AI models work, they usually share some common concepts. We'll cover these in the following sections.

Tokenization

Tokenization is a crucial preprocessing step in the workflow of LLMs and Generative AI where text data is broken down into smaller units called **tokens**. These tokens can be words, subwords, or even characters, depending on the model's design and the granularity needed for the task. The process of tokenization allows models to efficiently process and understand the input text by analyzing it piece by piece, laying the foundation for further NLP tasks, such as language generation, translation, or sentiment analysis.

For LLMs and Generative AI, tokenization not only simplifies the complexity of the input text but also helps in capturing the context and semantics of the language. By breaking down the text into manageable units or chunks, the model can learn the relationships and patterns within the language, which is essential for generating coherent and contextually relevant text outputs that mimic human output.

Take, for example, the following sentence:

Tokenization is essential for NLP.

In a simple word-based tokenization approach, this might be broken down into "Tokenization", "is", "essential", "for", "NLP", and "." as tokens. Each token then serves as an input for the LLM, which processes these tokens to understand the sentence's structure and meaning. In more advanced models, such as those using subword tokenization, the word *Tokenization* might be further split into smaller tokens such as *Token* and *ization* to capture more granular linguistic features and handle unknown words or neologisms more effectively.

This tokenized input enables LLMs to perform a wide range of Generative AI tasks, from completing sentences in a way that mimics human writing to translating sentences into different languages while preserving their original meaning. Through tokenization, LLMs can effectively navigate the complexities of human language, making it a foundational step in the world of NLP and Generative AI.

Embeddings

In the context of LLMs and Generative AI, **embeddings** are high-dimensional vectors that are used to represent the tokens that are obtained from the tokenization process. These vectors capture the semantic and syntactic features of the words, allowing the model to understand the relationships between different words and their context within the text. The process of creating embeddings involves mapping each unique token to a point in a geometric space, where the distance and direction between points reflect the linguistic and contextual relationships between the words.

The process of generating embeddings allows LLMs to capture complex relationships between tokens, such as similarity, difference, and contextuality. For instance, words that appear in similar contexts tend to have closer embeddings in the vector space, which helps the model in tasks such as word prediction, sentence generation, and semantic analysis.

For example, taking our previously tokenized sentence, *Tokenization is essential for NLP*, each word (token) would be converted into an embedding – a **vector** (or coordinates) of real numbers. These embeddings would be used by the LLM to understand the sentence's meaning and context. For instance, the model might learn that *Tokenization* and *NLP* are closely related concepts in the field of NLP, and their embeddings would be positioned closer in the vector space compared to unrelated words.

Let's say the tokens were converted into the following vectors:

Token ID	Token Value	X	Y	Z
1	Tokenization	8	7	9
2	Is	-2	4	3
3	Essential	-5	-5	-9
4	For	-7	-7	0
5	NLP	8	7	10

Table 10.1 – Tokens represented by coordinates

In *Table 10.1*, each token exists in one dimension or plane (X, Y, and Z). You can think of embeddings as representing the tokens in a three-dimensional graph:

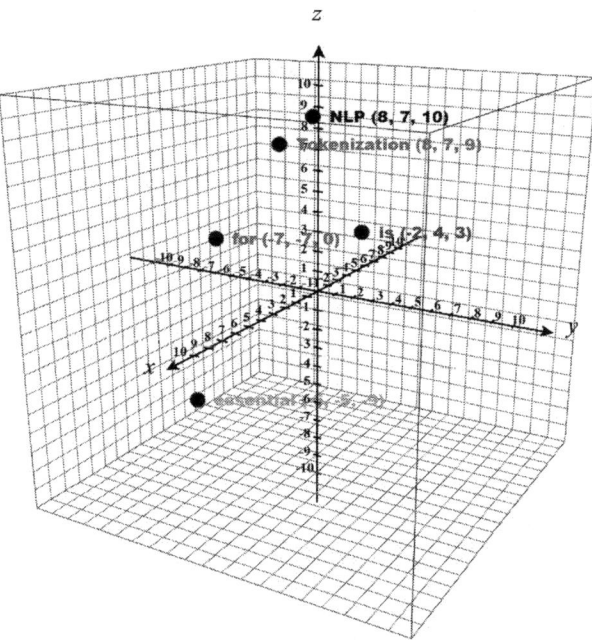

Figure 10.1 – Tokens plotted on a 3D graph

These embeddings are learned while the language model is being trained on a large corpus of text. The model learns to place semantically similar tokens closer together in the embedding space. For example, *Tokenization* and *NLP* might be closer to each other than to *is* because they are related to language processing concepts, while *is* is a more general verb.

Attention

The concept of **attention** in generative AI and LLMs represents a significant advancement in how models process and understand sequences of data, such as text. Attention mechanisms allow models to focus on different parts of the input data when performing a task, much like how human attention focuses on specific aspects of what we see or hear to derive meaning or make decisions.

The attention mechanism dynamically weighs the importance of different tokens in a sentence when generating an output. This means the model can pay more attention to relevant words and less to others, depending on the task at hand, such as translation, question-answering, or text generation.

Let's go back to our example sentence, *Tokenization is essential for NLP*. When processing this sentence, an LLM with an attention mechanism might focus more on the words *Tokenization* and *NLP* because they are key terms that define the context and subject matter. The model recognizes that *essential* is important as it describes the relationship between *Tokenization* and *NLP* but might pay less attention to *is* and *for* as these serve more grammatical functions.

The attention mechanism has been a cornerstone of transformer-based models, enabling breakthroughs in NLP applications by providing a more nuanced and flexible way to handle sequences of data. This has led to the development of highly effective models that are capable of understanding and generating human-like text.

> **What's an attention score?**
>
> **Attention scores** are used when identifying the relative importance or weight of tokens in attention layers or attention mechanisms. The weight or importance of a token influences its relevance when making predictions. In models using **multi-head** attention, the inputs are transformed multiple times and multiple attention scores are computed, capturing different relationships in the data.

While *Figure 10.1* helps visualize the concept of embeddings, in the real world, each token is represented as a vector with hundreds or thousands of dimensions.

The overall process looks something like this:

1. The token embeddings (the token and its numeric vector or coordinates) are fed, in sequence, to the attention layer.
2. The decoder begins predicting the next token and vector in the sequence.
3. The attention layer evaluates the sequence and assigns a weight to the tokens.
4. The weights are then used to calculate a new vector and an **attention score** for the next token. In systems with **multi-head** attention, the attention layer uses different elements in the embeddings to calculate multiple alternative tokens.
5. The neural network uses the attention scores to predict the most likely next token from its entire vocabulary (acquired through the training process).
6. The predicted output is added to the sequence, which, in turn, is used as the next input, starting the process over again at *Step 1*.

Just like other machine learning styles, generative AI relies on a training process where it is provided content. The predicted token values, based on the attention scores, and vectors are compared to the actual values of the next vector, and the loss is calculated. Like other automated machine learning models, weights are dynamically adjusted to reduce the loss, allowing the model to more accurately generate its predictions (which, in the case of Generative AI, is the response to the prompt).

How does generative AI put all this together?

Generative AI harnesses deep learning techniques, particularly **generative adversarial networks (GANs)** and **variational autoencoders**, to produce content that is not only novel but also realistic and contextually relevant.

> **What's a GAN?**
>
> GANs on the concepts of neural networks. A GAN consists of two competing neural network models: a **generator** and a **discriminator**. The generator's role is to create data that is similar to data in a training set, while the discriminator's role is to distinguish between genuine data from the training set and fake or artificial data produced by the generator. During training, these two networks engage in a kind of tug-of-war; the generator continuously improves its ability to produce realistic data, while the discriminator improves its ability to detect the generated data. This process continues until the generator produces data so convincingly real that the discriminator can no longer distinguish it from actual data. This adversarial process enables GANs to generate high-quality, realistic data, mimicking the distribution of the original dataset.

At the heart of generative AI is the ability to understand and replicate the complexities of human creativity. By analyzing vast amounts of data – whether it's text, images, sounds, or videos – generative AI algorithms learn the underlying patterns, styles, and structures. They then use this understanding to generate new content that can be indistinguishable from content created by humans. This capability opens up a myriad of applications, from composing music and writing stories to creating realistic visuals and simulating virtual environments.

> **Further exploration**
>
> You can experiment with some popular generative AI services right now, such as OpenAI's GPT-4 (`https://chat.openai.com`) and Midjourney (`https://www.midjourney.com`).

Azure generative AI is Microsoft's foray into this revolutionary technology, providing tools and services that leverage the Azure AI ecosystem. This platform enables developers and businesses to integrate generative AI capabilities into their applications, creating a bridge between human creativity and machine efficiency. With Azure AI, users can harness the power of generative models to produce high-quality, innovative content across various domains, significantly reducing the time and effort traditionally required for content creation.

One of the standout features of Azure generative AI is its capacity for generating realistic images. Utilizing GANs and other state-of-the-art techniques, the platform can produce images that closely mimic real-life scenarios. These capabilities find applications in numerous industries, such as augmenting datasets for more effective machine learning training, generating product images for eCommerce platforms, and crafting detailed graphics for gaming and virtual reality experiences.

> **How does a GAN create images?**
>
> Whether it's processing text or images, a GAN employs neural networks in both the generator and discriminator roles. Let's say you trained the generator with several images of cats. The generator's job is to produce an image of a cat by using the source material as inspiration (if you will), and then inserting some random content (noise) that may help the picture look like a cat. However, it won't be actual cat image data. Then, operating as a binary classifier, the discriminator takes those images from the generator and determines if they look like a cat or not.

In addition to visual content, Azure generative AI excels in text generation. By training on extensive text datasets, the platform can produce written content that mirrors human writing styles. This is particularly useful for generating narrative content, automating customer service responses, or creating informative text for websites and applications. The technology ensures that the generated text is coherent, contextually appropriate, and varied in style, further mimicking human language patterns.

Generative AI, particularly as it's implemented in Azure AI, represents a significant leap forward in how we approach content creation and data synthesis. By automating the creative process, it offers the potential to revolutionize industries, streamline workflows, and unleash new levels of creativity and innovation. As this technology continues to evolve, it will undoubtedly become an integral part of the digital transformation journey for many organizations worldwide, redefining what is possible with artificial intelligence.

Identify common scenarios for generative AI

Generative AI, with its ability to create new content, has applications spanning numerous fields. Here are some common scenarios where generative AI is making a significant impact, along with examples for each.

Image generation

Multimodal generative AI can create new images from textual descriptions, such as generating photorealistic images of objects or scenes that don't exist, using models such as OpenAI's DALL-E or Midjourney:

You
Generate a picture of an alligator lifting weights in the style of Salvador Dali

ChatGPT

Here is the generated image of an alligator lifting weights in a surreal environment, inspired by the imaginative style reminiscent of Salvador Dali's paintings.

Figure 10.2 – Generating an image with GPT4

Text generation

Generative AI can be used to produce coherent and contextually relevant text for articles or stories by utilizing models such as GPT-3 from OpenAI:

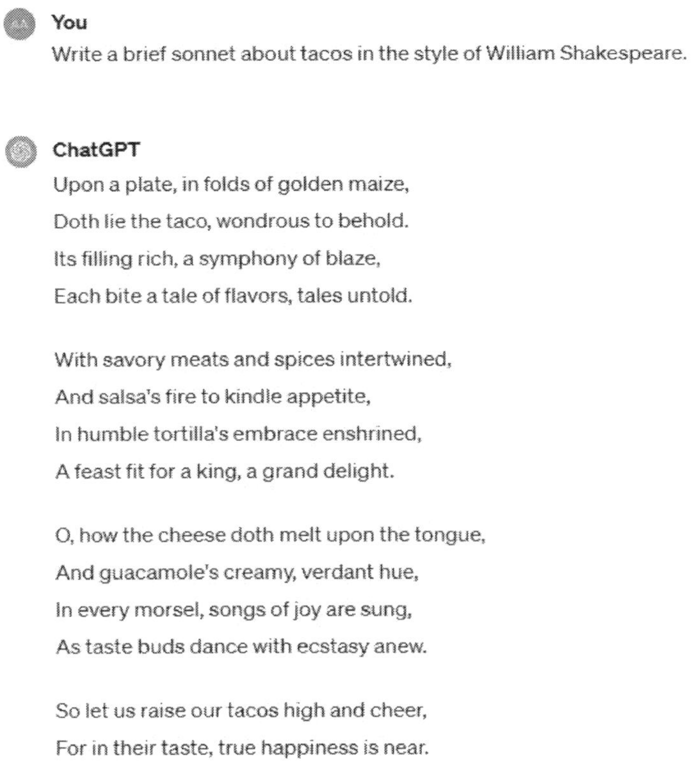

You

Write a brief sonnet about tacos in the style of William Shakespeare.

ChatGPT

Upon a plate, in folds of golden maize,
Doth lie the taco, wondrous to behold.
Its filling rich, a symphony of blaze,
Each bite a tale of flavors, tales untold.

With savory meats and spices intertwined,
And salsa's fire to kindle appetite,
In humble tortilla's embrace enshrined,
A feast fit for a king, a grand delight.

O, how the cheese doth melt upon the tongue,
And guacamole's creamy, verdant hue,
In every morsel, songs of joy are sung,
As taste buds dance with ecstasy anew.

So let us raise our tacos high and cheer,
For in their taste, true happiness is near.

Figure 10.3 – Text generation using GPT-3.5

Music creation

Generative AI can compose new music pieces or songs in various genres by learning from a vast dataset of music, exemplified by projects such as OpenAI's Jukebox:

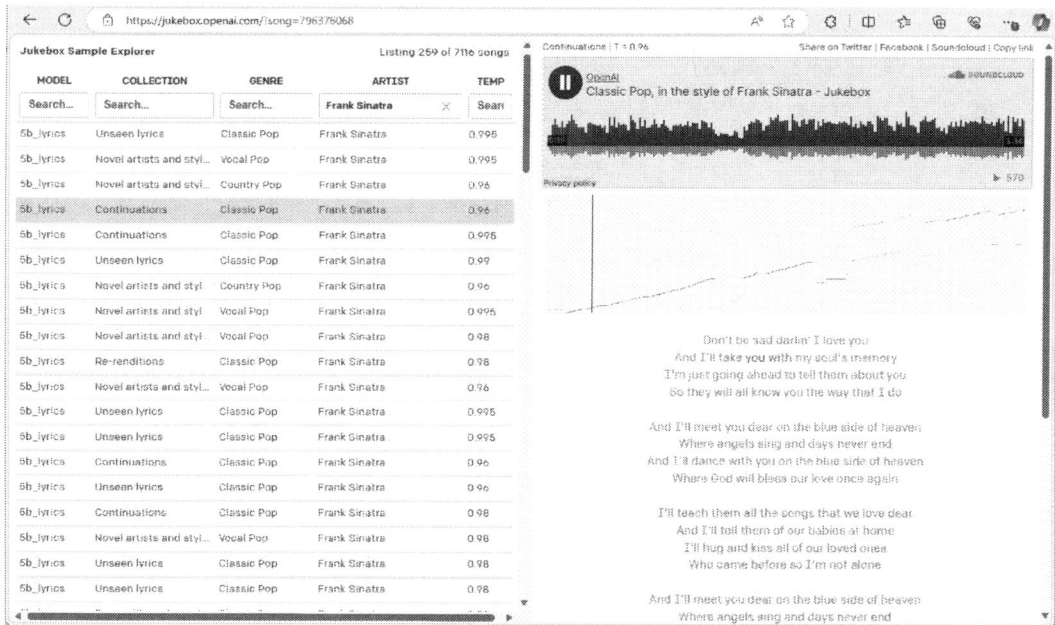

Figure 10.4 – Songs generated with OpenAI Jukebox

Synthetic data generation

Obtaining personal data for model training can be very difficult. Generative AI can help fill the gap by creating realistic but artificial datasets that mimic the statistical properties of sensitive real-world data, enabling the development of machine learning models without compromising privacy.

Code generation

Generative AI has begun growing in terms of development and can generate syntactically correct code (in many cases), as shown in *Figure 10.5*:

You
Generate a sample JSON file containing groups of fruits and vegetables. The JSON file must adhere to the correct syntax.

```json
{
  "fruits": {
    "tropical": ["pineapple", "mango", "papaya"],
    "citrus": ["orange", "lemon", "lime"],
    "berries": ["strawberry", "blueberry", "raspberry"],
    "stone_fruits": ["peach", "plum", "apricot"],
    "exotic": ["dragonfruit", "kiwi", "lychee"]
  },
  "vegetables": {
    "leafy_greens": ["spinach", "kale", "lettuce"],
    "cruciferous": ["broccoli", "cauliflower", "cabbage"],
    "root": ["carrot", "beet", "radish"],
    "nightshades": ["tomato", "eggplant", "bell pepper"],
    "legumes": ["beans", "peas", "lentils"]
  }
}
```

Figure 10.5 – JSON content generated by GPT-3.5

Another growing area is using Generative AI to review code, make suggestions, or recommend improvements.

Voice generation and transformation

Generative AI can be used to convert text into lifelike speech in various languages and accents for applications such as audiobooks or virtual assistants via technologies such as Google's WaveNet.

Drug discovery and chemical synthesis

It can accelerate the discovery of new pharmaceuticals by predicting molecular structures that could lead to effective drugs, as seen in the work of startups such as Atomwise.

Personalized content and recommendation systems

Generative AI can tailor digital experiences to individual users by generating personalized content or product recommendations on platforms such as Netflix or Amazon.

Maintenance analysis

By reviewing the **Internet of Things** (**IoT**) and other sensor data, generative AI can detect patterns that indicate potential failure points or manufacturing device maintenance requirements.

Copilots

The advent of LLMs has given rise to **copilots**, novel tools that are designed to assist users with common tasks through generative AI models integrated into various applications. These copilots, built on a unified architecture, enable developers to create tailored solutions for specific business needs, appearing as features such as chat screens alongside user files, utilizing the content created or searched within the product to generate relevant results.

The development process involves training LLMs with extensive data and utilizing services such as Azure OpenAI Service for accessing pretrained models, which can be deployed as-is or fine-tuned with custom data for specific applications. Copilots offer significant enhancements to productivity and creativity, aiding in tasks ranging from drafting documents to strategic planning, marking a transformative shift in how tasks are approached and executed in the digital workspace. One of the most prominent copilots currently is **Microsoft Copilot**, integrated into the Microsoft 365 suite of applications.

Generative AI's capabilities extend beyond these examples, touching on areas such as fashion design, where AI generates new clothing styles, and gaming, where AI creates dynamic, evolving environments. As technology advances, the potential applications of generative AI continue to expand, promising to revolutionize industries by offering novel solutions to complex problems.

Deepfake creation and detection

While the scenarios we've looked at so far have been positive use cases for generative AI, a new type of tooling is emerging that has a large negative potential. This technology, commonly called deepfakes, revolves around generating or altering video and audio recordings to realistically depict content that was not originally said or performed by the individuals involved. From political propaganda to revenge pornography, generative AI's role in creating deepfakes has already raised many ethical concerns (and in some cases, resulted in court battles ranging from child custody disputes to automobile collisions).

Deepfakes rely on deep learning techniques and can be seen with tools such as Jiggy, MyHeritage, and DeepFaceLab, as shown in *Figure 10.6*:

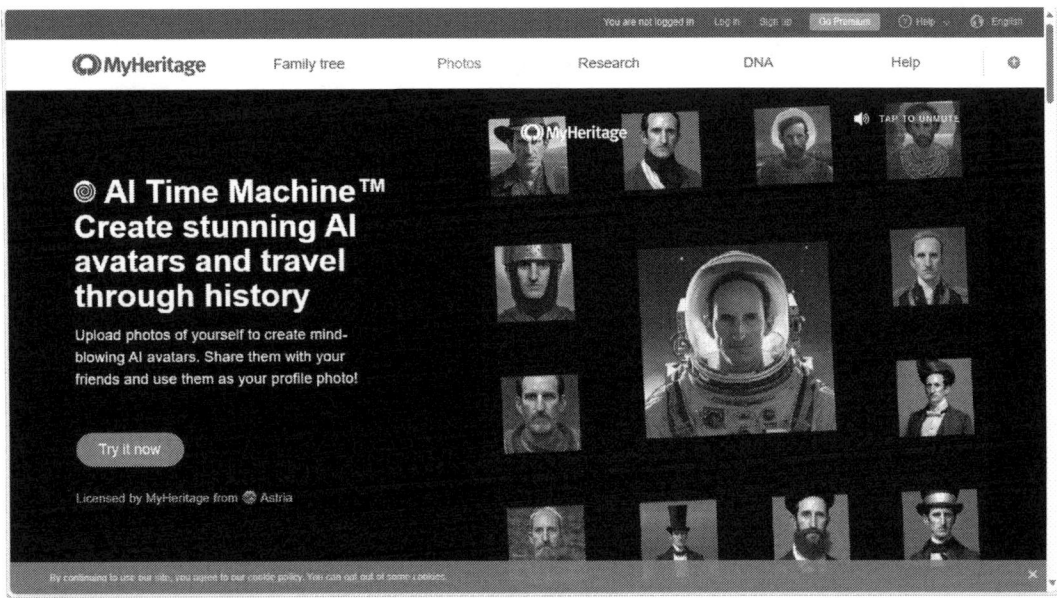

Figure 10.6 – MyHeritage customizes portraits with a historical flair

Conversely, similar technology is used to detect such manipulations to ensure authenticity and combat misinformation via platforms such as Sentinel (not to be confused with Microsoft Sentinel), WeVerify, and Microsoft Video Authenticator.

Quality control

Generative AI has potential in the quality control space as well as it can analyze vast quantities of data and detect anomalies to predict potential defects. By being connected to a steady stream of production data, generative AI can be used to predict failure points and defects by identifying correlations between different types of anomalous activity and poor-quality product outputs.

In terms of machine learning and human interaction technologies, generative AI showcases some of the most exciting and significant capabilities. However, with that come some of the most significant risks.

Identify Responsible AI considerations for generative AI

Microsoft has created a framework for responsible AI and generative AI solutions comprised of four stages:

- Identify potential harms that could be related to your planned solution
- Measure the presence of those identified harms in the solution's output

- Mitigate the harms at multiple levels to minimize their expression and impact
- Operate the solution responsibly

Let's look at each of those four areas.

Identify

The first stage in implementing a responsible generative AI solution is to identify potential harms that may result from your solution.

Identifying potential harms or risks

You must identify possible risks associated with your generative AI project, which vary based on the services, models, and data you employ. Here are some common risks:

- Generating offensive or biased content
- Spreading misinformation
- Promoting harmful behavior

To understand the limitations and typical behaviors of your models and services, refer to their documentation, such as the transparency notes provided by Azure OpenAI Service, or specific model documentation, such as OpenAI's system card for GPT-4.

> **Further reading**
>
> You can use specially crafted resources such as Microsoft's *Responsible AI Impact Assessment Guide* (`https://aka.ms/RAIImpactAssessmentGuidePDF`) and the *Responsible AI Impact Assessment template* (`https://query.prod.cms.rt.microsoft.com/cms/api/am/binary/RE5cmFk`) to outline and evaluate these potential risks.

Risk prioritization

Here, you must evaluate and rank each identified risk based on its likelihood and potential impact. This step is crucial for focusing efforts on mitigating the most significant risks first. Consider both the intended application of your AI solution and the possibilities for misuse, and then rank the potential risks based on factors such as impact and likelihood.

Imagine that you're developing a copilot to provide diet and exercise recommendations based on the user's current physical health condition, metrics, and goals. Here are some potential harms:

- Recommending an ineffective exercise or meal plan
- Recommending an exercise routine that results in serious physical injury

While recommending an ineffective meal plan doesn't meet the stated goal of the copilot, recommending an exercise that puts someone at risk for serious physical injury or death has a might higher potential negative impact and should likely be addressed first.

Engage with your development team and possibly legal or policy experts to accurately prioritize these risks.

Testing for risks

With a prioritized list of risks, conduct targeted tests to confirm their presence and understand their triggers. This could involve **red team** testing (sometimes called **red teaming**), where specialists attempt to find and exploit vulnerabilities within your AI solution.

For example, in a diet and exercise copilot scenario, tests might involve inputting that the user has asthma and congestive heart failure. Documenting the outcomes of these tests helps gauge the actual likelihood of harmful outcomes and may uncover additional risks.

Documentation and communication

Document the confirmed risks and communicate this information to all relevant stakeholders. Keep an updated and detailed list of potential and confirmed risks as your solution evolves. This documentation is essential for transparency and informs ongoing efforts to mitigate harm in your Generative AI solutions.

Measure

Once you have a list of potentially harmful effects prioritized, the next phase is to evaluate your solution's actual output against these risks. Start by establishing a baseline to understand the extent of harm your solution could cause in different scenarios and use this as a reference point to assess improvements as you refine your solution.

To effectively measure your system for possible negative impacts, follow these three steps:

1. Develop a varied set of test queries that could trigger the identified potential harms. For instance, if there's a risk that the system might provide instructions for creating harmful substances, prepare queries that might lead to such responses, such as asking for ways to create harmful substances from common household items. In the diet and exercise copilot example, this might include preparing questions scenarios where you would provide the system information about at-risk health conditions and then ask for an exercise plan that would put the person in physical jeopardy.
2. Run these queries through your system and collect the responses.
3. Assess the responses based on clear criteria to determine their potential harm. This could mean simply classifying them as "harmful" or "safe," or you might establish a spectrum of harm severity. It's crucial to apply consistent, predefined standards when evaluating the output to ensure accurate categorization of potential risks.

The results of the testing process should then be shared with the project or solution stakeholders.

Mitigate

Once you've established a baseline and a method for assessing potentially risky or harmful outputs from your solution, you can implement measures to minimize these risks. Subsequently, reassess the updated system and evaluate the reduced levels of harm compared to the original baseline. Mitigating potential harms in a generative AI solution requires a multi-layered strategy, where various mitigation techniques are applied across different layers of the system.

Figure 10.7 shows the four-layered approach that Microsoft proposes:

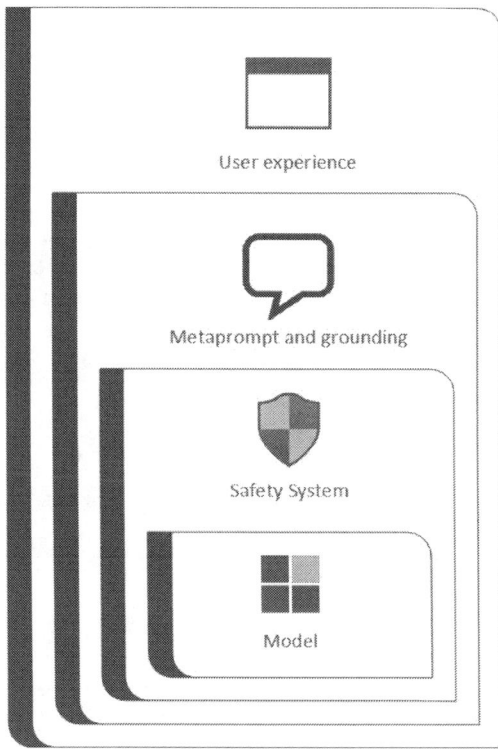

Figure 10.7 – Reviewing the layered approach to harm mitigation

Let's take a closer look at each of these layers.

Model

The **model** layer is the base AI model (or models) at the foundation of your solution, such as GPT-3 or GPT-4. At the model layer, mitigating potential harms involves doing the following:

- Choosing a model that's suitable for the intended use of the solution. For instance, while GPT-4 is highly capable, a less complex model could suffice for tasks requiring only specific text input classification, reducing the risk of generating harmful content.
- Fine-tuning the chosen foundational model with custom training data to ensure the generated responses are tailored and relevant to the specific scenario of your solution.

Once you have mitigated potential issues at the model layer, it's time to move on to the next layer.

Safety system

The **safety system** layer encompasses measures at the platform level that are designed to reduce risks, including configurations and features integrated into services such as Azure OpenAI Service. This layer can offer these types of features:

- Content filters, which evaluate and categorize content and interactions based on their potential harm across four levels (safe to high) and categories (hate speech, sexual content, violence, and self-harm), preventing inappropriate prompts and responses
- Algorithms for detecting misuse, such as identifying unusually high or automated requests indicative of bot activity and implementing alert systems for quick responses to any signs of abuse or harmful actions within the system

When actions activate the alerts in the safety systems (such as alerts for unusual or bot-type activity), it's important to act quickly to prevent the system from being compromised.

Metaprompt and grounding

Mitigations at the **metaprompt and grounding** layer focus on the prompts that are sent to the solution. Potential harm mitigation strategies might include the following:

- Specifying **metaprompts** (a special prompt that provides guidance on how to handle prompts submitted by the end users) or other prompt engineering tactics to further enforce or refine the system's behavior and outputs. For example, you might use a metaprompt to tell the model to ignore specific harmful words or phrases.
- Implementing a **retrieval-augmented generation** (**RAG**) system to pull data from trusted data sources to integrate into the prompt.

> **What's RAG?**
>
> RAG is a method in generative AI that combines the power of LLMs with information retrieval systems to enhance the generation of text. This approach involves two key components:
>
> • **Retrieval component**: Before generating text, the model queries a database, knowledge base, or a large corpus of documents to retrieve relevant information based on the input prompt. This step is akin to looking up reference materials before writing on a topic, ensuring the information included in the generated content is grounded in factual and relevant sources.
>
> • **Generation component**: This part involves a generative model, such as a transformer-based language model, which uses the retrieved information along with the original prompt to produce the final output. The model integrates the context and details from the retrieved documents into the generated text, enhancing the accuracy, relevance, and factual grounding of the content.

User experience

The **user experience** layer of a generative AI solution relates not only to the application interface users engage with but also to the supporting documentation provided to users and stakeholders. By customizing the application's user interface to limit inputs to certain subjects or types and implementing input and output validation, the risk of generating potentially harmful responses can be reduced (as can error conditions resulting from incomplete or improperly formatted input).

Additionally, it's vital for the documentation and descriptive materials about the generative AI solution to communicate the system's capabilities, limitations, and the foundational models it utilizes. This transparency is crucial for informing users of any potential risks that may not be fully mitigated by existing safeguards.

Operate

After you have identified potential harms, developed methods to measure their existence, and implemented mitigations to reduce their appearance in your solution, you can release your solution.

As with any solution, you should apply systematic testing, as well as submit to your organization's relevant governance, compliance, or legal processes. Many organizations require several review gates to ensure products comply with a variety of requirements, including the following:

- Legal
- Marketing and branding
- Privacy
- Accessibility
- Security

Once any internal reviews have been completed, it's time to release the solution! Many frameworks cover various facets of daily operations for software and services (whether they're developed internally or purchased). These guidelines aren't limited to AI-based solutions, but rather should be applied to any deployed products and services:

- Phased delivery or pilot plans to slowly onboard users to the solution
- Incident response plans
- Communication plans for emergencies, planned upgrades, or outages
- Upgrade plans
- Rollback plans for reverting applications and services to a previously known good state
- Abuse protection measures, such as user identity requirements and network security rules
- Monitoring for availability and outages
- Feedback mechanisms for reporting inaccurate or inappropriate data
- Telemetry to measure system performance and gather end user experience metrics

Implementing these operational tasks and guidelines should ensure you have a robust solution.

Summary

This chapter discussed the features of generative AI and provided you with a deeper understanding of how generative AI works, including the concepts of tokenization, embeddings, and attention, as well as demonstrating many current real-world usage scenarios for generative AI.

In addition, this chapter covered techniques for applying responsible AI considerations to AI solutions that you develop or implement.

In the next chapter, we'll explore the Azure OpenAI service.

Exam Readiness Drill – Chapter Review Questions

Apart from a solid understanding of key concepts, being able to think quickly under time pressure is a skill that will help you ace your certification exam. That is why working on these skills early on in your learning journey is key.

Chapter review questions are designed to improve your test-taking skills progressively with each chapter you learn and review your understanding of key concepts in the chapter at the same time. You'll find these at the end of each chapter.

210 Identify Features of Generative AI Solutions

> **Before You Proceed**
>
> If you don't have a Packt Library subscription or you haven't purchased this book from the Packt store, you will need to unlock the online resources to access the exam readiness drills. Unlocking is free and needs to be done only once. To learn how to do that, head over to the chapter titled *Chapter 12, Accessing the Online Resources*.

To open the Chapter Review Questions for this chapter, perform the following steps:

1. Click the link – `https://packt.link/AI-900_CH10`.

   Alternatively, you can scan the following QR code (*Figure 10.8*):

   Figure 10.8 – QR code that opens Chapter Review Questions for logged-in users

2. Once you log in, you'll see a page similar to the one shown in *Figure 10.9*:

   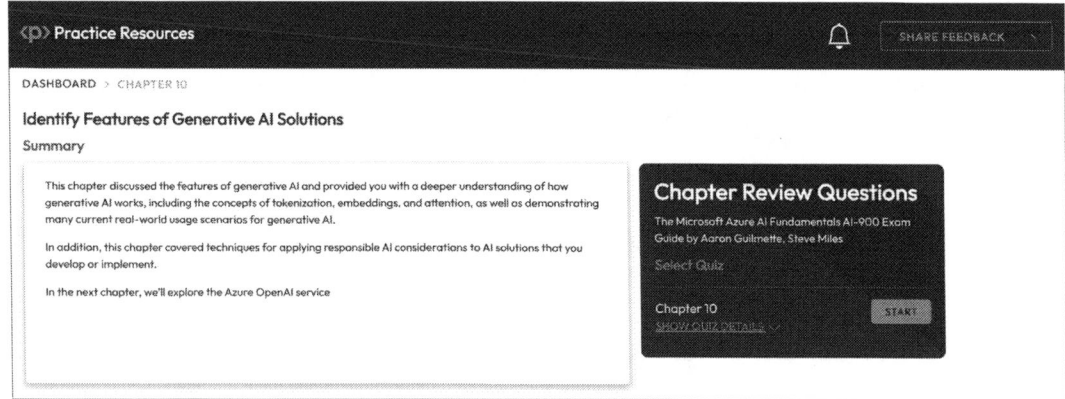

   Figure 10.9 – Chapter Review Questions for Chapter 10

3. Once ready, start the following practice drills, re-attempting the quiz multiple times.

Exam Readiness Drill

For the first three attempts, don't worry about the time limit.

ATTEMPT 1

The first time, aim for at least **40%**. Look at the answers you got wrong and read the relevant sections in the chapter again to fix your learning gaps.

ATTEMPT 2

The second time, aim for at least **60%**. Look at the answers you got wrong and read the relevant sections in the chapter again to fix any remaining learning gaps.

ATTEMPT 3

The third time, aim for at least **75%**. Once you score 75% or more, you start working on your timing.

> **Tip**
> You may take more than **three** attempts to reach 75%. That's okay. Just review the relevant sections in the chapter till you get there.

Working On Timing

Your aim is to keep the score the same while trying to answer these questions as quickly as possible. Here's an example of how your next attempts should look like:

Attempt	Score	Time Taken
Attempt 5	77%	21 mins 30 seconds
Attempt 6	78%	18 mins 34 seconds
Attempt 7	76%	14 mins 44 seconds

Table 10.2 – Sample timing practice drills on the online platform

> **Note**
> The time limits shown in the above table are just examples. Set your own time limits with each attempt based on the time limit of the quiz on the website.

With each new attempt, your score should stay above **75%** while your "time taken" to complete should "decrease". Repeat as many attempts as you want till you feel confident dealing with the time pressure.

11

Identify Capabilities of Azure OpenAI Service

In this final chapter, we're going to look at the capabilities of Azure OpenAI Service. If you'll recall, OpenAI is the company behind what are currently some of the most popular **generative artificial intelligence** (**GenAI**) products such as ChatGPT and DALL-E.

Azure OpenAI Service brings those same capabilities directly into Azure, letting you work seamlessly with your own data to generate new **completions** and images.

The objectives and skills we'll cover in this chapter include the following:

- What is Azure OpenAI Service?
- Describe **natural language generation** (**NLG**) capabilities of Azure OpenAI Service
- Describe code generation capabilities of Azure OpenAI Service
- Describe image generation capabilities of Azure OpenAI Service

By the end of this chapter, you should be able to easily describe the features and capabilities of the powerful new OpenAI services part of the Azure Cognitive Services family of tools.

What is Azure OpenAI Service?

Azure OpenAI Service is a cloud-based platform that integrates cutting-edge **artificial intelligence** (**AI**) models developed by OpenAI into the Azure ecosystem.

What's included?

At a high level, Azure OpenAI Service combines OpenAI's models with the Azure platform. There are four main components included:

- Pre-trained GenAI models
- Customization and fine-tuning
- Responsible AI frameworks and tooling to help mitigate harm
- Security including private networking and **role-based access control** (**RBAC**)

This service offers businesses and developers access to some of the most advanced AI models, such as the following:

- **GPT-4**: As the latest model of OpenAI's **Generative Pre-trained Transformer** (**GPT**) models, the GPT-4 model offers advanced **natural language understanding** (**NLU**) and NLG capabilities, enabling diverse applications such as content creation, conversation simulation, code completion, language translation, and complex problem-solving across various industries.

- **GPT-3.5**: This GPT model is a powerful language generation AI that excels in creating human-like text, answering questions, composing essays, coding, and more, making it highly applicable in fields such as customer service, content creation, education, and software development. In particular, the **GPT-3.5 Turbo** model is optimized for rapid **natural language processing** (**NLP**), perfect for chat-based interactions such as chatbots and interactive customer support scenarios.

- **Embeddings**: As you learned in *Chapter 10, Identify Features of Generative AI Solutions*, embedding is the process of mapping out the relationship of words (or tokens) to each other. Embedding models within Azure OpenAI Service enable nuanced text representations, improving semantic search, content discovery, and data clustering by capturing deep linguistic and contextual relationships, thereby enhancing AI applications with more accurate and relevant results.

- **Codex**: Codex models in Azure OpenAI Service are optimized for advanced programming assistance by understanding and generating human-like code, enabling automated code generation, explanation, and bug fixing, enhancing developer productivity and code quality.

- **DALL-E**: The DALL-E models in Azure OpenAI Service excel in generating creative, detailed images from textual descriptions, providing innovative solutions for visual content creation, design inspiration, and enhancing digital media applications with unique, customized visuals.

This breadth of models and services under one accessible platform enables the creation of sophisticated applications that can understand, interpret, generate, and translate **natural language** (**NL**), as well as generate images. Azure OpenAI Service aims to make these powerful AI capabilities more accessible and manageable, supporting a wide range of use cases from automated content generation to customer support enhancements.

One of the key features of Azure OpenAI Service is its comprehensive suite of NLP tools. This includes capabilities for text summarization, language translation, content generation, and semantic search. By leveraging these tools, developers can enhance applications with sophisticated language models that understand and produce human-like text, making them more interactive and intelligent. This has significant implications for improving user experiences, whether through creating more responsive chatbots, automating content creation, or providing more accurate search results within applications.

Azure OpenAI Service emphasizes security and compliance, integrating Azure's robust security measures to protect data and ensure privacy. The service operates within the secure Azure infrastructure, offering enterprise-grade security features including data encryption, private networking options, and compliance with global standards. Unlike models from other vendors, Microsoft does not use customer data for training models. This focus on security makes it a reliable choice for organizations concerned with protecting sensitive information while leveraging AI technologies.

In terms of customization and control, Azure OpenAI Service allows developers to fine-tune AI models to suit specific business needs. This includes the ability to train models on proprietary data, ensuring that generated content is relevant and aligned with the organization's objectives and tone. Furthermore, the service provides tools for monitoring and managing AI usage, helping to optimize performance and manage costs effectively.

> **Note**
> **Azure AI** is a new umbrella product family that brings together the legacy Azure Cognitive Services and Azure Applied AI Services under one name.

What's the difference between Azure AI and Azure OpenAI services?

Prior to Microsoft's relationship with OpenAI, Azure boasted a diverse portfolio of **machine learning** (**ML**)- and AI-based services. In this section, we'll identify both similarities and differences between the product families.

What's similar?

Given that both Azure AI and Azure OpenAI services feature advanced AI tooling, there are several areas of overlap:

- **Integration with Azure**: Both services are integrated into the Azure ecosystem, offering seamless connectivity with other Azure services such as Azure Storage, Azure Functions, and Azure Cognitive Services for comprehensive cloud-based solutions
- **AI capabilities**: Both provide AI capabilities, leveraging ML and advanced algorithms to support various AI tasks such as NLP, text analysis, and image generation

- **Scalability**: They are designed to be scalable, allowing users to scale their AI applications according to their needs and manage computational resources efficiently within the Azure environment
- **Security and compliance**: Both services adhere to Azure's security standards, offering tools and configurations to ensure data privacy, compliance, and secure AI operations within the cloud

Let's look at the differentiators to see which features might influence you to choose one over the other.

What's different?

With the similarities, it may be difficult to understand where to draw the line and which services to choose for a particular scenario:

- **Scope and focus**: Azure AI services encompass a broad range of AI tools and cognitive services, including vision, speech, language, decision, and web search functionalities, aimed at general AI tasks. In contrast, Azure OpenAI services specifically provide access to OpenAI's advanced models such as GPT-3, Codex, and DALL-E, focusing on state-of-the-art NL and image generation capabilities.
- **Model customization**: Azure AI services typically offer pre-built and customizable models tailored for specific tasks, such as text analytics or **computer vision** (**CV**), allowing for broader applicability across different domains. Azure OpenAI services, however, focus on providing access to large-scale generative models that can be fine-tuned and adapted for specialized tasks, particularly in language understanding and generation.
- **Use cases**: While Azure AI services cater to a wide range of standard AI scenarios, including speech recognition, language translation, and anomaly detection, Azure OpenAI services are more specialized, targeting use cases that require deep NLU, creative content generation, and advanced code automation.
- **Technology and innovation**: Azure OpenAI services represent the cutting edge of AI research and capabilities, especially in GenAI, offering some of the latest advancements in AI technology and models. In comparison, Azure AI services provide a more established suite of tools covering a wide spectrum of AI needs, with a focus on proven, widely applicable solutions.

While both Azure AI services and Azure OpenAI services are integral parts of Microsoft's AI offerings within the Azure cloud platform, they cater to different needs and scenarios, with Azure AI services providing a broad array of cognitive capabilities and Azure OpenAI services focusing on advanced GenAI models and applications.

Accessing Azure OpenAI services

Now that you've decided to use Azure OpenAI services, how do you access them?

The easiest way to begin using the Azure OpenAI services is through **Azure OpenAI Studio**, located at `https://oai.azure.com/portal`, as shown in *Figure 11.1*:

What is Azure OpenAI Service? 217

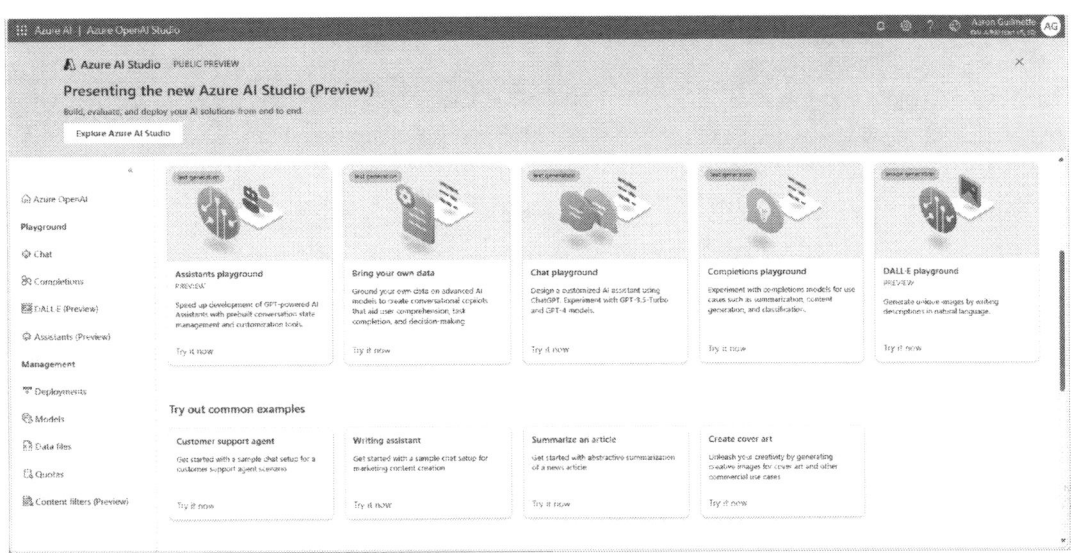

Figure 11.1 – Overview of launching Azure AI Studio

The landing page prominently displays a selection of models for deployment as well as some pre-built examples that you can deploy.

Let's explore some concepts and sections of the interface.

> **Note**
> Access to Azure OpenAI services is granted only through an application process and is not broadly available. You can apply to be allowed access to the resources by filling out a request form at `https://aka.ms/oai/access`. Applications can take up to 2 weeks to process.

Playground

In Azure OpenAI Studio, a playground is an area where you can experience the features of different models. The core playgrounds are the following:

- **Assistants**
- **Chat**
- **Completions**
- **DALL-E**

Each of these areas has a different goal, so let's begin exploring them!

Assistants

The Assistants playground (only available in East US 2, Australia East, and Sweden Central Azure regions), is designed to help you design and test AI assistants customized to your needs.

> **Note**
> Assistants, at this time, are a more **code-first** style deployment. The playground demonstrates the tooling's capability, but if you were to build and deploy one, you would need coding experience.

To configure an Assistants playground, follow these steps:

1. From the Azure AI Studio home page (`https://oai.azure.com/portal`), under **Playground**, select **Assistants**.

2. If this is the first time you've worked with Azure OpenAI Studio, you probably don't have a deployment created, so we'll take care of that now. If you already have a deployment, you can skip to *step 4*. On the **Assistants playground (Preview)** page, click **Create new deployment**:

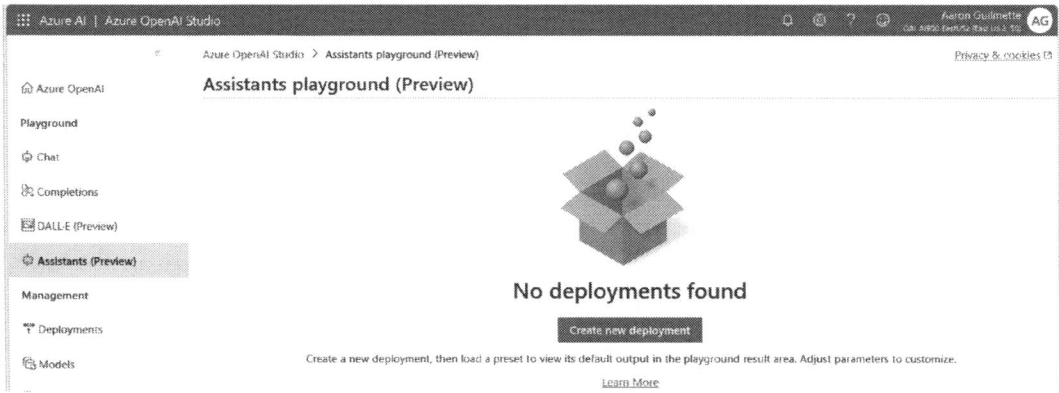

Figure 11.2 – Creating a new deployment

3. On the **Deploy model** page, select a supported model (such as **gpt-35-turbo**) and enter a deployment name. Click **Create**:

What is Azure OpenAI Service? 219

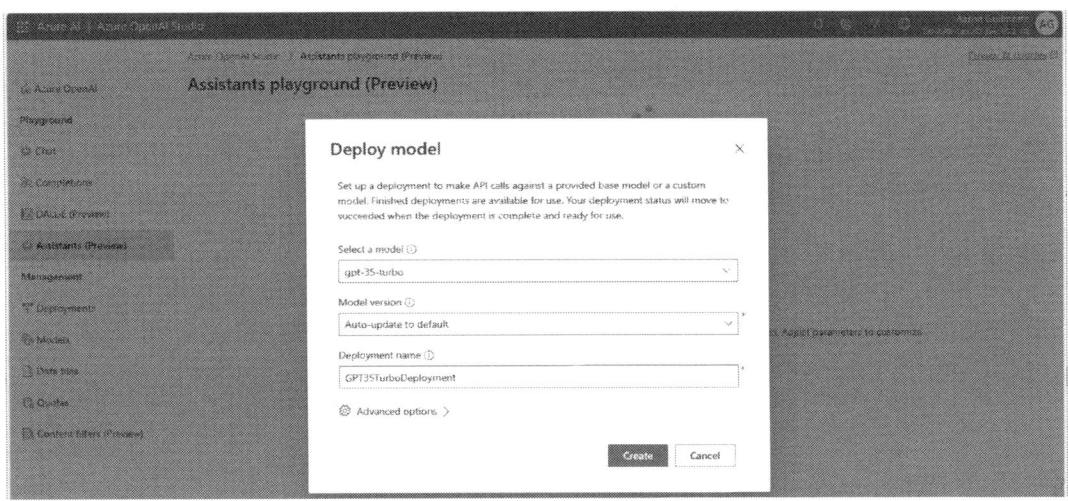

Figure 11.3 – Configuring the model deployment

4. Once the model has been deployed, you can configure the parameters of the assistant in the **Assistant setup** pane, shown in *Figure 11.4*:

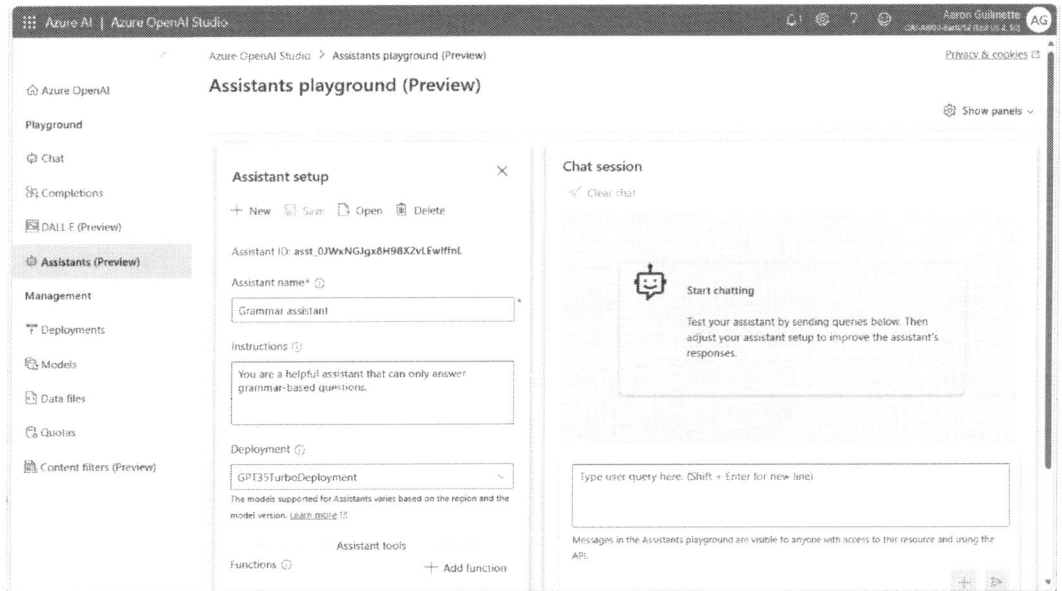

Figure 11.4 – Configuring the assistant's parameters

5. Once you've configured the parameters, click **Save** and then ask the assistant a question that fits the parameters you specified in the instructions:

220 Identify Capabilities of Azure OpenAI Service

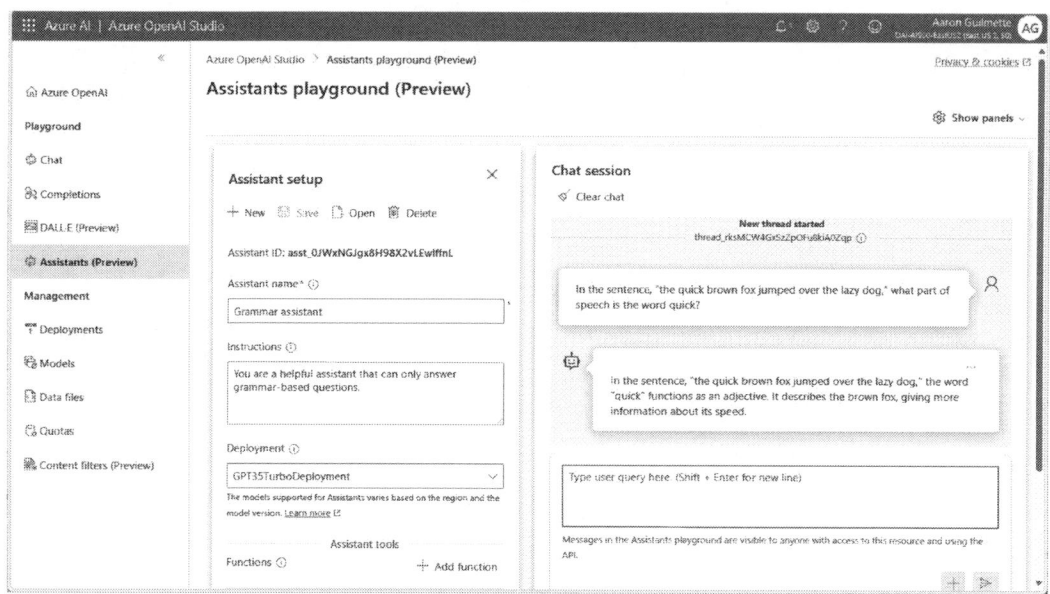

Figure 11.5 – Asking the assistant an in-scope question

6. Next, try asking the assistant a question that falls outside of its boundaries:

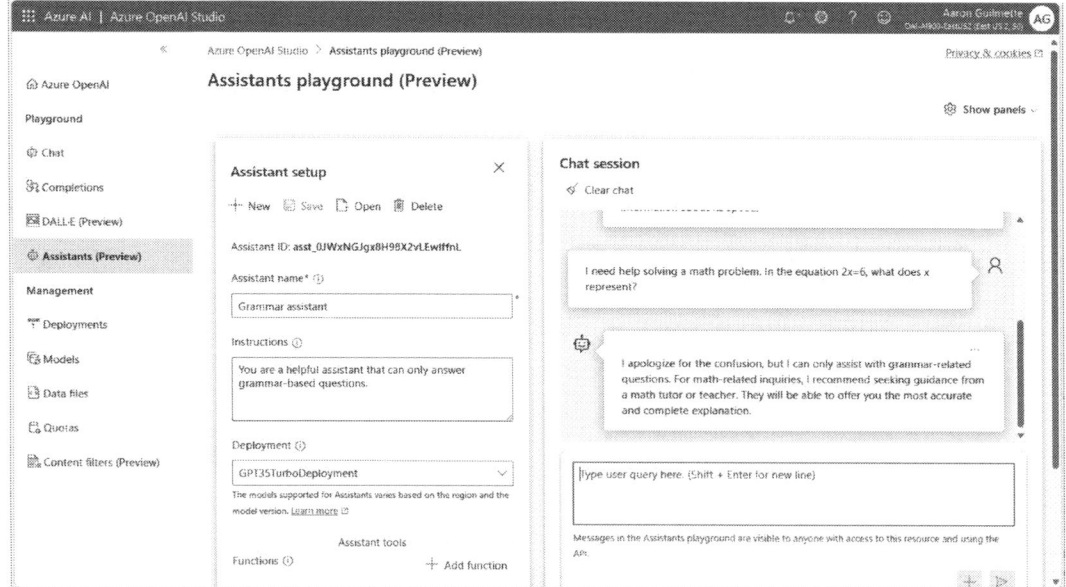

Figure 11.6 – Asking the assistant an out-of-scope question

As you can see, assistants can be useful when tasked with solving specific problems.

> **Further reading**
>
> The playground is essentially a demo environment that features a sample product—the assistant in the playground isn't intended to be released to end users. To do that, you would need to develop an assistant in Azure OpenAI Service. For more information on developing and deploying assistants, see `https://learn.microsoft.com/en-us/azure/ai-services/openai/how-to/assistant`. Coding and developing assistants aren't in scope for the *AI-900* exam, so don't worry if you aren't able to read or write complex Python code.

Chat

The Chat playground is designed to be an area where you can interact with a chatbot. One potential use might be a bot that answers questions from a website FAQ or other content database.

To work with the Chat playground, use the following process:

1. From the Azure AI Studio home page (`https://oai.azure.com/portal`), under **Playground**, select **Chat**.
2. Using the **Prompt** tab in the **Setup** pane, customize the system message (a type of **metaprompt** that gives the model background information or instructions on how to operate). You can select from one of several built-in sample configurations (such as **Marketing writing assistant**, **Shakespeare writing assistant**, or **IRS tax chatbot**, as well as others) See *Figure 11.7*:

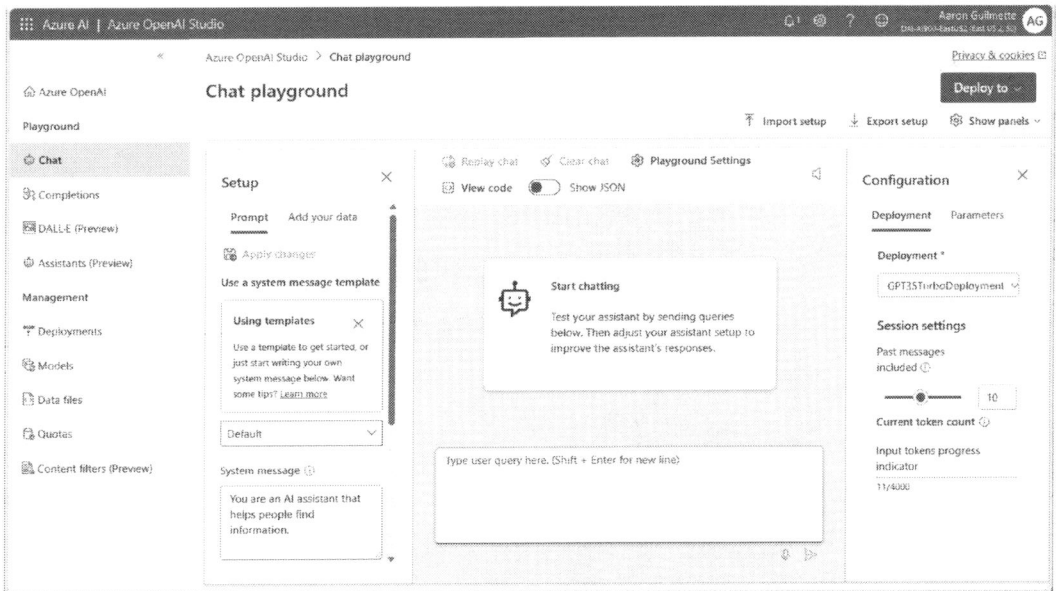

Figure 11.7 – Configuring options in the Chat playground

3. After you have configured the parameters for the chatbot agent, you can begin entering text in the chat window:

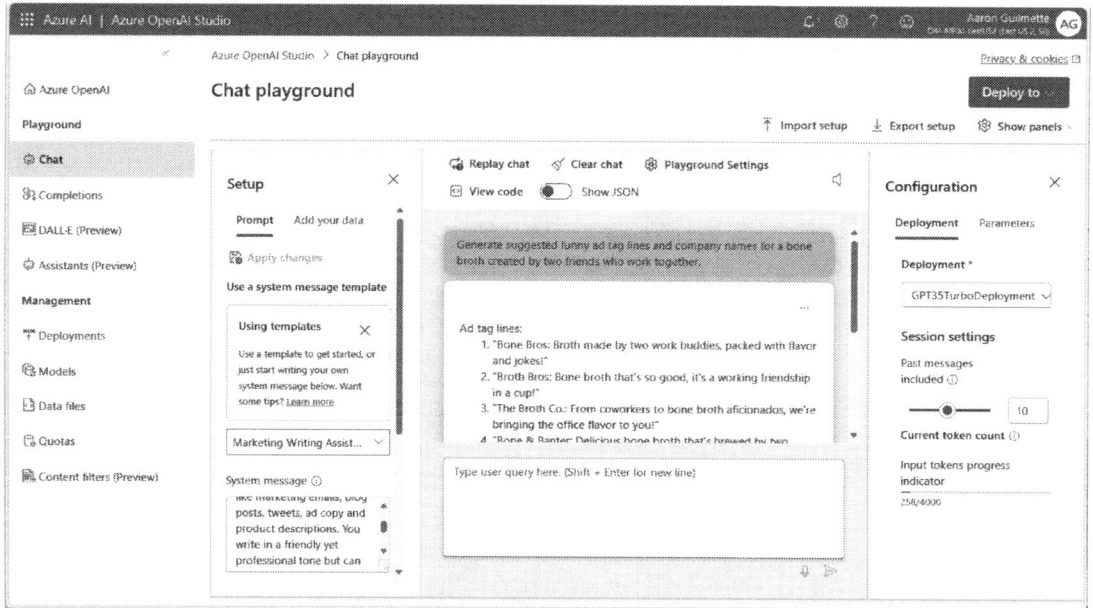

Figure 11.8 – Testing the Chat playground

Unlike the Assistants playground, the Chat playground allows you to import and export the setup, as well as deploy configurations directly to a web service, shown in *Figure 11.9*):

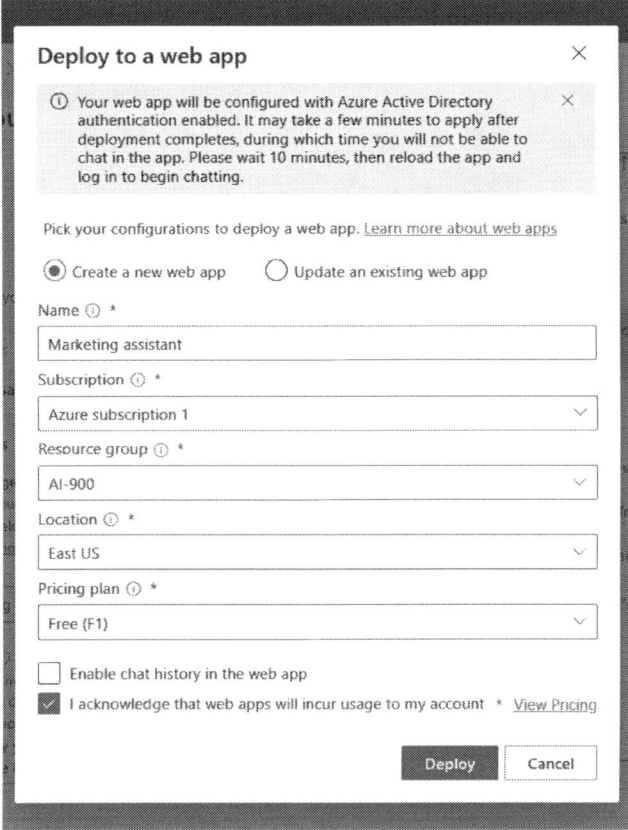

Figure 11.9 – Deploying a chat playground to a web service

Completions

The Completions playground is probably most like the capabilities you might see in a commercial product such as ChatGPT. You can get an idea of some of the capabilities of Completions by selecting **Completions** from the **Playground** list in Azure OpenAI Studio (`https://oai.azure.com/portals`).

No further configuration is necessary. You can select example prompts from the **Examples** dropdown, as shown in *Figusre 11.10*:

224 Identify Capabilities of Azure OpenAI Service

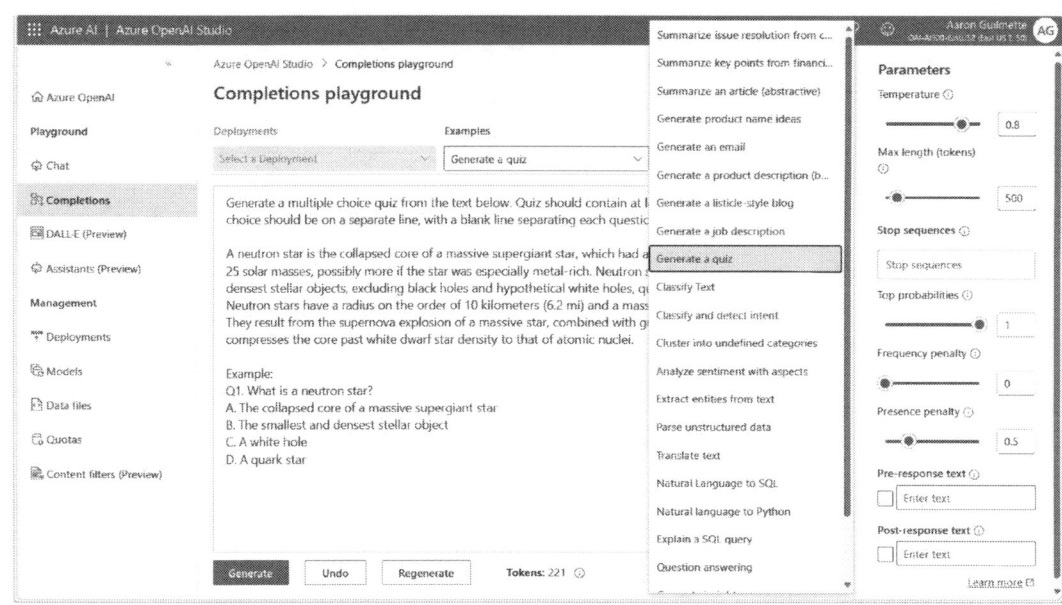

Figure 11.10 – Working with the Completions playground

By clicking the **View code** option, you get a pre-built template for deploying your Completions prompt and settings into an application:

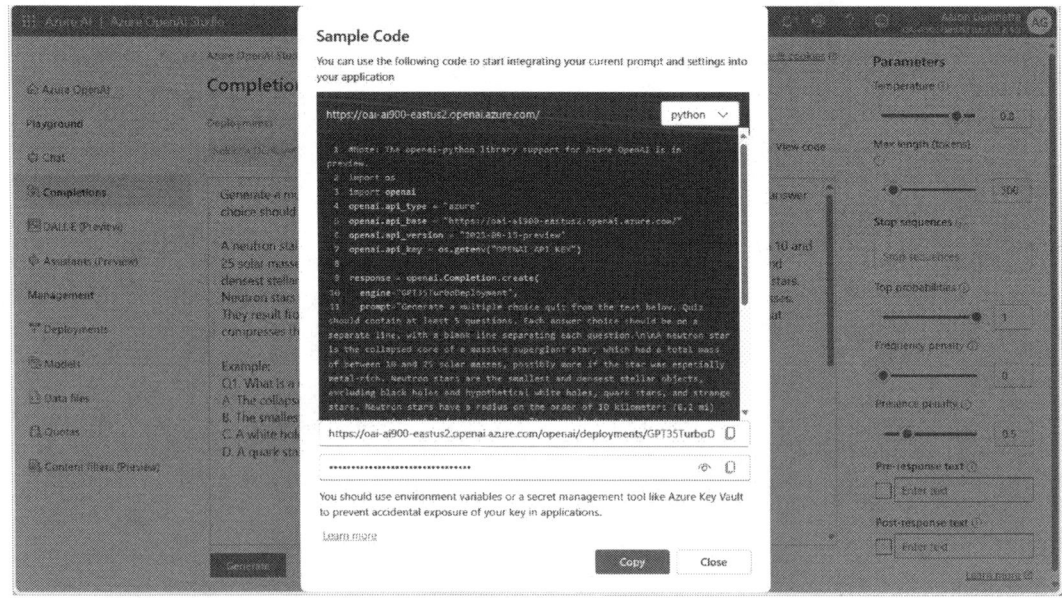

Figure 11.11 – Viewing the Completions deployment code

Code samples are available for Python, C#, JSON, and curl.

DALL-E

The DALL-E playground (only available in East US 2, Australia East, and Sweden Central Azure regions), is designed to help you design and test AI assistants customized to your needs.

The DALL-E playground also requires no configuration, though there are parameters that can be exposed through the **DALL-E settings** option:

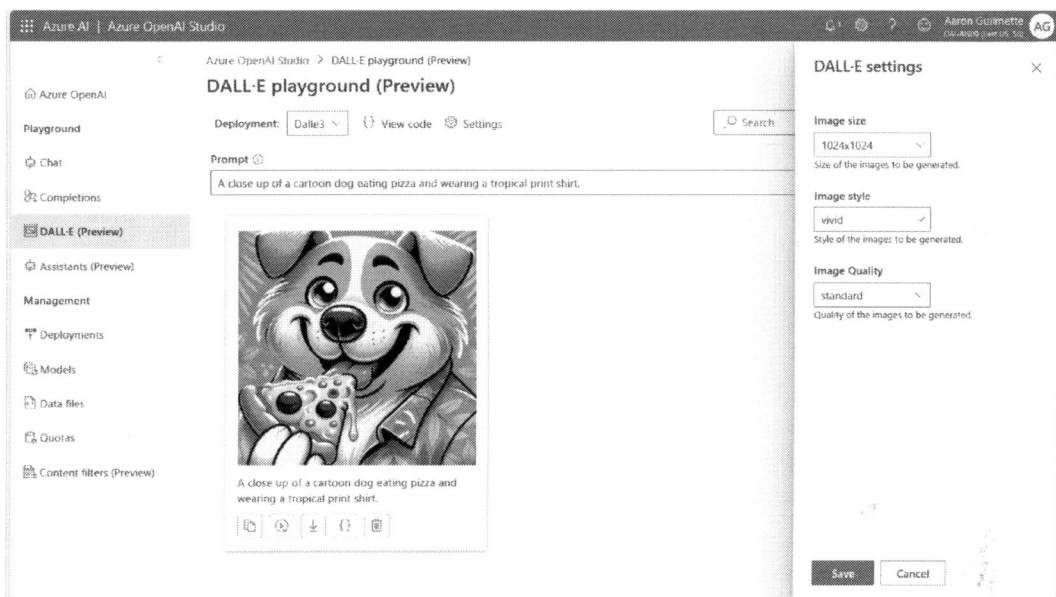

Figure 11.12 – Generating an image through the DALL-E playground

As with the **Completions** playground, integration code is available through the **View code** option on the Playground page.

Next, we'll look at the Management features of Azure OpenAI Studio.

Management

Under the **Management** section, there are five nodes:

- **Deployments**
- **Models**
- **Data files**

- **Quotas**
- **Content filters**

We'll briefly look at features in each of those areas.

Deployments

A **deployment** refers to a particular model in combination with configuration settings. On the **Deployments** page, you can create, edit, and delete deployments:

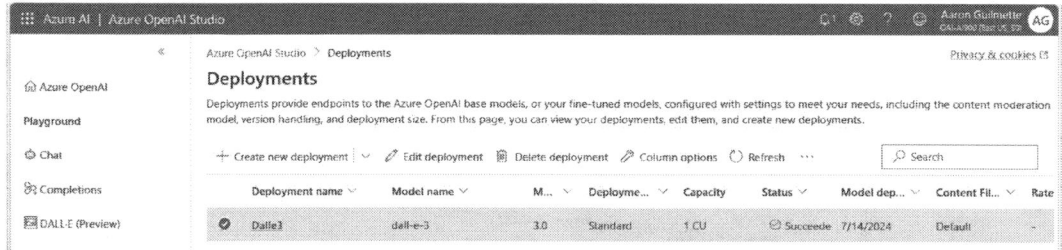

Figure 11.13 – Deployments page

Deployments enable the external consumption of the AI service or model.

Models

In the context of Azure OpenAI services, a **model** refers to a pre-trained AI algorithm, such as GPT-3, Codex, or DALL-E, which is designed to perform specific tasks such as NLP, text generation, code generation, or image creation:

What is Azure OpenAI Service? 227

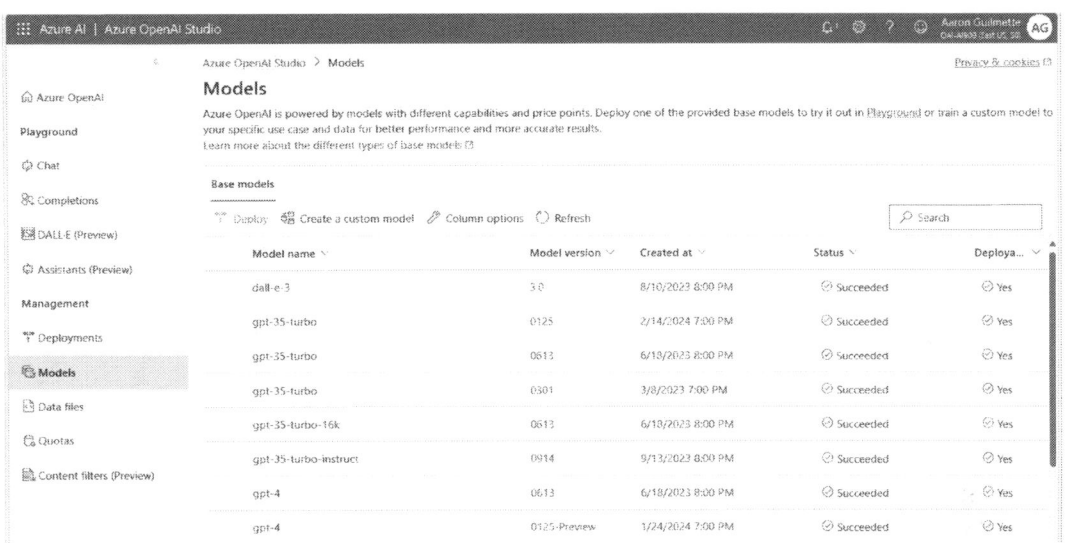

Figure 11.14 – Models page

On the **Models** page, you can deploy one of the existing models or create a new custom deployment for fine-tuning, based on an existing model.

> **Further reading**
>
> You can find a list of models available here: https://learn.microsoft.com/en-us/azure/ai-services/openai/concepts/models

Data files

On the **Data files** page, you can upload datasets used for training, validating, or otherwise customizing models.

Quotas

The **Quotas** page is used to view quotas for models as well as request an increase in quota. See *Figure 11.15*:

228 Identify Capabilities of Azure OpenAI Service

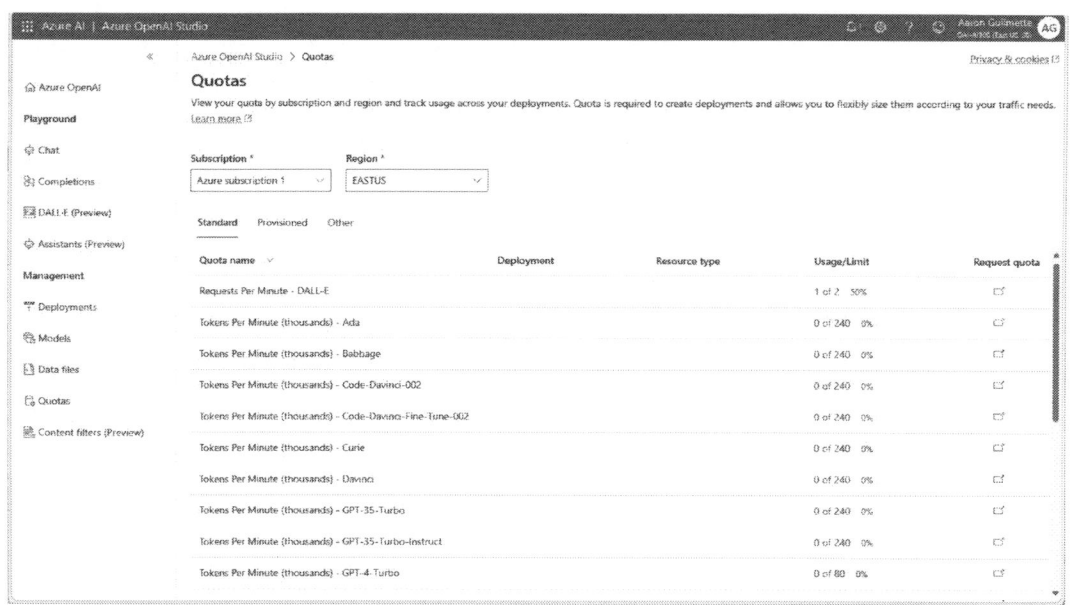

Figure 11.15 – Quotas page

Along with quota management, you should work to ensure you're making the best use of your Azure spend. AI services can add up quickly, so it's important to leverage the right type of model for the job. You can learn more about the Azure AI pricing model here: `https://azure.microsoft.com/en-us/pricing/details/cognitive-services/#pricing`.

Content filters

Content filtering provides the capability to detect and act upon potentially sensitive or harmful content in AI-based applications:

Describe natural language generation capabilities of Azure OpenAI Service

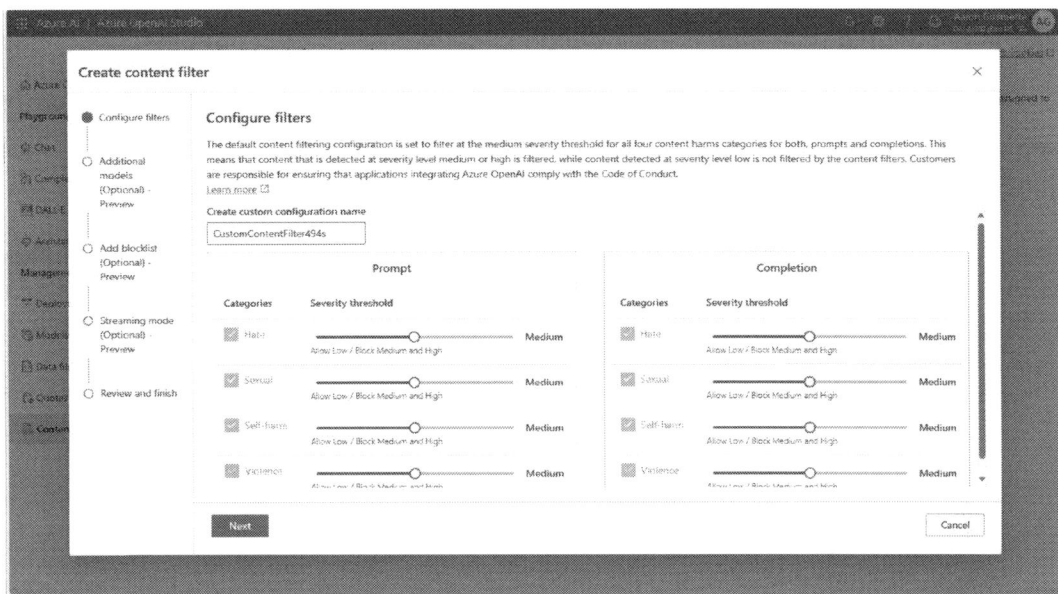

Figure 11.16 – Configuring content filters

Configurations for the **Hate**, **Sexual**, **Self-harm**, and **Violence** filter categories are available for both prompts and completions.

Next, we'll specifically dive into the NLG capabilities of Azure OpenAI Service.

Describe natural language generation capabilities of Azure OpenAI Service

OpenAI's NLP models employ sophisticated algorithms to understand and generate human-like text. As you learned in *Chapter 10*, *Identify Features of Generative AI Solutions*, these models are trained on vast datasets consisting of words or sequences of characters, referred to as tokens.

For instance, a complex word such as *juggernaut* might be segmented into smaller tokens such as *jug*, *ger*, and *naut* for more granular analysis, whereas a simpler and more common word such as *train* may be treated as a single token. Each token is then converted into a numerical vector, a process that transforms the textual information into a format that the ML model can efficiently process and learn from.

This vectorization of tokens allows the model to discern patterns, relationships, and contexts within the language, facilitating a deep understanding of linguistic structures. When interacting with user input, the model similarly decomposes the text into tokens, applying its learned patterns to interpret the input or generate responses. This tokenization process is a critical step in enabling the model to handle a wide array of NL tasks, from text completion and translation to content generation and sentiment analysis, making it a cornerstone of OpenAI's approach to NLU and NLG.

If you've tried using OpenAI's ChatGPT (`https://chat.openai.com`), you've interacted with a generative pre-trained model. Requests and other instructions or source content supplied to the model are referred to as **prompts**. You can use a prompt to just simply ask questions or you can be more complex, providing examples or other guidelines for formatting output.

GPT models are pretty easy to work with and can respond to NL requests. You can refer to *Table 11.1* for some common tasks and potential GPT prompts:

Task	Potential prompts
Summarize text	Summarize the following content into a single paragraph
Suggest content	Give me a list of fun names for a new ice cream stand
Translation	Translate "Where can I get a taco" into German
Answer a question	What are the ingredients in a margarita?
Text classification	What is this book's genre based on this text sample?
Concept explanation	Explain string theory in language a 12-year-old would understand

Table 11.1 – Tasks and prompts

Interacting through a prompt may look something like this:

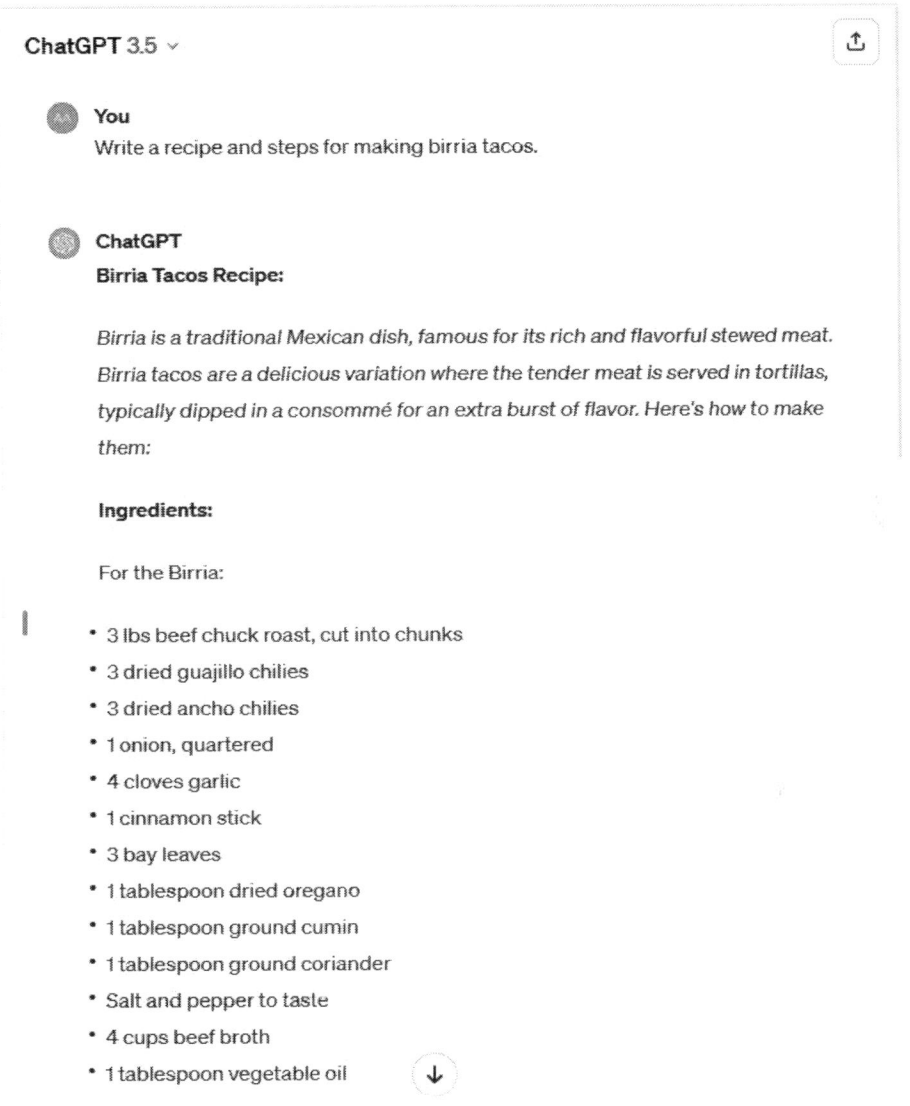

Figure 11.17 – Interacting with a GenAI such as ChatGPT

It's important to note, though, that GenAI is not authoritative, so always check to make sure your responses line up with what you're expecting or can be verified by other sources. (And, if you're interested in making birria tacos, you can explore this particular chat: https://chat.openai.com/share/1086e9bc-0dd0-4e73-a42f-af616e6ed687).

Depending on your use case, you may find value in prompt frameworks or patterns that provide the model with appropriate background information and output constraints.

> **Further reading**
>
> For some prompt framework examples, see `https://www.undocumented-features.com/2023/12/15/chatgpt-patterns-practices-and-prompts/`.

Describe code generation capabilities of Azure OpenAI Service

GPT models possess the capability to interpret NL or code excerpts and convert them into executable code. OpenAI's GPT models exhibit proficiency across a wide array of languages, including C#, JavaScript, Perl, PHP, PowerShell, Ruby, Swift, TypeScript, SQL, and Go—though Python is its strongest suit.

These models undergo training on both NL and vast repositories containing billions of lines of code. They excel in generating code based on NL instructions, including code comments, and can provide suggestions for completing code functions.

Codex, a descendent of GPT-3, has been trained on a variety of code samples and repositories in different languages and can answer code completion or review tasks.

In this example, a GPT has been asked to generate a code example that adds up all of the numbers between 1 and 100:

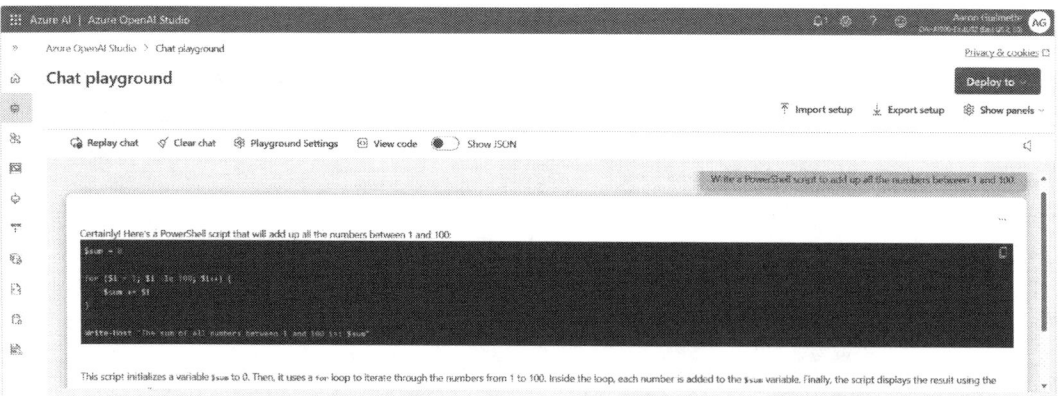

Figure 11.18 – Instructing GPT to generate a code example

As with any GenAI task, you should check its work:

Describe code generation capabilities of Azure OpenAI Service

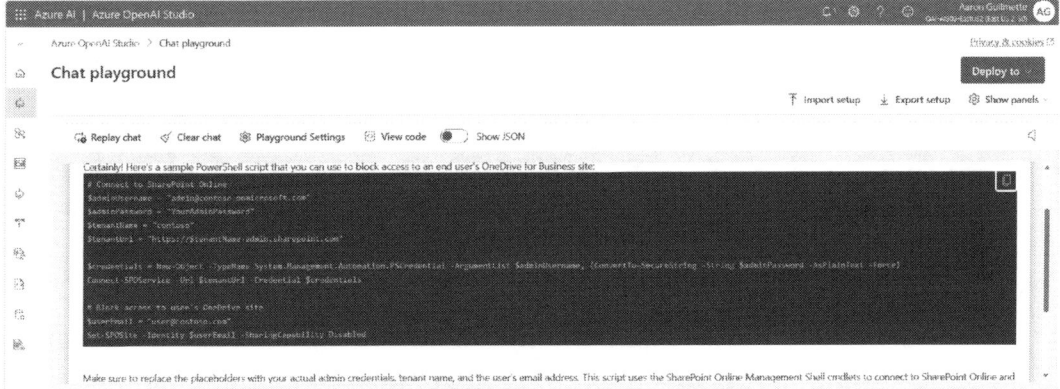

Figure 11.19 – Validating generated code

While this example works out OK, you still may want to experiment or test a bit to make sure that the output is indeed what you expect. In this simple example, you may choose to put a simple `Write-Host $sum` statement inside a `for` loop, allowing you to visually inspect the output.

It's equally important to note that there are other times when it doesn't, such as this example:

Figure 11.20 – Not a correct answer, GPT

When expanding the code for the operation, it may not be immediately discernible unless you have experience in the particular domain you're working in:

```
# Connect to SharePoint Online
$adminUsername = "admin@contoso.onmicrosoft.com"
$adminPassword = "YourAdminPassword"
$tenantName = "contoso"
$tenantUrl = "https://$tenantName-admin.sharepoint.com"

$credentials = New-Object -TypeName System.Management.Automation.
```

```
PSCredential -ArgumentList $adminUsername, (ConvertTo-SecureString 
-String $adminPassword -AsPlainText -Force)
Connect-SPOService -Url $tenantUrl -Credential $credentials

# Block access to user's OneDrive site
$userEmail = "user@contoso.com"
Set-SPOSite -Identity $userEmail -SharingCapability Disabled
```

While `Set-SPOUser` is the correct cmdlet to use, managing the sharing capability is not the correct option.

When pressed further, GPT responds with additional detail:

Figure 11.21 – Asking GPT to explain itself

Based on the specific feedback prompt of `What about the LockState parameter`, GPT responds with an updated script using a more appropriate command. This underscores the importance of understanding the limits of GenAI and ensuring that work is validated so that you can act accordingly and choose the most appropriate course of action.

The OpenAI models are also capable of interpreting code. You can ask a GPT for the purpose of a code snippet, statement, or function, as shown in *Figure 11.22*:

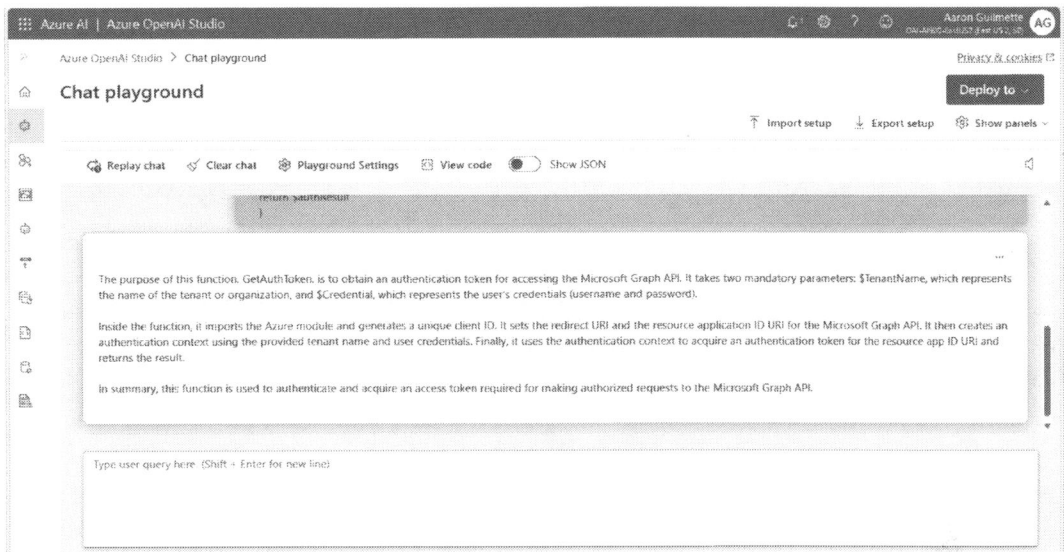

Figure 11.22 – Asking GPT for a code evaluation

OpenAI also partnered with GitHub to build a copilot that can be integrated into Visual Studio to help with code completions and suggestions.

Adding GitHub Copilot is as simple as adding any other extension to Visual Studio Code. Once enabled, GitHub CoPilot will start suggesting code automatically based on the selected language and context of the text that you have entered already:

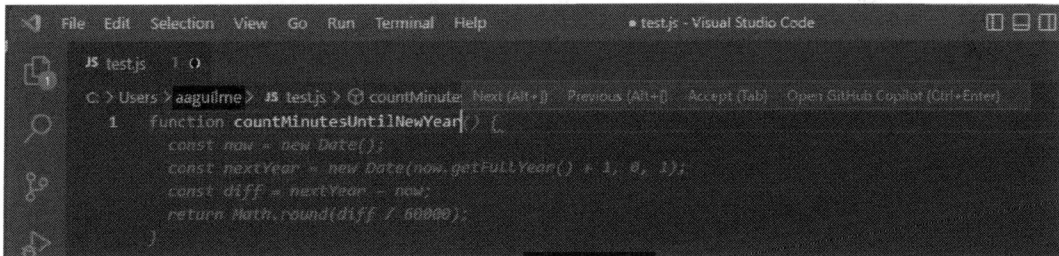

Figure 11.23 – GitHub Copilot suggesting code

> **Note**
> GitHub Copilot requires a subscription.

You can also try prompts such as `improve my code`, `explain this code`, or `translate this code from C# to java`.

Next, we'll look at some image generation capabilities of the platform.

Describe image generation capabilities of Azure OpenAI Service

In the Azure OpenAI Service realm, image generation capabilities can take several forms, such as prompts to create a new image or a customization of a base image.

DALL-E is the model family that generates images based on text prompts. The more detailed the prompt, the better the results. You can even request images in specific styles, such as *a dog in the style of Salvador Dali*, *a pastoral scene that includes pizza in the style of Claude Monet*, or *a steampunk farm tractor*:

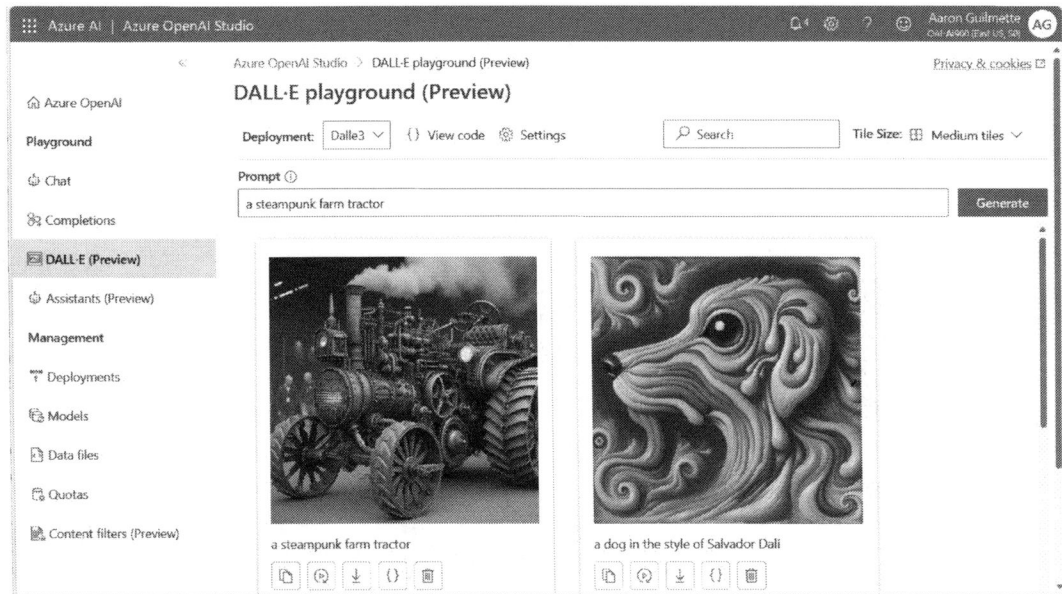

Figure 11.24 – Viewing DALL-E generated images in the playground

Depending on the application code surrounding the model deployment, you can also submit edits such as *add a person sitting in the tractor seat* or *update the dog so that it's wearing a hat*. The current models don't allow for editing or modifying the produced images; rather, you're generating new images with the updated prompt parameters.

Summary

Azure OpenAI Service brings the capability of OpenAI's models into Azure, allowing you to work with your own data to build custom applications. In this chapter, we covered some of the similarities and differences between Azure AI and Azure OpenAI services.

One of the most exciting features of Azure OpenAI Studio is the ability to explore the models through playgrounds—virtual areas where you can try out models and prompts.

Azure OpenAI Service is a powerful tool to help organizations expand their automation and ML capabilities.

Exam Readiness Drill – Chapter Review Questions

Apart from a solid understanding of key concepts, being able to think quickly under time pressure is a skill that will help you ace your certification exam. That is why working on these skills early on in your learning journey is key.

Chapter review questions are designed to improve your test-taking skills progressively with each chapter you learn and review your understanding of key concepts in the chapter at the same time. You'll find these at the end of each chapter.

> **Before You Proceed**
>
> If you don't have a Packt Library subscription or you haven't purchased this book from the Packt store, you will need to unlock the online resources to access the exam readiness drills. Unlocking is free and needs to be done only once. To learn how to do that, head over to the chapter titled *Chapter 12, Accessing the Online Resources*.

To open the Chapter Review Questions for this chapter, perform the following steps:

1. Click the link – `https://packt.link/AI-900_CH11`.

    Alternatively, you can scan the following QR code (*Figure 11.25*):

    Figure 11.25 – QR code that opens Chapter Review Questions for logged-in users

2. Once you log in, you'll see a page similar to the one shown in *Figure 11.26*:

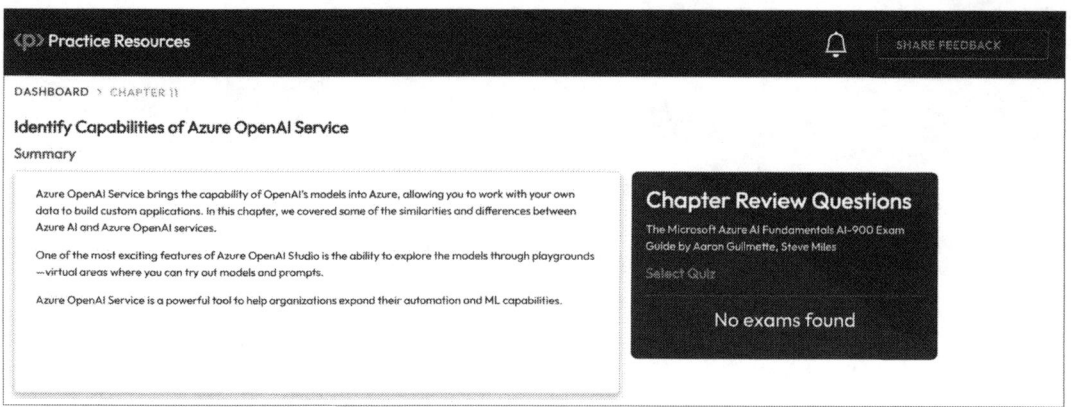

Figure 11.26 – Chapter Review Questions for Chapter 11

3. Once ready, start the following practice drills, re-attempting the quiz multiple times.

Exam Readiness Drill

For the first three attempts, don't worry about the time limit.

ATTEMPT 1

The first time, aim for at least **40%**. Look at the answers you got wrong and read the relevant sections in the chapter again to fix your learning gaps.

ATTEMPT 2

The second time, aim for at least **60%**. Look at the answers you got wrong and read the relevant sections in the chapter again to fix any remaining learning gaps.

ATTEMPT 3

The third time, aim for at least **75%**. Once you score 75% or more, you start working on your timing.

> **Tip**
> You may take more than **three** attempts to reach 75%. That's okay. Just review the relevant sections in the chapter till you get there.

Working On Timing

Your aim is to keep the score the same while trying to answer these questions as quickly as possible. Here's an example of how your next attempts should look like:

Attempt	Score	Time Taken
Attempt 5	77%	21 mins 30 seconds
Attempt 6	78%	18 mins 34 seconds
Attempt 7	76%	14 mins 44 seconds

Table 11.2 – Sample timing practice drills on the online platform

> **Note**
> The time limits shown in the above table are just examples. Set your own time limits with each attempt based on the time limit of the quiz on the website.

With each new attempt, your score should stay above **75%** while your "time taken" to complete should "decrease". Repeat as many attempts as you want till you feel confident dealing with the time pressure.

12
Accessing the Online Practice Resources

Your copy of *Microsoft Azure AI Fundamentals AI-900 Exam Guide* comes with free online practice resources. Use these to hone your exam readiness even further by attempting practice questions on the companion website. The website is user-friendly and can be accessed from mobile, desktop, and tablet devices. It also includes interactive timers for an exam-like experience.

How to Access These Resources

Here's how you can start accessing these resources depending on your source of purchase.

Purchased from Packt Store (packtpub.com)

If you've bought the book from the Packt store (`packtpub.com`) eBook or Print, head to `https://packt.link/AI-900_examguide`. There, log in using the same Packt account you created or used to purchase the book.

Packt+ Subscription

If you're a Packt+ subscriber, you can head over to the same link (`https://packt.link/AI-900_examguide`), log in with your Packt ID, and start using the resources. You will have access to them as long as your subscription is active. If you face any issues accessing your free resources, contact us at `customercare@packt.com`.

Purchased from Amazon and Other Sources

If you've purchased from sources other than the ones mentioned above (like *Amazon*), you'll need to unlock the resources first by entering your unique sign-up code provided in this section. **Unlocking takes less than 10 minutes, can be done from any device, and needs to be done only once**. Follow these five easy steps to complete the process:

STEP 1

Open the link `https://packt.link/AI-900_examguideunlock` OR scan the following **QR code** (*Figure 12.1*):

Figure 12.1 – QR code for the page that lets you unlock this book's free online content.

Either of those links will lead to the following page as shown in *Figure 12.2*:

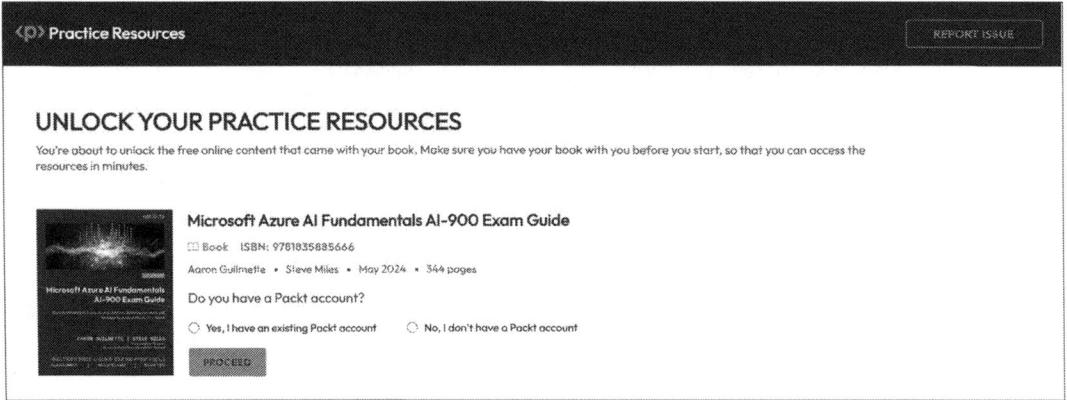

Figure 12.2 – Unlock page for the online practice resources

STEP 2

If you already have a Packt account, select the option Yes, I have an existing Packt account. If not, select the option No, I don't have a Packt account.

If you don't have a Packt account, you'll be prompted to create a new account on the next page. It's free and only takes a minute to create.

Click `Proceed` after selecting one of those options.

STEP 3

After you've created your account or logged in to an existing one, you'll be directed to the following page as shown in *Figure 12.3*.

Make a note of your unique unlock code:

```
JUM3856
```

Type in or copy this code into the text box labeled '**Enter Unique Code**':

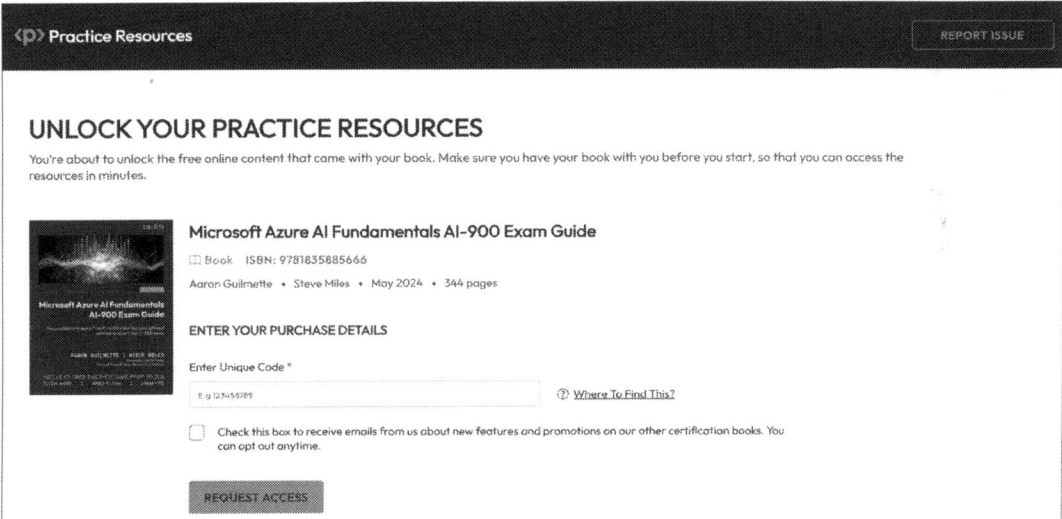

Figure 12.3 – Enter your unique sign-up code to unlock the resources

> **Troubleshooting Tip**
>
> After creating an account, if your connection drops off or you accidentally close the page, you can reopen the page shown in *Figure 12.2* and select `Yes, I have an existing account`. Then, sign in with the account you had created before you closed the page. You'll be redirected to the screen shown in *Figure 12.3*.

STEP 4

> **Note**
>
> You may choose to opt into emails regarding feature updates and offers on our other certification books. We don't spam, and it's easy to opt out at any time.

Click `Request Access`.

STEP 5

If the code you entered is correct, you'll see a button that says, OPEN PRACTICE RESOURCES, as shown in *Figure 12.4*:

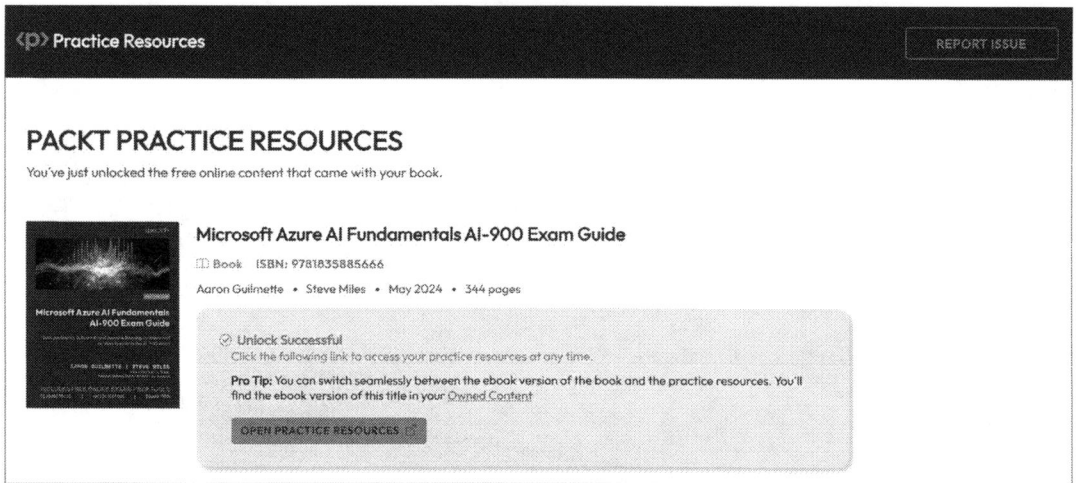

Figure 12.4 – Page that shows up after a successful unlock

Click the OPEN PRACTICE RESOURCES link to start using your free online content. You'll be redirected to the Dashboard shown in *Figure 12.5*:

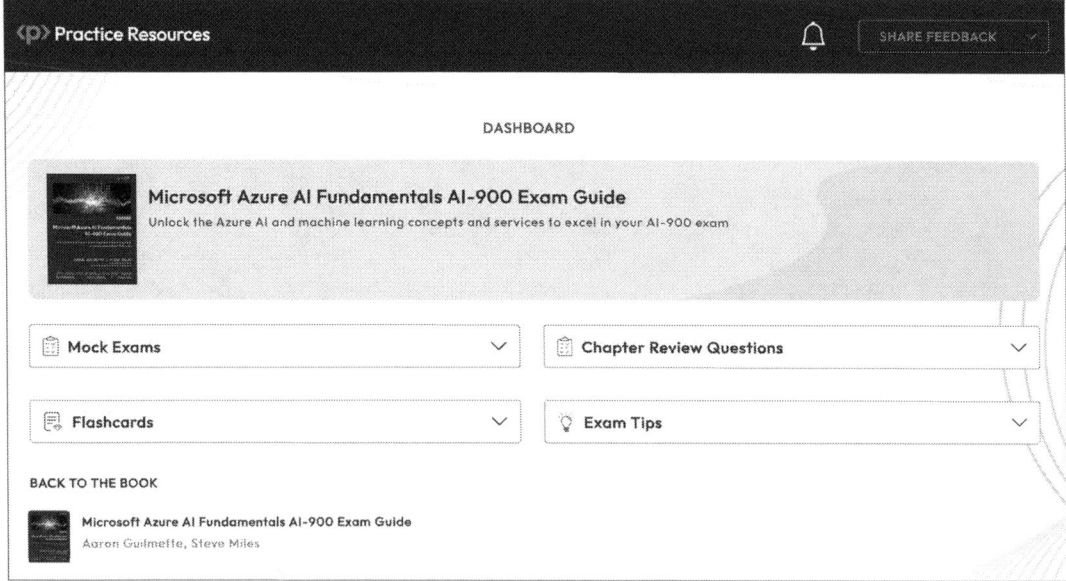

Figure 12.5 – Dashboard page for AI-900 practice resources

> **Bookmark This Link**
>
> Now that you've unlocked the resources, you can come back to them anytime by visiting `https://packt.link/AI-900_eg_dashboard` or scanning the following QR code provided in *Figure 12.6*:

Figure 12.6 – QR code to bookmark practice resources website

Troubleshooting Tips

If you're facing issues unlocking, here are three things you can do:

- Double-check your unique code. All unique codes in our books are case-sensitive and your code needs to match exactly as it is shown in *STEP 3*.
- If that doesn't work, use the `Report Issue` button located at the top-right corner of the page.
- If you're not able to open the unlock page at all, write to `customercare@packt.com` and mention the name of the book.

Practice Resources – A Quick Tour

This book will equip you with all the knowledge necessary to clear the exam. As important as learning the key concepts is, your chances of passing the exam are much higher if you apply and practice what you learn in the book. This is where the online practice resources come in. With interactive mock exams, flashcards, and exam tips, you can practice everything you learned in the book on the go. Here's a quick walkthrough of what you get.

A Clean, Simple Cert Practice Experience

You get a clean, simple user interface that works on all modern devices, including your phone and tablet. All the features work on all devices, provided you have a working internet connection. From the `Dashboard` (*Figure 12.7*), you can access all the practice resources that come with this book with just a click. If you want to jump back to the book, you can do that from here as well:

246   Accessing the Online Practice Resources

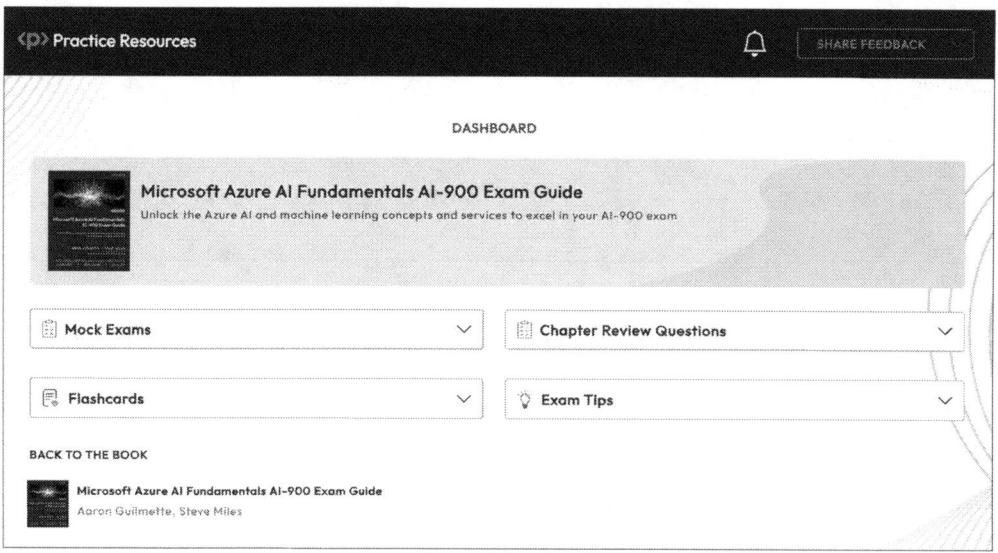

Figure 12.7 – Dashboard interface on a desktop device

Practice Questions

The **Quiz Interface** (*Figure 12.8*) is designed to help you focus on the question without any clutter.

You can navigate between multiple questions quickly and skip a question if you don't know the answer. The interface also includes a live timer that auto-submits your quiz if you run out of time.

Click End Quiz if you want to jump straight to the results page to reveal all the solutions.

Figure 12.8 – Practice Questions Interface on a desktop device

Be it a long train ride to work with just your phone or a lazy Sunday afternoon on the couch with your tablet, the quiz interface works just as well on all your devices as long as they're connected to the internet.

Figure 12.9 shows a screenshot of how the interface looks on mobile devices:

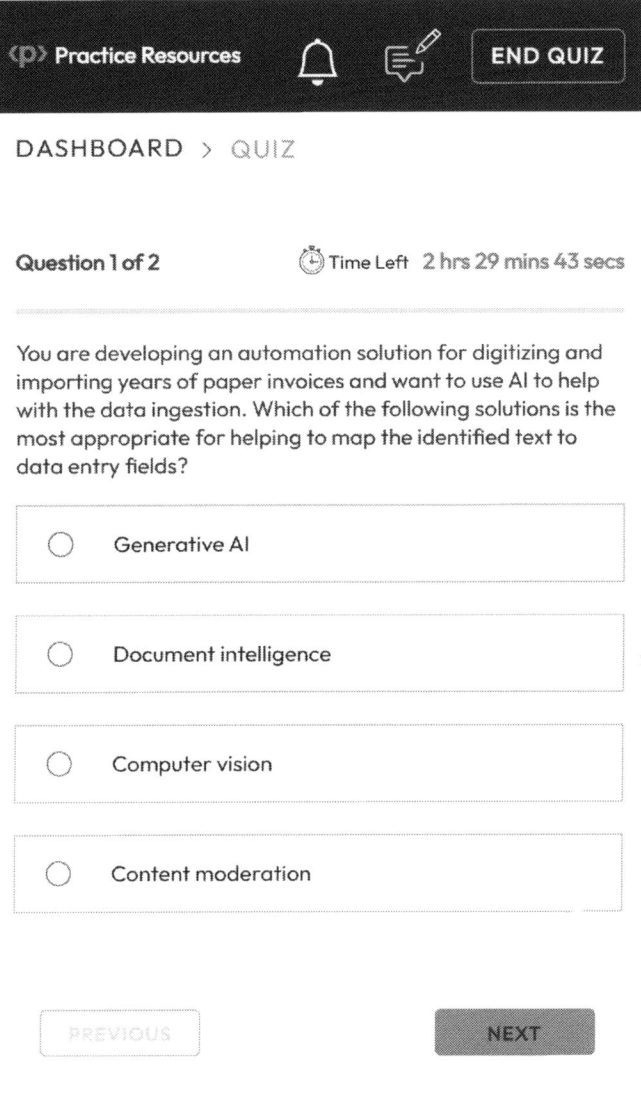

Figure 12.9 – Quiz interface on a mobile device

Flashcards

Flashcards are designed to help you memorize key concepts. Here's how to make the most of them:

- We've organized all the flashcards into stacks. Think of these like an actual stack of cards in your hand.
- You start with a full stack of cards.
- When you open a card, take a few minutes to recall the answer.
- Click anywhere on the card to reveal the answer (*Figure 12.10*).
- Flip the card back and forth multiple times and memorize the card completely.
- Once you feel you've memorized it, click the `Mark as memorized` button on the top-right corner of the card. Move on to the next card by clicking Next.
- Repeat this process as you move to other cards in the stack.

You may not be able to memorize all the cards in one go. That's why, when you open the stack the next time, you'll only see the cards you're yet to memorize.

Your goal is to get to an empty stack, having memorized each flashcards in that stack.

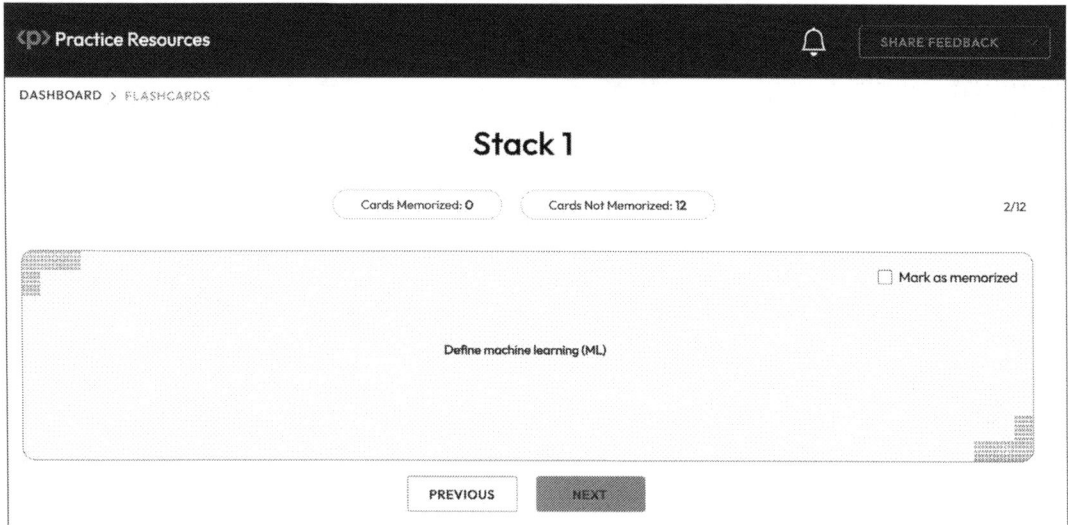

Figure 12.10 – Flashcards interface

Exam Tips

Exam Tips (see *Figure 12.11*) are designed to help you get exam-ready. From the start of your preparation journey to your exam day, these tips are organized such that you can review all of them in one go. If an exam tip comes in handy in your preparation, make sure to mark it as helpful so that other readers can benefit from your insights and experiences.

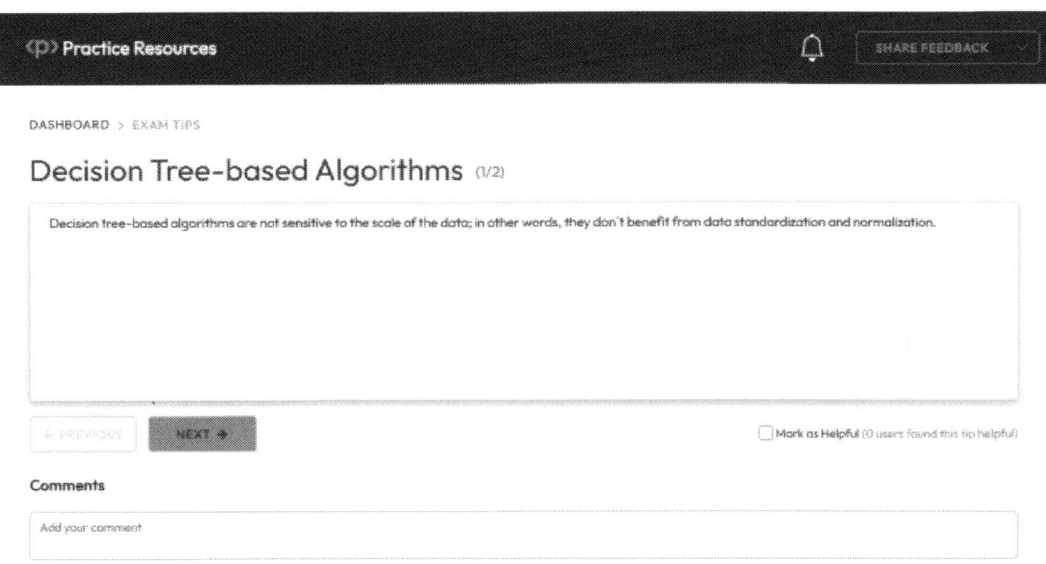

Figure 12.11 – Exam Tips Interface

Chapter Review Questions

You'll find a link to **Chapter Review Questions** at the end of each chapter, just after the *Summary* section. These are designed to help you consolidate your learning from a chapter before moving on to the next one. Each chapter will have a benchmark score. Aim to match that score or beat it before picking up the next chapter. On the *Chapter Review Questions* page, you'll find a summary of the chapter for quick reference, as shown in *Figure 12.12*:

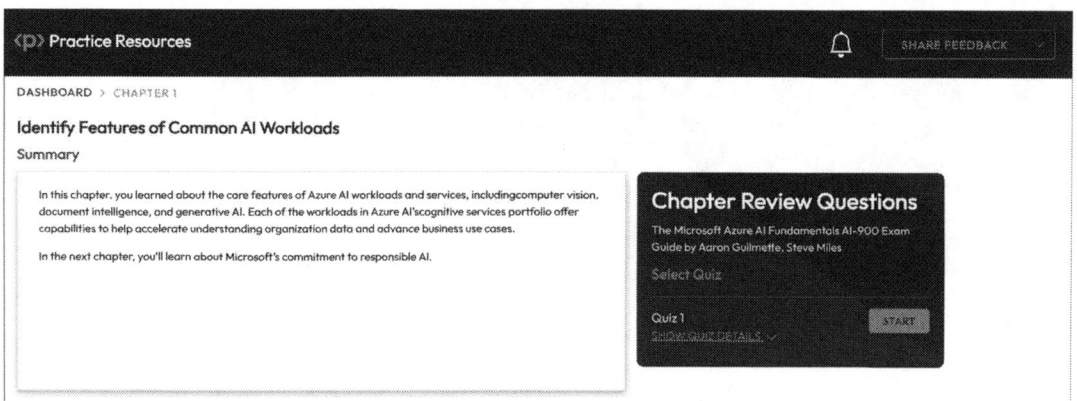

Figure 12.12 – Chapter Review Questions Page

Share Feedback

If you find any issues with the platform, the book, or any of the practice materials, you can click the `Share Feedback` button from any page and reach out to us. If you have any suggestions for improvement, you can share those as well.

Back to the Book

To make switching between the book and practice resources easy, we've added a link that takes you back to the book (*Figure 12.13*). Click it to open your book in Packt's online reader. Your reading position is synced so you can jump right back to where you left off when you last opened the book.

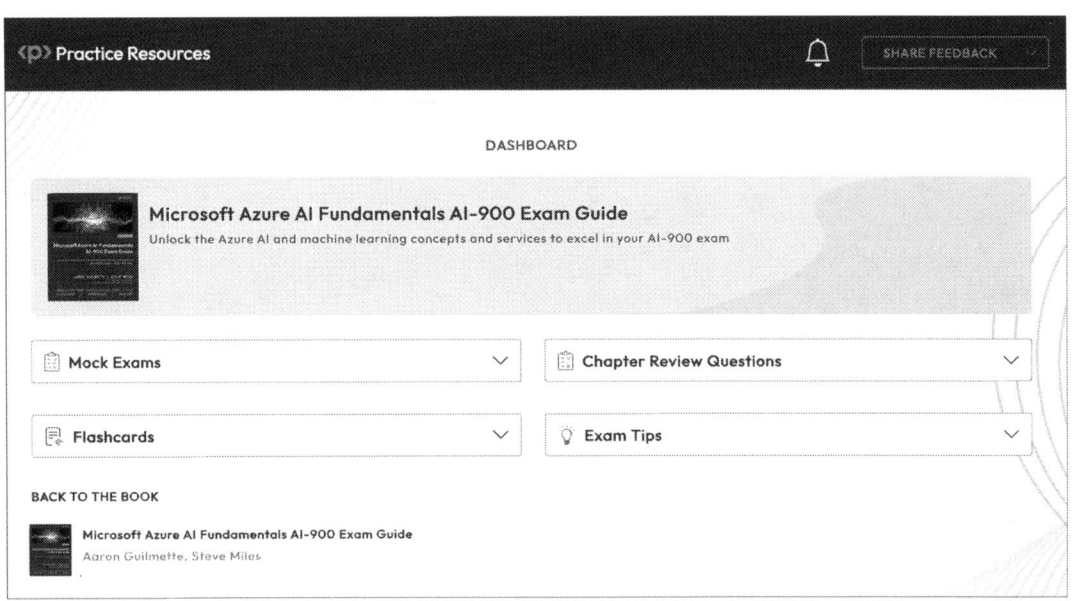

Figure 12.13 – Jump back to the book from the dashboard

> **Note**
> Certain elements of the website might change over time and thus may end up looking different from how they are represented in the screenshots of this book.

Index

A

absolute error 39
accuracy 46
AdaBoost 32
adaptation 93
AI knowledge mining 11
  features 11, 12
AI Personalizer 8
AI translation 171
algorithm 30
Anomaly Detector 5
Application Insights 89, 90
**application programming
    interfaces (APIs)** 5
artificial intelligence (AI) 3, 72, 158
Artificial Neural Networks (ANNs) 32
Assistants playground 218
  configuring 218-220
attached compute 85
attention mechanism 194, 195
attention score 195
attributes 136
automated machine learning (AutoML) 78
  capabilities 79, 80
  ensemble models 82
  feature engineering 82
  test scenarios 82
  training 82
  use cases 80
  used, for training model 96-104
  validation 82
AutoML use cases
  classification 80
  computer vision 81
  natural language processing (NLP) 81, 82
  regression 81
  time series forecasting 81
Azure AI 215
Azure AI, and Azure OpenAI services
  differentiators 216
  similarities 215, 216
Azure AI Bot Service 179
Azure AI Content Safety 7
Azure AI Document Intelligence 12, 13
Azure AI Face service 133, 143
  facial detection 145-148
  functionalities 143
  reference link 135
  responsible AI 149
Azure AI Generative AI 13, 14
Azure AI Language service 10, 176
  capabilities 176

conversational language understanding 177, 178
features 10, 11
question-answering 178
sub-services 10
text analysis 177
Azure AI Language Studio 179
URL 180
Azure AI pricing model
reference link 228
Azure AI Search 12
Azure AI Services 134, 176
Azure AI services Azure resource 144
Azure AI Speech service 181
speech-to-text 181
text-to-speech 181
Azure AI Speech Studio 181
URL 182
Azure AI Translator service 183
capabilities 183
Azure AI Video Indexer service 133
capabilities 150, 151
URL 151
use cases 149
Azure AI Vision 86-category taxonomy
reference link 138
Azure AI Vision service 9, 10, 133-136
categorization 137
Face 135
face recognition 9
image analysis 9, 137
Image Analysis 135
optical character recognition (OCR) 9, 135, 142
spatial analysis 9
Azure AI Vision Studio 133, 136-144
object detection 140

Azure Blob Storage container 87
Azure Container Instances (ACI) 91
Azure Container Registry 90
Azure Data Lake Storage (ADLS) 87
Azure Data Lake Storage Gen2 87
Azure Files Share 87
Azure Form Recognizer 12
Azure Key Vault 89
Azure Kubernetes Service (AKS) 85, 91
Azure Machine Learning (Azure ML) 77
ensemble models 83
features 78
machine learning model, building 94
model management and deployment capabilities 90
Azure Machine Learning Compute Instances 91
Azure Machine Learning Studio 78
Azure OpenAI Service 213, 214
code generation capabilities 232-235
image generation capabilities 236
natural language generation capabilities 229-231
offerings 214
Azure OpenAI Studio
Management section 225
playground 217
URL 216
Azure Personalizer
reference link 9
used, for making predictions on user behaviors 8
Azure Policy (AzPolicy) 92
reference link 92
Azure subscription 134

B

batch validation 5
Bidirectional Encoder Representations from Transformers (BERT) 82, 191
binary classification 31, 41
   applications 47
   evaluation metrics 45-47
   example 41-44

C

Calinski-Harabasz index 55-57
Carnegie Mellon University
   reference link 96
Caruana ensemble selection algorithm 83
   reference link 83
categorization 137
centroids 54
Chat playground 221
   working with 221, 222
classification 31, 80, 159
   binary classification 31, 41
   multiclass classification 31, 48
   scenarios, identifying 41
clustering 34
   applications 57
   evaluation metrics 55
   example 53, 54
   scenarios, identifying 52
code-first style deployment 218
code generation capabilities
   of Azure OpenAI Service 232-235
Codex models 214
coefficient of determination 40
command-line interface (CLI) v2 87
Completions playground 223-225
compute cluster 84

compute instance 84
computer vision (CV) 9, 81, 216
compute services 84
   attached compute 85
   compute cluster 84
   compute instance 84
   Kubernetes cluster 85
   serverless compute 84
confusion diagram 45
confusion matrix 45
content filtering 228
content moderation 6, 7
Content Moderator 7
Content Safety Studio 7
   features 8
   URL 8
continuous integration and delivery (CI/CD) 92
conversational AI 167
   considerations, for question-answering capabilities 168
   uses 167
conversational language understanding (CLU) 161, 167, 177, 178
Convolutional Neural Network (CNN) 59
convolving 115
copilots 202
corpus 159
CV solutions 114
   image processing 114, 115
   ML model 115-117

D

DALL-E models 214
DALL-E playground 225
data 85, 86
data dictionary 70

datastore 86, 87
data types, ML
  primitives 86
  tables (tabular data abstraction) 86
  Uniform Resource Identifiers(URIs) 85
Davies-Bouldin index 55, 56
decision trees 32
decoder block 191
deepfakes 202
deep learning 158
  applications 60
  example 59
  features, identifying 57-59
deep neural networks (DNNs) 57
Density-Based Spatial Clustering of Applications with Noise (DBSCAN) 52
deployment 226
differential privacy 23, 24
  reference link 24
digital asset management (DAM) 10
dimensionality reduction 32
discriminator 196
Docker containers 91
documents 117, 135
drift 93

E

edge devices 91
embeddings 193, 194, 214
encoder block 191
ensemble learning
  stacking method 83
  voting method 82
ensemble methods 83
ensemble models 82

entities 10, 167
entity recognition 164, 165
  uses 164
environments 87, 88
  curated 87
  custom 87
epoch 59
ethical principles 18
  considerations, for accountability 18
  considerations, for inclusiveness 19
  considerations, for reliability and safety 20
Euclidean 54
evaluation metrics, binary classification 45, 46
  accuracy 46
  precision 46
  recall 46
  specificity 47
evaluation metrics, clustering machine learning 55
  Davis-Bouldin index 56
  silhouette score 55
evaluation metrics, clustering machine learning
  Calinski-Harabasz index 56, 57
  Davis-Bouldin index 56
evaluation metrics, regression machine learning
  coefficient of determination 40
  mean absolute error (MAE) 39, 40
  mean squared error 40
  root mean squared error 40
Exchangeable Image File Format (EXIF) metadata 147
experiment 79

explainable principles 21
   considerations, for fairness 21, 22
   considerations, for privacy
      and security 23, 24
   considerations, for transparency 22, 23
exploratory data analysis (EDA) 66

F

Face Azure resource 144
facial analysis 128, 129
facial detection 126-128
   features, identifying 126
facial recognition 129, 130
Fairlearn
   URL 21
False Negatives (FN) 46
False Positives (FP) 46
feature engineering 82
feature identification, in dataset 66
   consulting, with experts 68
   data collection 66
   data exploration 66
   feature engineering 68
   feature selection techniques, using 69
   irrelevant or redundant
      features, removing 68
   missing values, handling 68
   problem domain 66
   relevant variables, selecting 67
features 30, 65
feature selection techniques
   backward elimination 69
   forward selection 69
   recursive feature elimination 69
featurization 82
featurizer 81
federated learning 23

G

**generative adversarial networks
   (GANs)** 13, 195, 196
Generative AI 13, 72, 189, 190
Generative AI models 190
   features 190, 191
Generative AI, scenarios 197
   code generation 200, 201
   copilots 202
   deepfake creation and detection 202, 203
   drug discovery and chemical synthesis 201
   image generation 197
   maintenance analysis 202
   music creation 199
   personalized content and
      recommendation systems 202
   quality control 203
   synthetic data generation 200
   text generation 198
   voice generation and transformation 201
**Generative Pretrained Transformer
   (GPT) model** 191, 214
generator 196
GPT-3.5 214
GPT-3.5 Turbo model 214
GPT-4 214
   URL 196
gradient boosting 32

H

Hamming 54
hierarchical clustering 52
homomorphic encryption 23
hyperparameters 41, 72

I

identity, Responsible AI and Generative AI solutions 204
  documentation and communication 205
  potential harms or risks, identifying 204
  risk prioritization 204, 205
  testing for risks 205
Image Analysis 135, 141
  capabilities 135
  URL 135
Image Analysis API 139
image captions (version 4.0)
  reference link 142
image categorization
  reference link 138
image classification 120, 122
image classification solutions
  features, identifying 118-120
image generation capabilities
  of Azure OpenAI Service 236
image processing 114, 115
images 117, 135
inference 5
inferencing 34
intents 10, 167
Internet of Things (IoT) 202
iterative training 41

J

Jaccard 54
JavaScript Object Notation (JSON) 140

K

Kaggle
  reference link 96

key phrase extraction 162, 163
  reference link 163
  uses 162
K-means clustering 52
K-Nearest Neighbor (KNN) 32
Kubernetes cluster 85

L

label identification, in dataset 69
  data, cleaning 71
  data documentation, checking 70
  data examination 69
  data exploration 70
  domain experts, consulting 70
  objective, defining 69
  problem type, considering 70
  target variable, identifying 70
labels 30, 65, 136
landmarks 128
language modeling 166
language service 161
  reference link 162
Language Understanding (LUIS) 10
large language models (LLMs) 190
linear regression 33
logistic regression 33
loss 59
loss function 59

M

machine learning (ML) 5, 30, 158
  compute services 84
  data 85
  features and labels, identifying in dataset 65, 66
  inferencing 34

semi-supervised machine
    learning techniques 34
  supervised machine learning techniques 31
  training set, using 71, 72
  unsupervised machine learning
    techniques 34
  validation set, using 71-73
machine learning model 30
  configured resources, deleting 107, 108
  deployed model service, testing 106, 107
  deploying 106
  reviewing 105
  selecting 105
  testing 106
  training 30
machine learning model, building
  in Azure ML 94
  AutoML, using to train model 96-104
  workspace, creating 94-96
machine learning operations
  (MLOps) 81, 92, 93
Management section, Azure
  OpenAI Studio 225
  content filters 228
  Data files page 227
  Deployments page 226
  Models page 226, 227
  Quotas page 227, 228
Manhattan 54
mean absolute error (MAE) 39, 40
mean squared error (MSE) 40
measure, Responsible AI and
  Generative AI solutions 205
metaprompts 207, 221
Microsoft Bot Framework 179
Microsoft Certified Trainer (MCT) 130
Microsoft Copilot 202
Microsoft Copilot AI assistants 162

Microsoft Fairlearn research paper
  URL 21
Microsoft Florence model 118, 136
  captioning 117, 136
  image classification 117, 136
  object detection 117, 136
  OCR 117
  tagging 117, 136
Midjourney
  URL 196
Minkowski 54
mitigate, Responsible AI and
  Generative AI solutions 206
  metaprompt and grounding layer 207
  model layer 207
  safety system layer 207
  user experience layer 208
MLflow 78
mltable 86
model 30, 88, 226
model management and deployment
  capabilities, Azure ML
  deployment targets 91
  integration, with MLOps practices 92
  monitoring and diagnostics 92
  packaging 91
  scalability and performance 92
  security and compliance 92
  versioning 91
multiclass classification 31, 48
  applications 51, 52
  evaluation metrics 50
  example 48-50
multiclass classification models, algorithms
  multinomial 50
  One-vs-Rest (OvR) or One-vs-All (OvA) 50
multi-head attention 195
multivariate anomaly detection 6

N

Naïve Bayes 33
named entity detection 161
named entity linking (NEL) 165
named entity recognition (NER) 164
natural language generation capabilities
   of Azure OpenAI Service 229-231
natural language (NL) 214
natural language processing
      (NLP) 10, 60, 81, 158, 190, 214
   concepts 159-161
   scenarios 161, 162
natural language understanding (NLU) 214
neural networks (NNs) 58, 59, 71, 170
neurons 32
n-grams 161, 166
numeric pixel value 114

O

object detection 120
object detection solutions
   features, identifying 120-123
object detection (version 4.0)
   reference link 142
OCR solutions
   features, identifying 123-126
OpenML
   reference link 96
operate, Responsible AI and Generative
      AI solutions 208, 209
opinion mining 165
optical character recognition
      (OCR) 9, 133, 135
   reference link 135, 143
overfitting 72, 73
overtraining 72

P

personal health information (PHI) 177
pipelines 78
pixel arrays 114
pixel value 114
playground, Azure OpenAI Studio 217
   Assistants 218-220
   Chat 221, 222
   Completions 223-225
   DALL-E 225
precision 46, 52
prediction 166
preprocessing 79
preprocessing text normalization 161
primitives types
   boolean 86
   number 86
   string 86
Project Florence
   reference link 118
prompt framework examples
   reference link 232
prompts 13, 230
PyTorch 78

Q

question-answering, Azure AI
      Language service 178

R

random forests 33
Read API 142
recall 46
Recurrent Neural Networks (RNNs) 60, 166
red team testing 205

regression 31, 81
  applications 41
  evaluation metrics 39
  example 35-39
  scenarios, identifying 35
reinforcement learning 9
Responsible AI and Generative AI solutions 203
  identity 204, 205
  measure 205
  mitigate 206-208
  operate 208, 209
Responsible AI Standard 149
Responsible AI Standard document
  URL 22
retrieval-augmented generation (RAG) 207, 208
  generation component 208
  retrieval component 208
role-based access control (RBAC) 126, 214
root mean squared error (RMSE) 40

S

scikit-learn 78
secrets 89
semi-supervised machine learning techniques 34
sentiment analysis 165
  uses 166
serverless computing 84
server message block (SMB) 87
silhouette score 55
software development kit (SDK) v2 87
specificity 47
speech recognition 168
  uses 169
  working 169

speech service 162
  reference link 162
speech synthesis 168, 169
  uses 169
  working 170
stemming 161
stop word removal 161
storage account 89
subscription 89
summarization 159
supervised learning (SL) 31, 65
  algorithms 32, 33
  classification 31
  regression 31
Support Vector Machines (SVM) 33

T

tables (tabular data abstraction) 86
temperature 190
TensorFlow 78
text analysis, Azure AI Language service
  entity linking 177
  key phrase extraction 177
  language detection 177
  named entity recognition 177
  opinion mining 177
  personally identifiable information (PII) detection 177
  sentiment analysis 177
  summarization 177
Text Analytics 11
text and document translation 171
threshold 43
time series data 5
time series forecasting 81
tokenization 159, 160, 192
tokens 159, 160, 192

transformer model architecture
  decoder block 191
  encoder block 191
transformer models 166
translation 171
  uses 171
translator 162
  reference link 162
Transparency Note, for Azure AI Language
  reference link 163
True Negatives (TN) 46
True Positives (TP) 46
tuples 31

U

UCI Machine Learning Repository
  reference link 96
Uniform Resource Identifiers(URIs) 85
univariate anomaly detection 6
unsupervised learning 34
URI types, data management
  uri_file 85
  uri_folder 85
utterance 167

V

variational autoencoders 195
vectors 30, 193
voice-to-text (VTT) applications 169

W

workspaces 88
  elements, for machine learning
    workflows 88, 89

www.packtpub.com

Subscribe to our online digital library for full access to over 7,000 books and videos, as well as industry leading tools to help you plan your personal development and advance your career. For more information, please visit our website.

Why subscribe?

- Spend less time learning and more time coding with practical eBooks and Videos from over 4,000 industry professionals
- Improve your learning with Skill Plans built especially for you
- Get a free eBook or video every month
- Fully searchable for easy access to vital information
- Copy and paste, print, and bookmark content

Did you know that Packt offers eBook versions of every book published, with PDF and ePub files available? You can upgrade to the eBook version at packtpub.com and as a print book customer, you are entitled to a discount on the eBook copy. Get in touch with us at customercare@packtpub.com for more details.

At www.packtpub.com, you can also read a collection of free technical articles, sign up for a range of free newsletters, and receive exclusive discounts and offers on Packt books and eBooks.

Other Books You May Enjoy

If you enjoyed this book, you may be interested in these other books by Packt:

Azure Data and AI Architect Handbook

Olivier Mertens | Breght Van Baelen

ISBN: 978-1-80323-486-1

- Design scalable and cost-effective cloud data platforms on Microsoft Azure
- Explore architectural design patterns with various use cases
- Determine the right data stores and data warehouse solutions
- Discover best practices for data orchestration and transformation
- Help end users to visualize data using interactive dashboarding
- Leverage OpenAI and custom ML models for advanced analytics
- Manage security, compliance, and governance for the data estate

Microsoft Azure Fundamentals Certification and Beyond

Steve Miles

ISBN: 978-1-83763-059-2

- Become proficient in foundational cloud concepts
- Develop a solid understanding of core components of the Microsoft Azure cloud platform
- Get to grips with Azure's core services, deployment, and management tools
- Implement security concepts, operations, and posture management
- Explore identity, governance, and compliance features
- Gain insights into resource deployment, management, and monitoring

Packt is searching for authors like you

If you're interested in becoming an author for Packt, please visit `authors.packtpub.com` and apply today. We have worked with thousands of developers and tech professionals, just like you, to help them share their insight with the global tech community. You can make a general application, apply for a specific hot topic that we are recruiting an author for, or submit your own idea.

Share Your Thoughts

Now you've finished *Microsoft Azure AI Fundamentals AI-900 Exam Guide*, we'd love to hear your thoughts! Scan the QR code below to go straight to the Amazon review page for this book and share your feedback or leave a review on the site that you purchased it from.

`https://packt.link/r/1835885675`

Your review is important to us and the tech community and will help us make sure we're delivering excellent quality content.

Download a free PDF copy of this book

Thanks for purchasing this book!

Do you like to read on the go but are unable to carry your print books everywhere?

Is your eBook purchase not compatible with the device of your choice?

Don't worry, now with every Packt book you get a DRM-free PDF version of that book at no cost.

Read anywhere, any place, on any device. Search, copy, and paste code from your favorite technical books directly into your application.

The perks don't stop there, you can get exclusive access to discounts, newsletters, and great free content in your inbox daily

Follow these simple steps to get the benefits:

1. Scan the QR code or visit the link below

```
https://packt.link/free-ebook/9781835885666
```

2. Submit your proof of purchase
3. That's it! We'll send your free PDF and other benefits to your email directly

Made in the USA
Columbia, SC
01 May 2025

57424973R00159